THE HIDDEN WORLD

THE HIDDEN WORLD

Deciphering Sacred Text and Unveiling Mind

T.J. ROSWELL

Harrox Cambit Press.

Harrox Cambit Press
63-66 Hatton Garden, Fifth Floor, Suite 23,
London, EC1N 8LE

Harrox Cambit Press and Harrox Cambit Books are part of Harrox Cambit Publishing House Limited.

Copyright © T.J. Roswell
www.tjroswell.com

T.J. Roswell has asserted his right to be identified as the author of this Work by the Copyright, Designs and Patent Act 1988.

First published in the United Kingdom by Harrox Cambit Press in 2023.
First published in the United States by Harrox Cambit Publishing House in 2023.

www.harroxcambit.com

A CIP catalogue record for this book is available from the British Library. ISBN 9781739506599

Harrox Cambit Publishing House is the authorised representative in EEA, USA, Canada and Australia.

Copyright © 2023 by T.J. Roswell

All rights reserved. No part of this book may be reproduced in any manner whatsoever without written permission except in the case of brief quotations embodied in critical articles and reviews.

First Printing, 2023

Praises for

The Hidden World

Roswell questions traditional interpretations of the Quran in this nonfiction debut... However critical of conventional religion the book may be, it nevertheless approaches the Quran with a profound appreciation that makes the text relevant to modern readers both inside and outside the faith.

A well-researched, accessible reinterpretation of Quranic teaching.

- Kirkus Reviews.

Roswell's approach is to share close readings of key Quranic verses and stories, like that of Adam, with attention paid to Quranic Grammar, breakdowns of root words and etymologies, and explications that interested lay readers will be able to follow. ... Discovering ancient psychological wisdom from the Quran. Its goal: the peace that comes with a higher consciousness.

- BookLife Reviews.

Roswell's The Hidden World... aims to analyze the Quran from a psychological perspective.

...his book should nonetheless spark debate and introspection among readers.

- BlueInk Reviews.

The Hidden World's linguistic analysis of the Qur'an leads into unique exegetical arguments....

Using a fresh interpretation of the Qur'an to encourage positive psychological self-orientation, The Hidden World forwards unique exegetical arguments for awareness around mental instability.

-Foreword and Clarion Reviews.

Preface

When we explore the Arabic Quran, shorn of the shackles of conventional interpretations and literalist perspectives, we stumble upon an ancient fountain of wisdom that provides an astute dissection of human psychology. Instead of just a manual for religious observance, the text metamorphoses into an insightful charter on the complex tapestry of the human mind, presenting profound enlightenment on diverse facets such as self-awareness, social understanding, and the stewardship of relationships.

This age-old philosophical treatise lays bare the ongoing conflict within the human psyche between affirmative and damaging thought processes. It offers intricate strategies for vanishing destructive mental patterns, fostering psychological well-being. The teachings transcend the material plane to engage with the more abstract dimension of cognition and emotion. This recasting of the Arabic Quran offers the reader an uncharted journey into understanding the depths of the human psyche from a vantage point of ancient wisdom.

Introductory Remark

I do not align myself with any particular ideological or philosophical school of thought or hold any political or religious ties to individuals, groups, or organisations. The motivation behind this book is not to single out, criticise, or condemn any specific religion, tradition, culture, or person. Instead, my objective is to delve deep into the teachings of the Quran, presenting my research and understanding from a stance that is not influenced by traditional religious or literalist perspectives.

This book aims to provide an unbiased interpretation, shedding light on the Quran's teachings from a unique angle without prejudice or hidden agendas. I aim to share my findings and offer fresh insights, hoping they will stimulate thoughtful reflection and discussion.

DEDICATION

To my late father, the beacon of free thought and boundless inspiration behind these pages. An intellectual, poet, artist, and ever-curious spirit, he danced gracefully on the edges of conventional religious norms, daring to question where many would merely accept. His courage to seek truth beyond rituals and his encouragement to challenge rather than conform laid the foundation for this work. In his memory, I tread the path of inquiry and introspection.

To my loving mother, the beacon that guided me through life's most tumultuous storms. Her unwavering spirit, teaching me never to surrender, irrespective of life's trials and tribulations, has been my compass. This book is a testament to her strength, resilience, and indomitable spirit.

To my cherished wife, the anchor that steadfastly held our home. Her generous heart and selfless dedication gave me the freedom and tranquillity to transform thoughts into words and pages. Her love and support have been this endeavour's silent but potent forces.

This book is a humble offering to all of them, a small token of gratitude for their immense contributions to my life and work. Their love and support are the lifeblood that fuels my spirit, ambition, and creativity.

Contents

Preface vii
Introductory Remark viii
Dedication ix

1. The Introduction — 1
2. The Primer — 30

I
THE CORE PSYCHOLOGICAL CONCEPTS

3. Human Psychology in Quran — 48
4. The Pair in Psyche — 59
5. The Exposed and Hidden Components of Psychology — 68
6. The Innate Desires and Determinations — 88
7. Elevated and Base Consciousness — 98
8. Adam and The Forbidden Tree — 117
9. The Garden of Eden and Hellfire — 146
10. The Book — 162
11. The Introspection — 177
12. The Signs — 204
13. The Inner Voice — 214

| 14 | The Life and Death | 225 |

2
THE PRACTICAL IMPLICATIONS & EI

15	Thoughts A Quranic Perspective	240
16	Types of Personalities in Quran	261
17	Pathways to Cognitive Rectification	272
18	Emotional Intelligence	295

Epilogue — 305
Notes — 309
About The Author — 313
Index — 315

I

The Introduction

My Path to Self-Discovery

"The mind is like an iceberg, it floats with one-seventh of its bulk above water." Sigmund Freud.

What is the essence of God,? How can we envision God's form? Does God possess a specific gender? Is God's existence tangible? And if so, where does God reside? These questions arise in our minds, questioning why God seems distant from his creation. I observe the diversity of interpretations of God's nature within organised religions, leading me to ponder the actual reality behind these varied forms. The concept of religion beckons me to explore its true essence and why constructed deities or fabricated divinities are worshipped across different faiths.

Contemplating the forces governing our destiny, I question the influence of an unseen and unproven power. I find ourselves constrained by countless limitations, with God seemingly involved in the most mundane aspects of our lives: what we consume, how we dress, and even our thoughts. I struggle to comprehend why God interfered with our sexual orientation and relationships. This raises deeper inquiries about divine judgment and the connection between our life choices and eternal fate, whether in paradise or hell.

These reflections on heaven and hell touch the core of human existential concerns, prompting us to question the very fabric of morality and the underpinnings of our beliefs. At the heart of these musings lies the quintessential quest for freedom, the freedom to live authentically without the looming spectres of divine rewards or punishments. What if one's moral compass is not anchored in religious doctrine but in personal values or communal harmony? If the pursuit of an authentic life is divorced from divine considerations, it challenges the traditional paradigms of morality that many religious doctrines uphold. Such introspection might lead some to live a life guided by intrinsic values rather than extrinsic religious promises or threats. It underscores the need for personal agency in determining one's ethical path, free from the constraints of prescribed religious orthodoxy.

A further contemplation emerges as I question our autonomy and the ability to lead our lives according to our desires. I contemplate the paradox of a mighty creator allowing his creation to engage in conflict, even leading to violence and bloodshed in his name. I yearn for divine intervention to resolve these conflicts, bringing lasting peace.

These profound inquiries lead us to question the validity of the prevailing notions of God as defined by world religions. I seek to understand whether these concepts accurately reflect reality or a confusion or deliberate manipulation obscures a more profound truth. Alas, despite my pursuit of answers, satisfactory explanations to these and other related questions often elude me.

As someone with a deeply religious upbringing, intertwining religion and human psychology has long piqued my curiosity. As I matured and sought clarity from elders and religious intellectuals, I often found their explanations lacking in coherence and depth. Early on, it became apparent that many lacked genuine understanding and merely adhered to predetermined religious tenets. Notably, many had stifled their cognitive faculties in deference to religious orthodoxy. Within the Islamic tradition, certain questions are deemed heretical or blasphemous and labelled as Kufr. Venturing into such inquiries is believed to lead one astray from religious confines and often results in societal backlash, sometimes even aggressive coercion. As a result, many knowledgeable individuals in religious circles, restrained by apprehension, curtail their inquisitiveness. Prominent religious figures have even gone so far as to declare logic and reason as instruments of Satan, drawing parallels to Satan's questioning of God regarding his obedience to Adam.

These questions undeniably resonate in the minds of many. Yet, religious doctrines often urge us to dismiss them, to remain within their ideological boundaries. Essentially, these inquiries can be perceived as catalysts, tools that challenge established beliefs, freeing our minds from conventional constraints. Engaging our intellect and confronting these questions can liberate us from religion's mental restraints, alleviating the weight of guilt and fear of divine retribution. From personal encounters and dialogues with devout followers across diverse religious spectrums, I've discerned that deep faith in supernatural deities often necessitates a suspension of free, logical, and rational thought. Such surrender of critical thinking seems indispensable for unwavering belief.

Religion and Childhood

Religions typically find their roots in our lives during childhood, a phase when we're naturally predisposed to accept narratives without critical scrutiny. This stage, characterised by an evolving sense of logic and reason, becomes an ideal juncture for embedding religious doctrines in the malleable minds of children. Recognising this, many religious traditions prioritise early indoctrination. The inherent wisdom behind this strategy seems clear: once these young minds mature and hone their critical faculties, it becomes considerably more challenging to align them with specific religious tenets, be it Islam, Hinduism, Christianity, Judaism, or any other faith.

Arguments based on Logical Fallacies

During my intellectual explorations, I discerned a prevalent tactic adopted by many religious scholars and their adherents: the employment of logical fallacies. Notably, despite their extensive learning, some erudite religious figures occasionally resort to these fallacies in their discourses. Rather than fostering genuine inquiry and discernment, these fallacious arguments serve more as tools for persuasion. Instead of anchoring their debates in empirical validation or facilitating rational discourse on faith and divinity, they fall back on these flawed reasoning techniques.

Such stratagems may encompass circular reasoning (wherein the argument's conclusion is embedded within its premise), appeals to authority (proclaiming the veracity of a claim solely based on its endorsement by a reputed entity), or ad hominem attacks (undermining an argument by targeting the proponent's character rather than the argument's substance).

Some may posit a scenario to substantiate their stance: Imagine a footballer demanding comprehensive knowledge about the sport—its genesis, inception of rules, or the creation of the ball—before indulging in a match. In their portrayal, while other players might seek the joy of the game, this hypothetical player insists on comprehensive answers. The inference suggests that one needn't grasp every facet of a concept to appreciate or employ it, a logic extended analogously to various life elements like food or water.

Another oft-employed fallacy is the causality argument. Scholars might reference technological marvels, querying if they emerged spontaneously, aiming to bolster creationist claims.

Of course, playing a game or understanding the origins of food does not determine one's destiny in terms of heaven or hell. Even if one is interested in seeking answers to these questions, they can satisfy their intellectual curiosity. These matters differ from religious beliefs, which assert that adhering to certain practices makes one righteous and failing to do so makes one a sinner. Subscribing to the notion of a supernatural entity or endorsing fantastical narratives seemingly grants one a badge of righteousness. Conversely, diverging from these beliefs earns individuals labels of heresy or apostasy, supposedly making them worthy of divine disapproval or condemnation.

While such fallacies can be persuasive to those already inclined to believe, they do not necessarily contribute to a deeper, more nuanced understanding of religious texts or philosophies. Therefore, it is crucial for individuals to develop their critical thinking skills and question these fallacies when encountered, fostering a more enlightened and informed religious discourse.

Metaphysics Arguments

Adherents of faith often seek metaphysical reasoning when they struggle to articulate the rational basis for their beliefs, rituals, and traditional practices. This defence mechanism further solidifies the psychological barrier, obscuring the path to objective understanding and enlightenment.

To enrich the discussion, let's explore a few examples of metaphysical religious arguments that contrast with established scientific principles:

- *Creationism vs. Evolution:* One of the most well-known controversies involves the concept of Creationism, the belief that the universe and life originated from specific acts of divine creation, as opposed to Evolution, a scientifically established theory that explains the origin and development of life through natural processes and selection pressures over billions of years.
- *Miraculous events:* Numerous religious traditions advocate for the manifestation of miracles that seemingly contravene established natural laws. Instances such as reviving the deceased, treading upon the water, bifurcating the sea, or tales of aerial primates, elephants, mythical creatures like unicorns, and the splitting of the moon or countless similar phenomena are presented. These events often characterised as transcending the boundaries of conventional science, physics, and biology, are attributed to religious figures purportedly endowed with divine capacities.
- *Predestination vs Chaos Theory and Quantum Physics:* Some religious doctrines believe in predestination, suggesting that all events in the universe are foreknown and ordained by divine power. This contrasts with scientific principles

such as Chaos Theory and Quantum Physics, by "Deterministic Nonperiodic Flow". *Journal of the Atmospheric Sciences* (Lorenz, E. N. 1973 20(2), 130-141) and "*Die gegenwärtige Situation in der Quantenmechanik (The present situation in quantum mechanics)*" (Schrödinger, E. (1935), *Naturwissenschaften*, 23(49), 807-812), which suggests inherent unpredictability and randomness at fundamental levels of the universe.

The interplay between early religious conditioning, the use of logical fallacies, and deeply entrenched metaphysical beliefs highlights a systemic effort by religious institutions to stifle scientific reasoning and objective analysis. This framework acts as a 'barrier', obstructing the unfettered pursuit of knowledge and curtailing the exercise of rational scepticism. Such obstructions can impede the journey towards self-realisation and intellectual development. Consequently, a pressing need emerges for a harmonious fusion of scientific inquiry with spiritual belief, ensuring that one's faith does not impede personal and collective progress.

The Nature of Truth

Truth is often perceived as subjective, varying from one individual to another, specifically regarding faith and beliefs. Each person holds their own understanding of reality, making it challenging to establish a universal definition.

Truth is a complex philosophical idea that has been explored, debated, and discussed by numerous scholars and thinkers throughout history. Following are some key figures that engage with the notion of relative or subjective truth:

1. Nietzsche often delved into the nature of truth and knowledge. In his works, he suggested that all truths are interpretations influenced by various factors and are, therefore not absolute. Refer to his essay *"On Truth and Lies in a Nonmoral Sense"* (F. Nietzsche, 1873).

2. Wittgenstein discusses the nature of language and meaning, suggesting that our understanding (and thus, our grasp of "truth") is inextricably linked to the way we use language in specific contexts. *"Philosophical Investigations,"* (L. Wittgenstein, 1953).

3. Kuhn posits that scientific paradigms shift over time, and what one generation takes to be true in a particular scientific context might be replaced or revised by future generations based on new data or perspectives. *"The Structure of Scientific Revolutions"*, (T. Kuhn, 1962).

4. Focault explores how knowledge and "truth" are constructed by power structures and discursive practices. He challenges the idea of objective, timeless truth, suggesting instead that truths are products of historical and social contexts. *"The Archaeology of Knowledge"*, (M. Foucault, 1969).

5. As a pragmatist philosopher, Rorty believed that truth was not an objective correspondence with the world but was more about what works best in practice. See his work *"Philosophy and the Mirror of Nature."*, (Richard Rorty, 1979)

While exploring various faiths, I engaged in Bible study groups, interacted with multiple Christian denominations, delved into Hinduism, and participated in Islamic sect discussions. These experiences enriched my perspective, allowing me to appreciate the Truth as perceived by different beliefs and traditions.

It is not my prerogative to impose my understanding on others or to belittle anyone's deeply held beliefs. This book aims to objectively examine ancient wisdom, specifically in the context of Arabic Quran, without contesting or undermining any religious convictions or their associated divine entities. The primary aim of this work is to encourage readers to reflect upon and question their own truths and convictions.

The Similarities

Through my quest for knowledge and an unbiased approach to reading and learning, I have reached the following conclusions:

- The fundamental essence of major religious philosophies is remarkably similar, focusing primarily on human psychology.
- The older the religious scripture, the purer and spiritually oriented its teachings tend to be.
- Modern texts within religions often distort the original ancient wisdom and philosophies. They are frequently written to justify or make sense of current religious practices, traditions, and rituals within their respective faiths, drawing inspiration from the cultural and traditional contexts in which they originated.
- Surprisingly, I have discovered similar themes, patterns of storytelling, characters, and plots in contrasting religions, such as the Abrahamic religions and Hinduism.
- Ancient philosophies were often conveyed through parables. The characters, events, and situations within these parables were magnified to emphasise the significance of various aspects of human psychology. Over time, these characters and stories in ancient scriptures evolved into literal figures and events, ulti-

mately giving rise to religious traditions, stories, and associated rituals.

It's plausible that, just as Africa is frequently recognised as the cradle of humanity, there could be a singular source of the profound wisdom present in the Quran, Vedas, and other ancient sacred texts. Over the course of history, this foundational knowledge may have been influenced and nuanced by regional and cultural variations.

OR such universal insights might emerge from profound introspection, regardless of cultural or geographical background. This is reminiscent of numerous instances in scientific history where unconnected researchers, working independently, arrive at identical conclusions, underlining the universality of certain truths and ideas.

These insights have led me to recognise the underlying similarities and common threads among different religions. They allow me to view them through a broader lens and discern the psychological insights embedded within their teachings.

Furthermore, by approaching the core texts of ancient philosophies without the influence of traditions and rituals, one would discover a common wellspring of wisdom. This wisdom, when explored, provides profound insights into the intricacies of human psychology, an essential focus of this book. By stripping away the layers of cultural practices and dogmas, readers can access the timeless knowledge at the heart of these ancient teachings. Through this lens of understanding human psychology, these texts' true essence and value can be revealed.

The Human Psychology and Vedas

The Vedas, among the oldest sacred texts, encompass a wide range of topics, including philosophical discourses, hymns, and rituals. Many verses can be interpreted as referring to the innate divinity within humans and aspects of psychology, although the language is often allegorical or symbolic. Below are some quotes from the Vedas which can be seen in light of human psychology and the idea of the divine residing within us:

Rigveda: "Truth is one; the wise call it by many names." (Rigveda 1.164.46)

This quote underscores the universal nature of truth and could be interpreted as an understanding that diverse paths can lead to the same inner truth or realisation.

Atharvaveda: "Man in his ignorance identifies himself with the material sheaths that encompass his real self."

This touches upon the human tendency to associate with the material or external world, neglecting the inner self or consciousness.

Yajurveda: "Lead me from the unreal to the real. Lead me from darkness to light. Lead me from death to immortality." (Yajurveda 40.17)

This well-known mantra, the Asato Ma Sadgamaya, can be seen as a plea to move from ignorance to self-realisation, from unawareness to recognising the divine within.

Samaveda: "Let my mind be firmly grounded in my speech, and my speech be firmly grounded in my mind."

This can be interpreted as an alignment of thought, speech, and action – an integral part of understanding one's psyche.

The Vedas are profound, and their teachings, often metaphorical, can be interpreted in numerous ways. Many believe that the Vedas emphasise 'Atman' (the soul or self) as being a part of 'Brahman' (universal soul or God). This connection could be seen as an affirmation of the divine within each individual.

Human Psychology and The Bible

The Bible contains many verses that touch upon human psychology and the idea that God is within us or closely connected to us. Here are some verses from both the Old and New Testaments:

Following are some of the verses from the Old Testament.

Genesis 1:27: "So God created mankind in his own image, in the image of God he created them; male and female he created them."

This passage speaks to the inherent divinity within humans, suggesting a deep connection between man and God.

Jeremiah 31:33: "But this is the covenant that I will make with the house of Israel after those days, declares the LORD: I will put my law within them, and I will write it on their hearts. And I will be their God, and they shall be my people."

Here, the "law" written on hearts can be seen as an internal moral compass, suggesting that God's guidance is within each person.

Following are some of the verses from the New Testament.

1 Corinthians 3:16: "Do you not know that you are God's temple and that God's Spirit dwells in you?"

This explicitly mentions the idea that God's Spirit, or the divine, resides within individuals.

1 Corinthians 6:19: "Or do you not know that your body is a temple of the Holy Spirit within you, whom you have from God?"

Again, the concept of the body as a temple reiterates the idea of the divine residing within.

Romans 8:11: "But if the Spirit of Him who raised Jesus from the dead dwells in you, He who raised Christ Jesus from the dead will also give life to your mortal bodies through His Spirit who dwells in you."

This speaks to the spiritual connection and the power of the Spirit within believers.

Luke 17:21: "Nor will people say, 'Look, here it is,' or 'There it is,' because the kingdom of God is in your midst."

Often interpreted as the kingdom of God being within individuals or among them, pointing again to the idea of the divine's close connection with humanity.

These verses, among others in the Bible, can be interpreted to shed light on human psychology and our intrinsic connection to the divine. As with any religious text, understanding and interpretation can vary, and deeper insights often come from comprehensive study and reflection.

The Ancient Chinese and Greek Philosophies

The venerable sages of ancient Chinese and Greek civilisations have bequeathed profound insights into the human psyche and the innate divinity that resides within. Their treatises on self-awareness and inner wisdom have not only stood the test of time but also laid the foundational bedrock upon which contemporary philosophical thought and theories are constructed.

The wisdom of Tao Te Ching, Zhuangzi, and Confucius enriches Ancient Chinese philosophy. Tao Te Ching, often attributed to Laozi, is a foundational text for Taoism, emphasising harmony with the Tao, a cosmic force representing the ultimate order of the universe. Zhuangzi, a seminal figure in Taoist philosophy, offered profound reflections on nature, freedom, and the relativity of human experiences. Confucius, meanwhile, brought forth a philosophy grounded in ethical and moral principles, emphasising respect for tradition, righteousness, and societal harmony. Together, these thinkers have indelibly shaped the philosophical landscape of China and beyond.

Laozi (Lao Tzu) in the "Tao Te Ching":
Knowing others is wisdom; knowing the self is enlightenment. (Tao Te Ching, Chapter 33). The Tao that can be told is not the eternal Tao; The name that can be named is not the eternal name." (Tao Te Ching, Chapter 1) - This can be interpreted as the Tao (or the Way) being an intrinsic, indefinable quality within and beyond all things.

Zhuangzi: "Happiness is the absence of striving for happiness." - This reflects an understanding of inner contentment and psychology.

Ancient Greek philosophy, birthed in the cradle of Western thought, boasts a lineage of legendary thinkers who laid foundational principles for diverse fields of inquiry. Socrates, revered for his dialectic method, challenged conventional wisdom and emphasised the pursuit of genuine knowledge through questioning. His pupil, Plato, expanded on these ideas, creating allegories such as the Cave to explore reality and knowledge while establishing the famed Academy in Athens. Aristotle, a student of Plato, furthered philosophical discourse by classifying knowledge by penning treatises on ethics, politics, and natural sciences. Their collective efforts have been pivotal in shaping the intellectual trajectory of the West and continue to resonate in modern philosophical debates.

Socrates:
"The unexamined life is not worth living." (Plato's "Apology", 38a5-6)
"To know thyself is the beginning of wisdom." - This quote, while popularly attributed to Socrates, aligns more with the Delphic maxim "Know thyself."

Plato:
"The measure of a man is what he does with power." (Plato, "Republic")
"All learning has an emotional base." (Plato, "The Republic") - This emphasises the interrelation of emotion and cognition, touching upon psychology.

Plotinus in the "Enneads": "The One is perfect because it seeks nothing, lacks nothing, and rests in itself." (Enneads, V.5.12) - Here, the One or the Good is seen as an eternal, divine principle.

Heraclitus:
"Character is destiny." - This phrase captures the essence of human psychology and fate being intertwined.
"Listening not to me but to the Logos, it is wise to agree that all

things are one." - Heraclitus speaks of the Logos, an organising principle or divine reason inherent in the cosmos and human soul.

While notable parallels may exist between various ancient philosophies, as we have discussed above, I've chosen not to centre our discourse on these likenesses. They are fascinating and warrant a deeper exploration, but such an examination falls outside the scope of this particular narrative. Maintaining the integrity and focus of our primary subject matter is a conscious decision.

A Journey Stifled at the Outset: The Paradox of Unchallenged Faith.

For a prolonged period, I found myself wrestling with the problem of whether investing time in exploring ancient religious texts was a worthwhile endeavour, given my perception of all religions as constructs of human ingenuity. I pondered the merit of devoting precious hours to scrutinising manuscripts crafted by individuals of antiquity.

Nonetheless, an epiphany dawned upon me. In our ceaseless quest for knowledge, the sum of our understanding, manifested in our observations, aural experiences, readings, and learning, is, in essence, a by-product of cumulative human endeavour. Every novel idea, philosophical standpoint, and innovative breakthrough extends or evolves from pre-existing knowledge. Researching in isolation, with an expectation of conjuring something from the void, is inherently flawed. I concluded that a treasure trove of ancient wisdom may lie within these texts. The accurate measure of this wisdom can only be gauged through a commitment of time and intellectual energy to decipher them. It was crucial to refrain from emulating the widespread mentality where individuals unflinchingly proclaim the verity of their faith while discounting others without earnestly probing into the potential wisdom they might impart (an archetypical religious mindset, wouldn't you agree?).

In addition to this, the demands of my professional life and familial obligations were significant barriers to penning this book. Reconciling the pressures of full-time employment with domestic responsibilities created an arduous scholarly investigation and authorship environment.

Yet, a persistent thought has echoed within me for as long as I can remember, suggesting that ancient texts, particularly the Quran, harbour deeper meanings than their conventional interpretations. This suspicion was only strengthened whenever I encountered the stringent stance held by various Islamic schools of thought: the Quran should never be approached without its historical and traditional contexts, preferably only under the tutelage of a qualified teacher. The rationale? Venturing alone might result in misinterpretation and potentially stray the reader from their faith. This caution, almost verging on a warning, piqued my curiosity. What truths lay within these scriptures that stirred such caution and unanimity among diverse Islamic sects? What could be so potent in the text to necessitate such concerted efforts to dictate its reading and comprehension?

Despite all such roadblocks and limitations, I was resolute in articulating my thoughts and insights as comprehensively as possible within this work.

The reason I chose to focus on the Quran in this exploration, as opposed to other ancient texts, stems from my personal background: I grew up in an environment where the Quran was deeply revered. Venturing into the study of other scriptures would have required overcoming additional challenges, particularly in terms of language and cultural understanding, making the Quran a more immediate and familiar choice for me.

Further impetus for selecting the Quran comes from recognising that existing literature seldom delves deep into its teachings. Predominantly, available works either offer interpretations and justifications for traditional narratives and the Quran's origins or strive to pinpoint its weaknesses. In my view, neither approach adequately unearths the Quran's wisdom free from preconceived bias. Thus, an exploration of the Quran, approached with open-minded curiosity, promises to unveil the profound insights it may harbour.

Why is it Essential?

As we explore this book, it becomes pertinent to highlight the rationale behind interpreting the Quran in the manner attempted herein. If this premise is already lucid for you, please feel free to go ahead with the next chapter.

A significant portion of Quranic literature firmly anchors explanations within the context of historical figures, scenarios, incidents, and epochs. Alternatively, they lean on modern, traditional exegesis, purporting to clarify Quranic verses. Regrettably, such methodologies often fail to capture the essence and the actual message inherent in the Quranic wisdom.

Perusing an array of books on the Quran and Islam, authored by Muslim, non-Muslim, and ex-Muslim researchers and scholars alike, I discerned a pervasive pattern. Their interpretations invariably tether to established historical narratives, commentaries, or explanations, and at times, even draw influence from speeches and commonplace literature that's widespread in the Islamic world. A book by a Muslim or non-Muslim scholar that approaches the Quran without preconceptions, independent of history or established commentary, is yet to come to light.

As such, my approach may be seen as novel, if not the first attempt, at elucidating the Quran using solely the Quran. While this method might seem unconventional and diverges from standard practices, I firmly believe this is the only path to unveil the Quran's message truly. Whether entrenched religious bureaucracies and institutions and their steadfast gatekeepers will accept this approach is another debate. The answer is rather apparent, is it not?

Regardless of their acceptance, history bears witness to individuals who have comprehended and adhered to the Quran in this very manner. Though they are few, often marginalised, and live in fear of religious persecution, they have encoded the essence of the Quranic message through their poetry, proverbs, spiritualism, mysticism, and fictional characters, indirectly conveying the message to humanity. Within this group, I place all spiritually inclined individuals, Sufis, and mystics within the Islamic world.

For over two decades, I've been engaged in discussions and debates about the Quran and religion within my familial and friendly circles. Persistent encouragement from loved ones to contribute publicly to eradicating religious intolerance, extremism, and fanaticism has been a recurrent theme. If reading this book enables a single individual to liberate themselves from religious boundaries and limitations and view the Quran from a non-traditional vantage point, I would consider my effort worthwhile.

The Religions

According to the Oxford English Dictionary (OED), one of the most authoritative sources on the English language, the term "religion" is defined as:

"The belief in and worship of a superhuman controlling power, especially a personal God or gods".

As defined by the Encyclopaedia Britannica, religion can be understood as the human response to those elements in the individual and the universe that transcend the ordinary and every day. It typically encompasses practices, behaviours, beliefs, and institutions that relate humanity to the supernatural or the sacred. Religion often serves as a framework through which individuals interpret their experiences and derive meaning, purpose, and ethical guidelines. One can discern shared paradigms across the global tapestry of religions, encompassing rituals, narratives, symbols, and ethical imperatives. Yet, in a testament to their distinct identities, many maintain an exclusivist stance, often perceiving divergent beliefs as erroneous.

From my perspective, all religions are manufactured constructs developed based on geographical regions' specific faiths, traditions, and cultures. Throughout history and even today, religions have been used to control the human mind. Religious institutions have employed concepts such as sin, purity, righteousness, and endless restrictions on human life, including eating, clothing, relationships, and business.

The relationship between religion and statecraft and the idea that religion can be employed as a tool for political control has been a subject of study and speculation by many scholars and historians. While it's crucial to understand that this perspective does not apply universally to all religions or all eras, several notable books have explored this concept:

"The End of Faith: Religion, Terror, and the Future of Reason" by Sam Harris. Harris presents an argument about the dangers of faith and organised religion, touching upon its use as a control mechanism.

"The God Delusion" by Richard Dawkins. Dawkins delves deep into the harmful aspects of religious belief. He touches upon the idea that religion can be a tool for control, among other topics.

"The Prince" by Niccolò Machiavelli. While not solely about religion, Machiavelli's political treatise offers advice on governance and power, suggesting at times that rulers might manipulate religion for state purposes.

"A History of God: The 4,000-Year Quest of Judaism, Christianity, and Islam" by Karen Armstrong. Armstrong delves into the history of the three major monotheistic religions, providing insights into their evolution and how rulers have used them.

"The Power and the Glory: Inside the Dark Heart of Pope John Paul II's Vatican" by David Yallop. Yallop investigates the political machinations inside the Vatican, suggesting ways in which religious power can intermingle with political objectives.

"Under the Banner of Heaven: A Story of Violent Faith" by Jon Krakauer. Krakauer investigates religious extremism in the United States, hinting at how faith can be harnessed for specific, sometimes violent, ends.

However, as this book's primary focus lies elsewhere, we should confine our discussions to the main themes. Engaging too deeply in the intricacies of religion and politics might detract from our central subject. Still, it's always enlightening to be aware of the broader contexts in which our main discussion resides.

All religions assert that their scriptures serve as the manual for humanity, likening them to operating instructions for manufactured equipment or machinery. Intriguingly, humans considered the most intelligent and conscious species on this planet, require a manual from an imaginary divine power to navigate their daily lives. It raises questions worth pondering.

Furthermore, it is noteworthy that multiple religions exist, each with its scriptures or manuals for humanity. Humanity has never reached a consensus or collectively followed a single scripture, yet we continue to function. We manage to navigate life without such uniformity.

Many religions believe that a time will come when everyone will follow their specific religion or face dire consequences. These concepts often form the basis of apocalyptic narratives, the second coming of religious figures such as Jesus Christ or Mehdi, or avatars' appearance in polytheistic religions. While this subject is beyond the scope of this book, extensive scholarly work and research have been undertaken on such topics for those interested in exploring further.

The issue with religions and belief systems is that they are rooted in imaginary stories, miracles, and supernatural phenomena. They often rely on metaphysics, abstract theories with no factual basis, to justify their beliefs. I advocate for the freedom of individuals to believe in any imaginary character or story as they wish, as long as it does not harm others. However, when these beliefs lead individuals to view fellow human beings as infidels, impure, disgusting, or enemies, it becomes problematic. Regardless of how religions view themselves, such as being "a way of life," organised religions based on scriptures tend to share essential and inherent commonalities centred around hate and restrictions.

Interestingly, although religions claim to be based on love, it is undeniable that some of the greatest atrocities throughout human history have been committed in the name of religion. I believe humanity will continue to suffer until it liberates itself from the shackles of these religions. This realisation motivates me to contribute my part, without fear and regardless of the outcome, by at least writing and expressing my perspective.

On Authorship in Sacred Texts and the Notion of Divinity.

In my scholarly assessment, religious scriptures predominantly emerge from human endeavours rather than divine orchestration. The notion that an omnipotent, omniscient entity responsible for the vast expanse of the universe would resort to written means—subject to interpretation—to communicate with its creations seems implausible. A rational mind might find it challenging to reconcile with this perspective. Instead, I perceive the true marvel to be the evolution of human consciousness. I believe these sacred texts are manifestations of this very consciousness, articulated in diverse ways.

There's much speculation regarding the initial authorship of the Quran. While this debate falls outside the purview of this work and often sidetracks from primary discourses without reaching any consensus, I approach it with circumspection. Nonetheless, based on my extensive study and contemplation, I've formulated a hypothesis:

Many ancient texts, such as the Quran, Vedas, and others, lack attributed authors. However, contrary to religious assertions, their absence doesn't affirm their divine origin unequivocally. A plausible explanation, grounded in my understanding, is that these doctrines were orally transmitted across epochs. With the advent of writing technologies, these orally preserved tenets were transcribed, making pinpointing their inception or original composers arduous.

Moreover, another perspective worth considering is the possibility that once religions institutionalised and adopted specific ancient philosophies at their heart, there might have been a deliberate erasure of original authors. This could strategically position these scriptures with an air of divine origin, furthering religious objectives.

I must reiterate, though, that the genesis and purported sanctity or divinity of these scriptures are not the focal points of this book. It's paramount that I delineate my boundaries here. However, I remain confident that those intrigued by this subject will embark on their scholarly quests to delve deeper into it.

If one explored similar themes in academic discourse, some potential references could be investigated. Note that these references might not perfectly align with the content, but they offer critical perspectives on the authorship and origins of religious texts:

"*God: A Human History*", (Aslan, Reza, 2017). This book delves into the history of humanity's belief in God and suggests that the divine reflects human consciousness.

"*An Introduction to Hinduism*". Cambridge University Press. (Flood, Gavin D, 1996). It offers a comprehensive overview of Hinduism and discusses the Vedas and their transmission.

"*Beyond the Written Word: Oral Aspects of Scripture in the History of Religion*", (Graham, William A. (1987). Explores the transition from oral to written in religious traditions, discussing the implications and complexities of this shift.

"*What is Scripture? A Comparative Approach*", (Smith, Wilfred Cantwell, 1993). This text critically examines the concept of "scripture" across various religious traditions, addressing questions of authority, authenticity, and interpretation.

"*The Interface Between the Written and the Oral*", (Goody, Jack, 1987). An exploration of the dynamics between oral traditions and their written counterparts in various cultures and historical contexts.

"*The Case for God. Vintage*".(Armstrong, Karen, 2009). Armstrong examines the history of religious beliefs, providing insights into the human conception of divinity and the evolution of faith traditions over time.

The Organisation of the Book

My journey of exploration, research, and understanding of the Quran has led me to realise that it encompasses not only deep and profound psychological insights but also practical implications for our daily lives. Each concept discussed in the Quran has a direct and valuable connection that can be experienced and applied immediately once its psychological context is clear.

Unlike most books that focus solely on theoretical or practical aspects, I have tried to discuss both in separate sections. This approach allows readers to relate better the concepts presented in this book to their own lives and experiences.

Part 1: The Core Psychological Concepts in The Arabic Quran

In this section, I delve into the psychological philosophy of the Quran. I provide detailed discussions and explanations on well-known topics, exploring their connections to human psychology.

Part 2: The Practical Implications and EI

The book's second part examines how these core concepts can be practically applied to various aspects of our everyday lives. I discuss their relevance to different areas and offer insights on how they can positively influence our actions and choices.

This part will also focus on how the wisdom found in the Quran can be used to enhance emotional intelligence. I explain how understanding and applying Quranic teachings can contribute to developing higher emotional intelligence competence and lead to a more prosperous and fulfilling life.

By organising the book into these parts, I aim to provide readers with a comprehensive understanding of the psychological and practical dimensions of the Quran's wisdom and its potential for personal growth and transformation.

2

The Primer

The Innate Curiosity

"There are many ways to be free. One of them is to transcend reality by imagination, as I try to do." Anais Nin.

My formative years included an impactful experience of watching "The Ten Commandments," a Hollywood film, alongside my late father. The movie's influence was considerable, sparking a curiosity that led me to question the authenticity of the biblical narratives it depicted. For each query I put forth, my father would affirm that the events also found mention in the Quran. Consequently, I was puzzled about why we had two distinct books and two different religions if the narratives were identical, and I wondered if we should all align with Christianity. The responses provided by my father, predictable in their assertion that the Bible had been altered while the Quran remained pristine, temporarily allayed my curiosity.

However, my quest for understanding was not quelled. Throughout my late teenage years, I explored the Quran in-depth, seeking clarity through its translations. As I delved deeper, the complexities only seemed to increase. This journey introduced me to several individuals and groups who professed direct guidance from the Quran. Associating with them, I hoped to enhance my understanding, only to soon discern that they constituted a cult distorting Quranic interpretation to serve their purposes. Their interpretations of Quranic verses oscillated between literalism and metaphorical or spiritual interpretations based on their convenience. This characteristic, I observed, was not exclusive to them but was a common trait among various religions—switching between literalism and metaphors in interpreting their religious texts wherever they encountered challenges in providing physical justification.

Amongst these experiences and for numerous other reasons, the inquisitive spark within me continues to drive my pursuit of knowledge. I remain determined to find my path in either rejecting these texts or understanding them in their original essence, as they were intended to be perceived.

In my upbringing, my family had a mixed understanding of the Quranic stories, blended with traditional and literalist interpretations. However, I have come to recognise that true wisdom lies beyond the confines of traditionalism and literalism. Practices like reciting verses and using them to purify water or food were standard in my household and appeared in similar forms across various religions. Yet, I began to view these practices with scepticism, finding them more akin to superstitions rather than inspiring rituals.

As my curiosity grew, I explored different avenues of knowledge, including scientific perspectives. I aligned myself with a scientific school of thought that suggests the universe does not rely on a divine entity for its existence and operation. From this vantage point, our beliefs and actions on Earth hold limited significance on the vast cosmic scale.

The universe has existed long before us and will continue long after we are gone.

The concept of God, as developed by humans, originates in our search for meaning and understanding. Exploring the nature of God and the idea of existence warrants a separate exploration that requires careful consideration and analysis. While I may touch upon these subjects briefly throughout the book, a comprehensive examination of the concept of God itself would be a separate endeavour deserving of its dedicated work.

In essence, I intend to approach ancient texts, particularly the Quran, with an open mind and a desire to uncover their underlying wisdom. I aim to transcend the limitations of tradition and literalism, seeking a deeper understanding of human psychology and the profound insights embedded within these scriptures.

Guidance for Humanity?

The phrases "Guidance for Humanity" and "Salvation" have been the source of significant misconceptions and have fuelled countless evils throughout history. The claim by religions that their scriptures guide all of humanity inherently implies that those who disagree are misguided. This notion has led to religious bloodshed and continuous conflicts between different belief systems and even within the same religion, among other sects interpreting the exact text in various ways.

Drawing upon the Quran as a case in point, its verses are intricately woven in classical Arabic, a linguistic realm foreign to many, including many native Arab speakers. The depth and philosophical richness embedded within its lines often elude even those well-versed in the language. This begs the question: How can a text, so complex in its linguistic form and thus largely inaccessible to the global populace, serve as a universal guide for all humanity? Paradoxically, even some staunch proponents assert the Quran's universal applicability but struggle to grasp its profound essence, further complicating the claim of its all-encompassing guidance.

To counter these arguments, religions often introduce the concept of "Salvation." They acknowledge that there has never been a time in human history when the entire population followed a single faith or scripture, and it is improbable to occur in the future. Thus, they propose the idea of salvation, stating that while one may escape punishment for sins in this life, they will face torment in the afterlife, and only their religion can save them from eternal damnation. In reality, this approach is a way for religions to escape the burden of proving the divinity of their scriptures, shifting the responsibility to the afterlife. When religions resort to these arguments, it can be seen as an admission of defeat against rational reasoning.

The bitter truth is that no single religious scripture can guide all of humanity. While there may be elements of goodness or badness within each of them, it does not confirm their divinity. The concept of divinity itself raises significant questions. The claim made by religions to represent an almighty creator who has brought forth the vast and wondrous universe yet remains unable to reveal itself and end the conflicts caused by different interpretations of divinity by organised religions.

At its core, my proposition is straightforward: these revered texts are essentially repositories of ancient insights into human psychology. Historically, storytelling was a potent medium to convey messages, using allegorical characters symbolising diverse facets of human cognition, emotions, and wisdom. However, as time progressed, the allegorical essence of these narratives faded, leading to their literal interpretations. Although these ancient treatises have invaluable knowledge, their teachings are not a one-size-fits-all solution. As not everyone resonates with the nuances of philosophy or psychology, similarly, not everyone might find chemistry, mathematics, or computer science appealing. A connoisseur of poetry might be indifferent to chemical equations, while a mathematician might be unenthused by journalism. Hence, asserting that a single text —in mathematics, biology, or any discipline — serves as a universal guidepost for all humanity seems overly ambitious and lacks nuanced understanding.

The idea and claim of organised religions that humans, the most intelligent and dominant species on this planet, are helpless without these religious scriptures or that they will become morally corrupt without guidance is absurd. Other species on this planet, lacking our level of intelligence and consciousness, do not require such advice to manage their day-to-day lives. These claims and beliefs only denigrate humanity's intellect, intelligence, and consciousness.

In this book, I propose that the Quran does not explicitly delve into the intricate details of social, cultural, and legal matters, such as marriage, divorce, inheritance, and civil or criminal laws. Instead, I argue that these aspects of human relationships and societal functioning are products of human understanding, mutual agreement, and the evolving needs of a cohesive society.

Throughout history, human societies have developed and refined laws and regulations through shared experiences, knowledge accumulation, research studies, and adaptations to changing socioeconomic and environmental conditions. These legal frameworks are not static but rather dynamic systems that continuously evolve to meet the needs of a progressing society. Various factors shape them, including scientific and technological advancements, emerging facts, and the pursuit of justice and equity.

While religious traditions may claim divine intervention in law and governance matters, I assert that human agency and collective decision-making are integral to developing a just and harmonious society. As I interpret it, the Quran focuses more on fundamental principles of how human psychology works through a philosophy of introspection rather than providing explicit instructions for every societal facet.

By acknowledging the significance of human reason, societal consensus, and the ceaseless pursuit of knowledge, we can cultivate a progressive society that adjusts its laws and regulations in response to its inhabitants' evolving needs and circumstances. This book aims to delve into this perspective, fostering critical thinking and encouraging readers to reflect on the intersection of emotional intelligence, interpersonal relationships, and engagement with the external world.

By examining the Quranic wisdom and drawing connections to emotional intelligence, this book aims to empower readers to enhance their understanding of human psychology and develop the skills necessary for effective relationship management. Through thought-provoking discussions, we will explore how emotional intelligence can positively influence our interactions, decision-making processes, and overall well-being.

In doing so, I hope to stimulate a shift in perspective, encouraging individuals to embrace emotional intelligence as a vital component of personal growth and societal progress. By embracing critical thinking and open-mindedness, we can foster an environment that values empathy, understanding, and harmonious coexistence in an ever-changing world.

The Traditionalism

Traditionalism, in broad terms, refers to a philosophy or attitude that emphasises the importance of preserving established customs, practices, and values against the backdrop of modernity and change. It is rooted in a belief that there's inherent wisdom in traditions accumulated over generations and that these traditions should be adhered to and respected. This standpoint often contrasts with progressive or modernist views, which are more open to change and adaptation. Traditionalists argue that established norms and practices have stood the test of time for good reasons, providing stability and a sense of identity. Such a stance can manifest in various realms, from art and literature to politics and social norms. The tension between traditionalist and modernist perspectives has been a recurrent theme in cultural and philosophical discourses, especially in societies undergoing rapid transformation (Hobsbawm, Eric, and Terence Ranger, eds. The Invention of Tradition; Gellner, Ernest. Nations and Nationalism). It's worth noting that while traditionalism can offer continuity and a sense of belonging, critics argue it can also impede innovation and adaptability.

Religious traditionalism refers to the adherence to and preservation of foundational religious doctrines, practices, and interpretations that have been handed down through generations. This perspective often resists innovations or revisions to religious beliefs, emphasising ancient scriptures' authority and early religious leaders' teachings. Rooted in the idea of the "perennial philosophy," traditionalists believe that at the heart of the world's religions lies a set of unchanging truths, and these core principles should be maintained rigorously. In this context, religious traditionalism can be seen as a response to the rapidly changing world, offering stability and continuity by maintaining religious practices in their most original or "pure" form (Nasr, Seyyed Hossein.

Traditionalism: Religion in the Light of the Perennial Philosophy). Such an approach can sometimes clash with modernist or reformist views within the same religious tradition, leading to tensions between maintaining orthodoxy and accommodating contemporary sensibilities (Asad, Talal. Formations of the Secular: Christianity, Islam, Modernity).

Cultures and societies take pride in their unique traditions and values, which can contribute to their distinctiveness. Embracing and preserving core values can be beneficial in specific contexts. However, when it comes to interpreting ancient scriptures like the Quran, Bible, Vedas, or ancient Chinese texts, the stronghold of traditionalism can hinder the true wisdom embedded within these philosophies.

I firmly believe that these ancient scriptures contain profound ideas and insights about human psychology and spiritual experiences. However, interpreting them solely within the confines of traditionalism limits our understanding and appreciation of their true wisdom. To unlock the depths of these scriptures, it is necessary to break free from the shackles of conservatism and approach them with fresh perspectives and open minds. Only then can we fully grasp the profound philosophies they offer and apply them to our modern lives.

The Literalism

Literalism, in the realm of textual interpretation, particularly in religious or legal documents, emphasises understanding texts in their most immediate and overt meanings, setting aside metaphorical, symbolic, or nuanced readings. Such an approach sharply contrasts with more expansive interpretive or allegorical methods incorporating broader contexts or cultural subtleties. Scholars in hermeneutics—the study of interpretative principles—identify literalism as a key perspective in decoding texts. While some religious scholars advocate for a strictly literal reading of scriptures, viewing it as the path to doctrinal purity (as highlighted in Stanley Fish's "Is There a Text in This Class? The Authority of Interpretive Communities"), critics argue that this narrow lens may bypass the layered, multifaceted wisdom encapsulated in these texts, especially when decontextualised from their historical or cultural roots (as articulated by Paul Ricoeur in "Interpretation Theory: Discourse and the Surplus of Meaning").

Nevertheless, I posit that even the traditional and literal readings of religious texts stem from human interpretation. This very notion underscores that such texts inherently invite various interpretations. As such, these scriptures should be permitted an introspective analysis, anchored solely within their own framework, unhindered by external commentaries or the bindings of historical and traditional contexts.

Foundational narratives such as Adam and Eve, Noah's Ark, Moses's confrontation with Pharaoh, and tales of angels, Satan, and the eternal struggle between good and evil, particularly concerning life after death and the Day of Judgment, are intrinsic to the Judeo-Christian and Islamic traditions. Those entrenched in literalism perceive these stories as genuine historical events, staunchly embracing a face-value reading of scriptures.

Often, religious establishments champion these literalist and traditionalist perspectives, advocating for strict adherence to such readings as an essential component of their doctrinal integrity and continuity. Deviating from these entrenched views is frequently met with apprehension, sometimes even labelled as heretical or blasphemous. In certain instances, these deviations have been met with forceful resistance or direct harm. Thus, readers approaching the Quran without shedding these literalist or traditionalist interpretations might find the perspectives in this book somewhat challenging.

The Deep Impact

The convention of interpreting the Quran from a traditionalist and literal perspective is profoundly shaped by the Bible and Judeo-Christian traditions. In the Judeo-Christian readings of Biblical texts, events, characters, places, and situations are interpreted literally, often correlating them with real-world personalities, events and places. This same principle has been applied to Quranic interpretations by most scholars. Any deviation from this approach is often labelled as heresy. This method of Quranic interpretation arises from a dominant belief among traditionalists and literalists that the Quran serves as both an extension and refinement of the Judeo-Christian theological narrative. Consequently, these influences strongly tint their translations, leading them away from a neutral interpretation of the Quran's foundational message.

It is pivotal to underscore that this book doesn't delve into religious politics or historical distortions. Further, references to the Bible or Judeo-Christian traditions aren't made with the intent to diminish their value. Their mention only highlights the extent to which historical Quranic interpretations by most Muslim scholars may have been influenced, deliberately or inadvertently, by these traditions. This work presents a unique lens through which to view the Quran, celebrating it as a testament to human consciousness and a reservoir of profound insights into human psychology. Approaching the Quran with this viewpoint allows us to unearth its inherent wisdom, moving beyond the confines of conventional and literal readings.

The Interpretation

The Quran repeatedly asserts its clarity and ease of recall. While traditional scholars cite verses like 54:17,22,32,40 to highlight the straightforward nature of the Quran in Arabic, they also warn against approaching it without guidance, often invoking verse 2:26, albeit arguably out of its intended context. The Quran, interestingly, never claims to misguide its readers.

It appears that these scholars' insistence on adhering to conventional interpretative norms stems from a latent apprehension: a direct reader might unearth the Quran's core essence. Such discovery could challenge established, literal interpretations they perceive as foundational to the faith.

Central to the challenge of Quranic understanding is an over-reliance on external elucidations. Themes like Allah, Prophets, Angels, Jins, Islam, Muslim, Books, and the like are often presented devoid of context, supplemented by exegeses, tales, or even mythologies derived from entrenched schools or sects shaped by regional customs and legends. These external accounts become interwoven with our belief systems, falsely deemed as Quranic in origin. In this book, I deliberately leverage the Quran itself for clarifications, striving to offer an alternative lens.

A predominant concern is how Quranic Arabic terms are translated, often framed within a traditional context rather than adhering strictly to their foundational dictionary definitions.

Take the term "Nafs" (نَفْسٍ), for example. At its root, it denotes "Soul" or "Psyche." Yet, its application in various contexts sometimes extends to a physical entity, an enduring essence post-mortem, or in contexts like Nafs-e-Wahid, occasionally alluding to the figure of Adam.

Another illustrative example is the word "ilm" (ع ل م). Fundamentally, it signifies "knowledge." However, its derivative (العالَمين) in the Quran, which in a direct sense implies one who has knowledge, is frequently rendered as the "Lord of the Worlds."

Such semantic shifts in the interpretation of Quranic terms commonly arise in translations. These nuances often reflect a deeper entanglement with, and perhaps even an influence from, other religious traditions previously discussed.

The Quran intimates in 25:33 that its verses' optimal interpretation emerges from within its pages. Armed with an understanding of its interpretative principles, readers can independently find guidance in its verses. The efficacy of this methodology is, of course, for my readers to discern.

Predominant Quranic translations frequently intertwine with historical personas and traditions. Such entanglements, I contend, obstruct the discernment of the Quran's intrinsic message. However, this doesn't detract from the value of historical context or literal renderings. This book's essence isn't to contradict existing interpretations but to impartially scrutinise Quranic verses using the text's self-referential framework. I urge readers, as they peruse this work, to momentarily set aside entrenched interpretations, enabling a purer engagement with the Arabic Quran's essence.

The Parables and Storytelling

Stories hold a cherished position in religious narratives as they straddle dual facets. Firstly, they spotlight the physical attributes and persona of characters, a perspective commonly embraced by the general populace. Conversely, a deeper, metaphorical lens often promoted by erudite religious scholars seeks the allegorical meanings embedded in these tales. As Campbell (1968), in his seminal work "The Hero with a Thousand Faces", elucidates, these allegorical narratives dissect the dichotomy of good and evil in human psychology, offering a mirror to their tangible manifestations in the real world. Such stories, imbued with these dual meanings, have indelibly sculpted the human psyche, serving as catalysts for both historical transgressions and philanthropic ventures.

The inherent propensity of the human mind to assimilate knowledge through tales cannot be overlooked, irrespective of the historical veracity of these narratives. Bruner (1991), in his exploration of "The Narrative Construction of Reality", avers that storytelling's potency is rooted in its capacity to impart potent tenets to its recipients. This mode of communication, story-telling, is a linchpin in human societies, universally permeating diverse realms like politics, religion, science, commerce, and beyond. The observation by Simmons (2001) in "The Story Factor" reinforces this sentiment, suggesting that accomplished leaders invariably harness the art of storytelling to galvanise and lead.

Each narrative unfurls against a backdrop populated by characters whose deeds and traits are either lauded or admonished based on their role within the story's framework. It's these characters, with their intricate emotions and nuanced reactions to circumstances, that bear the story's core message to its audience, a principle detailed by Booker (2004) in "The Seven Basic Plots: Why We Tell Stories".

The Transcendence

The Quran presents its teachings through parables, examples, and abstract concepts beyond literal interpretation. Characters, places, and terms mentioned in the Quran, such as Angels, Demons, Jinns, Satan, Hell, and Paradise, are symbolic representations of abstract or unseen (Al-Ghaib) concepts. The Quran emphasises the need to break free from traditionalist and literalist views to understand its profound psychological philosophy truly.

By transcending traditionalism and literalism, one can unlock the Quran's more profound wisdom and message. This wisdom may have relevance and applicability to all individuals interested in exploring ancient wisdom's psychological philosophies. The Quranic parables utilise relatable characters to convey profound messages beyond physical aspects, leading to spiritual transcendence and a deeper understanding of human psychology.

The Language of Root Words

The language of the Quran is Pre-Classical Arabic, which primarily existed as an oral and regional language with various dialects. The structure of the Arabic language is based on root words, where a base word carries the semantic content and affixes (prefixes and suffixes) are added to form new words. The idea is that the base word and its inflected forms maintain the same core meaning.

However, it is essential to note that although Quranic Arabic follows the principles of a root word language, it no longer strictly adheres to these principles due to the evolution of Arabic into modern Arabic. The connection between the derivative words and their root word meanings may not always be apparent in modern Arabic.

When a single root word has multiple diverse meanings that do not directly relate to the essence of the root word, it challenges the notion that Arabic is solely a root word language. We should not mislead people into thinking that Arabic strictly adheres to root word meanings when the derivatives have disconnected meanings.

Translators of the Quran often have preconceived established meanings in their minds before undertaking the translation work. This can lead to confusion among readers. Overhauling the entire translation of the Quran is a challenging task, as it requires a comprehensive review of the established meanings and a fresh approach to accurately convey the true essence of the words in their respective contexts.

The daunting task of redefining the Quran's translation cannot be undertaken lightly; it demands a meticulous reassessment of entrenched meanings and a fresh, unbiased perspective to ensure the faithful conveyance of each word in its appropriate context. This task's magnitude necessitates a gradual approach, dissecting the Quran topic by topic, thus peeling back the layers of centuries-old interpretations to reveal the core of its timeless wisdom.

I

The Core Psychological Concepts

PART 1

THE CORE PSYCHOLOGICAL CONCEPTS IN ARABIC QURAN.

3

Human Psychology in Quran

The Nafs in Quran

"Who looks outside, dreams; who look inside, awakes." Carl Jung

In the Quran, the term "Nafs" is often rendered as "soul," a translation that has persisted in traditional and literalist interpretations of the text. This term is also frequently used interchangeably with other terms such as "person," "self," "Adam," "human," and "mankind." Yet, the Quran employs separate and distinct words for these notions, suggesting that the definition of "Nafs" has been moulded to accommodate traditional perspectives. Consequently, this elasticity of meanings has been exploited to harmonise with traditional and literal readings and to draw parallels between Quranic verses and Biblical narratives.

Etymological and Lexical Analysis.

"Nafs" is an indefinite feminine singular noun and is in the genitive case (مجرور). The noun's triliteral root is nūn fā sīn (ن ف س).

- Arabic English Lexicon, by E.W. Lanes. Vol 8, Page 2827: **The Soul, the spirit, the vital principle, the soul of intellect or reason, which is taken away during sleep.**
- The Hens Wehr Dictionary of Modern Arabic, by The Hans Wehr. Page 1155: **Soul, Psyche, and Human Mind.**
- The word Nafs with all its variations repeated 298 times in 270 verses in Quran. (Please refer to the notes for details).

The equivalence between the terms "soul" and "psyche" is rooted in etymology and historical usage. In many dictionaries and scholarly references, "psyche" is derived from the Greek word for "soul." For example:

Merriam-Webster Dictionary, the definition of Psyche is, "The soul, self, or personality of an individual", "The human soul, spirit, or mind".

Oxford English Dictionary (OED) described the Psyche as "The human soul, spirit, or mind", "The totality of elements forming the mind; the self or individual as a mental and emotional being".

It's worth noting that "psyche" in modern usage, especially in psychological contexts, has come to refer more broadly to the human mind or the seat of human consciousness and its processes. However, its origins tie it directly to the concept of the soul.

In academic literature, the term "soul" frequently corresponds with the concept of the "psyche." Although lexicon entries for both terminologies may converge, the prevalent interpretation of the "soul" is predominantly shaped by "The Deep Impact" (discussed in previous chapters) and cinematic portrayals, suggesting its endurance beyond physical demise. Notably, empirical and rational validations for this perspective remain absent, yet this notion remains a central part of most religious doctrines. This understanding has also seeped into translations and interpretations of the word "Nafs" in Quranic texts.

In most instances, the word "Nafs" is accurately translated in line with its true meaning, as the context of the verse does not allow for misinterpretation. However, in many other cases, the meaning is distorted to align with traditionalist narratives. This practice extends to numerous root words in the Quran, and it is one of the reasons why many schools of thought and scholars within the Muslim world emphasise the need for a religious teacher to guide the understanding of the Quran. These teachers often aim to suppress any contradictions in meaning that may arise.

It is important to note that this discussion is not intended to criticise or defame anyone. Instead, it serves as a background to explain why different translations of the Quran present varying interpretations of a single Arabic root word. Ideally, the meaning of a word should remain consistent throughout the book.

Moving forward, I will adopt the term "Psyche" to represent the Arabic word "Nafs" (نفس) to maintain consistency and alignment with the contextual meaning of all Quranic verses. This term remains in harmony with the intended message of these verses. It serves as a critical concept in unlocking the profound wisdom of this remarkable

Arabic Quran, which can be viewed as an artistic exploration of human psychology.

Quran and Human Psychology

Based on my research and understanding, I believe the Quran primarily focuses on human psychology. It provides insights into the mind's inner workings and offers guidance on how to comprehend, observe, and regulate its various states and phases. The ultimate goal is to achieve balance within the mind, where emotions and intelligence are under maximum control.

This balanced state is essential for directing internal energy towards attaining success (known as "Falah") and peace ("Salam") in life. It is important to note that success, as defined in the Quran, refers not solely to material wealth or achievements but to a state of mental equilibrium, stability, and inner peace.

Throughout the Quran, verses are presented as abstract parables and examples intended to facilitate our understanding of the different forces and energies at work within our psyche. By gaining a deeper understanding of these forces and their interactions, we can enhance our ability to govern our own psyche.

This improved understanding of our psyche and the comprehension of these forces and energies within every individual contributes to developing higher levels of Emotional Intelligence (EI). As a result, we can foster better relationships and cultivate harmony within our social circles, ultimately leading to collective peace.

If we liken our physical body to hardware, our psychology can be seen as the software that our consciousness shapes. While understanding and studying the Quran is one way to gain insights into the workings of this software, it is not the only path available. Various other sources, books, and philosophies offer valuable wisdom on the functioning of the human mind, some of which may provide equally comprehensive and accessible perspectives.

During my research, I noticed that translators often use the word "Soul" for "Nafs" when they need to be contextually accurate in the Quran. They rarely use "Psyche" instead. This might be because most people don't associate "Soul" with the idea of the human psyche.

Now let's try and understand what Al-Quran is discussing about this Word. Understanding this word and the subject may hold the key to understanding the Quran's actual wisdom. As Quran proclaimed:

75:14 Man can see, observe (understand/comprehend/aware/realise) his own Psyche (Nafs).

Traditional readings suggest that the verse predicts a future day of judgment where individuals will face divine assessment. Yet, another interpretation of the Quran highlights a personal 'day' when people gain the ability for self-reflection, allowing them to examine their own psyche. This significant moment, or 'day,' occurs when someone becomes acutely aware that their life's experiences and inner emotions are deeply linked to their own choices. This realisation can be viewed as their personal day of judgment, a time when they understand the consequences of their actions and become their own evaluators.

This perspective can be illustrated using everyday life situations: when you grasp the complete picture of a problem, you're better equipped to make informed, balanced decisions. The same principle applies in a court of law, where a judge, presented with both sides of a case, makes a judgement under the law. Hence, the verse hints at the notion of self-accountability, which is unlocked when one can introspect and assess their actions.

It's important to highlight that a fundamental aspect of the traditional interpretation of Judgement Day is the envisioned capacity it bestows upon individuals to retrospectively assess their lives with objectivity, discerning the outcomes of their decisions and actions.

Upon closer introspection, one might ponder: is it truly necessary to wait a designated day to harness such introspective capability? Could one's individual "Judgement Day" manifest at the onset of deep self-reflection on one's psyche, understanding its repercussions on one's history, current state, and future trajectory? When this understanding dawns, that very moment marks the beginning of one's personal Judgement Day, where one effectively becomes one's own adjudicator.

Let's explore some verses where the context does not allow for twisting the meaning of the word "Nafs". Please note that these verses are provided for reference purposes only, and we will focus on examining if any interpretation other than "soul/psyche" fits within the given context.

*39:41 Verily We have revealed the Book to thee in Truth, for (instructing) mankind. He, then, that receives guidance benefits his **soul**: but he that strays injures his **own soul**. Nor art thou set over them to dispose of their affairs.*

*5:104 O ye who believe! Guard your **souls**: If ye follow (right) guidance, no hurt can come to you from those who stray. The goal of you all is to Allah: it is He that will show you the truth of all that ye do.*

*6:104 Now have come to you, from your Lord, proofs (to open your eyes): if any will see, it will be for (the good of) his **own soul**; if any will be blind, it will be to his own (harm): I am not (here) to watch over your doings.*

7:205 *And do thou (O reader!) Bring thy Lord to remembrance in* **thy (very) soul**, *with humility and in reverence, without loudness in words, in the mornings and evenings; and be not thou of those who are unheedful.*

Throughout the aforementioned verses, the term "Nafs" is aptly translated as Soul, synonymous with a person's Psyche. This exemplifies the intrinsic elegance of the Arabic Quran and literature at large. When translators, for whatever reason, veer from the original essence of a concept, inconsistencies inevitably emerge. To cloak these inconsistencies, they may manipulate other parts of the text to fit their interpretation. While the adapted translation might suit certain contexts, it cannot be consistently applied without contradiction. Thus, translators sometimes default to the correct interpretation when it poses no threat to conventional or literalist narratives but alters it where it suits their agenda. This practice leads to a single Quranic term having varied and occasionally opposing translations.

The depiction of Psyche (Nafs) in Quranic translations is frequently marred by misinterpretation, obscuring its genuine essence. To navigate this challenge, I recommend a fundamental strategy: resort to esteemed Arabic dictionaries to derive the true meaning of root words. Although these dictionaries might list several meanings for a particular root, it's vital to opt for the one that resonates with the Quran's overarching narrative and ensures coherence across its verses.

Consider the term Nafs (Psyche), which recurs 270 times in the Quran. By uniformly interpreting it as Psyche across all instances, we can decipher the profound insights encapsulated in the Quran. Recognising the intricacies surrounding the term Nafs in Quranic translations is imperative. Its genuine core has faced numerous misrepresentations over time. Embracing this understanding will aid in preserving the word's authenticity and elucidating its true intent within the Arabic Quran.

The human psyche, a multifaceted and intricate entity, encompasses many dimensions and elements. It is imperative for us to delve into each of these components to grasp their functionality and interconnectedness truly. By understanding these intricacies, we can better comprehend how they collaboratively mould our character and behavioural patterns. Such insight not only enriches our knowledge of the self but also offers clarity on the diverse factors that underpin our individual personalities.

The subsequent two sections will provide a concise exploration of the components of the human psyche, both from a psychological standpoint and from the perspective of the Arabic Quran. Given that this book is centred on depicting the human psyche within the Arabic Quran, this theme will serve as the primary anchor for our discourse. This dual examination aims to bridge contemporary psychological insights with the Quranic portrayal, ensuring a comprehensive understanding of the topic at hand.

Components of Human Psychology

Human psychology, at its core, seeks to understand the intricate interplay of various facets that constitute human behaviour and cognition. Cognitive processes, such as perception, memory, decision-making, and problem-solving, lay the foundation for understanding and interacting with the world of Cognitive psychology. *"Appleton-Century-Crofts"*, (Neisser, 1967). Emotions, ranging from happiness to sadness, anger to fear, are pivotal in influencing our reactions to external stimuli and can deeply impact our well-being *"The nature of emotion: Fundamental questions"*, (Ekman & Davidson, 1994). Social interactions and the need for belonging significantly shape our behaviour and thought processes, emphasising the importance of social context in psychological outcomes, *"The need to belong: Desire for interpersonal attachments as a fundamental human motivation. Psychological Bulletin"*, (Baumeister & Leary, 1995). Motivation drives our actions, providing purpose and direction to our endeavours, *"The "what" and "why" of goal pursuits: Human needs and the self-determination of behaviour. Psychological Inquiry"*, (Deci & Ryan, 2000). Additionally, the unconscious mind, as theorised by *"The unconscious"*, Freud (1915), operates below our level of awareness but can profoundly influence our behaviours and choices. Together, these components provide a comprehensive framework for understanding the multifaceted nature of human psychology.

Components of Human Psychology in Quran

The Quran elucidates several fundamental elements of human psychology. Among these are the intrinsic desires inherent in humanity, the vigour and resolve to manifest these desires into action, the cognitive capacity to conceptualise, cultivate, and refine thoughts and ideas, and the vast repository of memory that archives our experiences channelled through our sensory perceptions. An examination of these elements is facilitated through an exploration of pertinent Quranic verses.

4:1 O **Mankind** be cautious from your **Lord (Rabb)**. He has created you from a **single or one Psyche**. From that (One Psyche), he makes its **pair/spouse (Zauj)** and radiates/spreads/broadcasts from them many Rijal **(Men)** and Nisa **(Women)**. Be conscious of Allah to whom you consult and the **Womb..** Indeed, **Allah** is watchful of you.

16:72 Allah place for you all **pairs in your own Psyches**. And from your pairs made your sons and grandsons. And give you pure food. Still, they believe in falsehood. And cover/conceal the gifts of Allah.

32:13 And if we had willed, all **Psyches** given guidance. But the word from me will come into effect. I will surely fill Jahanum(Hell-fire) from **Jinn** and **Naas** altogether.

30:8 Do not they ponder in their **own Psyche** how we have created/evolved **Heavens and Earth** and whatever in between them with truth, for a known period. But majority of the agitated minds conceal the meeting with their Lord.

To analyse this verse, it is essential to understand the concepts of **Allah/Rab, Taqwa, Naas (mankind), Zauj (spouse), Rijal (man), Nisa (woman), Adam, Jinn and Insaan, Heaven and Earth etc.** Each of these concepts will be explored in their respective chapters within this book, except Allah/Rab, which merits a separate book dedicated to its understanding of the Arabic Quran. However, in the context of this book, Allah/Rab can be understood as the sacred inner consciousness inherent in every human being. While I will not delve into this concept in great detail here, I will touch upon it throughout the book to help readers grasp its significance.

Indeed, as we delve deeper into more Quranic verses if you still find yourself unsure about the translation of "Nafs" as psyche, I encourage you to apply the biblical concept of Adam and Eve whenever you encounter "Nafs" and its pair. This could help dispel any lingering doubts and expand your comprehension of the material under discussion. This process facilitates a more layered understanding, allowing you to compare and evaluate different perspectives.

Summary

In this chapter, the term "Nafs" from the Quran is examined, traditionally denoting the human soul or psyche. Dictionary definitions often equate the soul with the human mind, personality, or psyche. Contrary to prevalent religious assertions, there exists no empirical or logical evidence to suggest that the soul persists as a distinct entity after a physical death. Contemporary psychological research identifies several facets of the human psyche, including cognitive processes like perception, memory, decision-making, and problem-solving, as well as emotions. Correspondingly, Quran 4:1 alludes to various elements of a singular psyche, characterising them as the "pair of the psyche," encompassing terms like rijal/nisa, among others.

4

The Pair in Psyche

THE COMPONENTS OF HUMAN PSYCHE

The Zauj of Nafs

"Logistikon (Reason) is the rational, logical, and thoughtful part of the soul". Plato.

In the previous chapter, we explored the concept of Nafs or Psyche and how it is created as a pair. It is essential to delve into the Quranic perspective on the pair of the human psyche to gain a deeper understanding of the Quranic philosophy concerning human psychology and the workings of the mind.

Before we delve into the details of the psyche's pair, it is essential to note that this pair is an integral part of the psyche itself. As mentioned in Quranic verses like 4:1, the pair of the psyche is created from within the psyche, indicating that it is not something external to it. Additionally, it is crucial to understand that in the context of the Quran, the concept of creation does not solely refer to the physical creation of the world or human beings. As you progress through this book, you will better understand how the Quranic notion of creation pertains to the realisation of various aspects of human psychology, including psychological processes, emotions, and feelings. These processes arise and cease within the human mind instantly, as exemplified by the Quranic phrase "Be and it is" (Kun, Fa Yakun).

The term "Zauj" or pair, when mentioned with the Nafs-e-Wahid (Single Psyche), is often associated with Eve, who is the wife of Adam, in biblical traditions. However, it is essential to note that there is no specific mention of the pair or spouse being Eve in the Quran. This association with Eve is a concept borrowed and propagated in various translations, but it is not explicitly stated in the Quran.

To truly understand the Quranic context, we need to look beyond these borrowed concepts and focus on the meaning within the Quran. Through careful analysis of the Quranic text, we can better understand the intended message and the significance of the term "Zauj" with the Nafs-e-Wahid or Single Psyche.

Etymological and Lexical Analysis.

A noun and possessive pronoun. The noun is masculine and is in the accusative case (منصوب). The noun's triliteral root is zāy wāw jīm (ز و ج). The attached possessive pronoun is third person feminine singular.

- Arabic English Lexicon, by E.W. Lanes. Vol 3, Page 1265: Coupled, Paired, e.g. in marriage where souls get coupled or united with their fellows.
- The Hens Wehr Dictionary of Modern Arabic, by The Hans Wehr. Page 447: To pair, couple, join in pairs of couples, to double, germinate, to employ parallelism, to use in parallel construction.
- This word, with all its variations, is repeated 81 times in 72 verses in Quran.

In the religious context, it is commonly believed that God has created everything in pairs, typically understood as male and female. However, in the Quranic sense, the concept of a pair is not limited to male and female relationships. It encompasses a broader understanding that pairs can consist of active/passive or exposed/hidden processes, abilities, emotions, thoughts, and other psychological components.

In this Quranic perspective, a pair represents a harmonious association between two elements that complement each other and form a complete picture or process. The understanding of pairs in the Quran goes beyond the traditional sense of gender and explores the interplay of various psychological aspects.

As we delve into the verses surrounding this subject, we will gain further clarification and insight into the Quranic concept of pairs and their significance in understanding human psychology.

*36:36 Glory to him who have created (evolved) everything in pairs which this earth grows and **in their Psyches**, but they have no knowledge of it.*

In this verse, it is evident that there is a pair within our own psyche that we are unaware of. If the traditional interpretation associates this pair with Adam and Eve or physical male and female, it raises the question of why the verse states that there are pairs in the psyche of which we do not know. The reason is that we are unaware that a single psyche and its pair, which is also a part of the psyche, are the essence from which mankind is created. It is important to note that Adam himself is a product of the human psyche. We will explore this concept in later chapters to gain a deeper understanding.

Let's see another verse to clarify that it is not Adam and Eve that Quran is referring to.

*30:21 And from his signs that he has formed/created **pair in your psyche** so that you find tranquillity with them. He has placed between you affection and mercy. Within it is the signs/ayat for those who ponder/think carefully/reflect/consider.*

The pair of psyche created within us serves the purpose of finding inner peace and tranquillity when we consult with it. This process involves deep thinking and realisation within each individual. However, many people are unaware that engaging in deep thought, utilising one's intellect and mental energies with a positive mindset, can cleanse and purify one's psyche.

Traditionalists and literalists often interpret this deep thinking process as solely referring to sexual intercourse between physical male and female couples. They mistakenly believe that sexual gratification is what the above verse is referring to. However, the verse clearly states that the pair referred to is not a physical couple but the internal pair within the psyche (Nafs). It is through the process of careful contemplation and deep thinking that one can achieve the tranquillity and peace mentioned in the verse.

Quran does not discuss physical urges and desires such as sex, reproduction, hunger, and excretion. These are natural processes essential for the survival of any species, including humanity. Quran's message goes beyond these basic instincts and aims to convey more profound wisdom and guidance to human beings. Distortions and misinterpretations have unfortunately obscured the true message of the Quran, diverting attention away from its deep teachings.

*16:72 Allah place for you all **pairs in your own Psyches**. And from your pairs made your sons and grandsons. And give you pure food. Still, they believe in falsehood. And cover/conceal the gifts of Allah.*

To understand this verse, first, refer following verse.

6:20 Those to whom we have given the book, they recognise it as their own sons. Those who are in a loss with their psyche they will not believe/are not secure.

The book in the verse is not the physical Arabic Quran, as one does not recognise it as their offspring. Instead, it symbolises our internal book, composed of our thoughts, memories, and consciousness. If we introspect and close our eyes, we can access and read the contents of this book, which are the native thoughts, memories, feelings, and emotions stored within our own psyche. The recognition of this internal book is akin to recognising something familiar, like one's own offspring. This stems from the fact that the memories and experiences we've garnered over the years emanate directly from our own psyche. It signifies the deep connection between our conscious self and the contents of our psyche.

In verse 16:72, the same concept is discussed. The psyche and its pair, representing stored knowledge and memories, give rise to multiple thoughts. These thoughts are metaphorically depicted as the offspring or descendants of the psyche and its pair. Since the psyche and its pair are integral parts of the overall psyche itself, the offspring of a psychological process can only be thoughts. In the Quran, these thoughts are further referred to as thought communities or "Qaum" (which we will explore in subsequent chapters).

The working mind or psychology generates ideas through these thought processes, regardless of whether they are positive or negative. The Quran emphasises the process of purification (Zakah) and striving (Jihad) to condition the mind and enable the purification of these thought processes. This purification aims to transform these thoughts into positive and righteous manifestations, akin to the righteous children of the psyche and its pair.

The physical Quran in Arabic, with its chapters and verses, is a compilation of the ancient philosophy of the human psyche presented in written form. However, the actual book that is universally understood by all individuals, regardless of their language, race, traditions, or belief systems, is the one that resides within themselves. This inner book refers to the individual's consciousness, which contains the power of thoughts and energies. The Quran acts as an expression that aims to inspire and establish a connection between human beings and their inner book, encouraging them to explore and harness the potential of their own consciousness.

*7:189 It is he who has created you all from **Single Psyche** and place from it its pair so it can rest with it. When he(psyche) is overwhelmed, it carries a lightweight with it. When it gets heavy, they call Allah to conclude/complete it a proper (practical thought) so that we will be thankful.*

In this passage, the psychological process involving the pair of psyches is further explained. The impregnation of ideas and thoughts into the psyche represents a psychological process. The objective of every individual is to ensure that this process is completed most beneficially and validly. It is similar to how half-formed ideas can cause more harm than good. Therefore, any idea or thought that arises in the mind should be held within the psyche until it matures before it is acted upon. The maturation process involves consulting the sacred inner consciousness, gathering relevant facts and information to support and nurture the idea, and analysing its implementation's potential advantages and disadvantages. The idea or thought can reach maturity and benefit the individual through this process.

This psychological process is a part of our daily lives, where we generate thoughts, nurture them, and strive to express them in the most suitable, applicable, and valid manner. The objective is to derive personal benefits and achieve desired outcomes.

This process applies to any thought, idea, discussion, or mental activity, whether it is related to our personal or professional life. As the faculty that generates thoughts, the mind engages in careful analysis, internal brainstorming, and extensive contemplation. We consider all possible outcomes to the best of our abilities, drawing from our experiences, knowledge, and observations. Ultimately, we refine our thoughts into practical actions. When these actions lead to favourable outcomes, we experience a sense of mental satisfaction and peace.

Even setting aside the precise messages of the aforementioned verses, aren't these actions already embedded in our daily routines? Don't we routinely contemplate the pros and cons of every significant decision in our lives? Don't we seek pertinent information to validate or refute the choices we've made? Viewed through this lens, the Quran isn't introducing a novel concept. It's simply articulating common sense, which aligns with what objective introspection would reveal. This introspective essence is also central to the Quran's teachings.

The segment of the psyche we associate with wisdom is termed the 'pair' of the psyche. This counterpart remains concealed and can only be awakened and optimally utilised for our benefit through profound introspection. This process is alluded to in the aforementioned verses, which describe the ensuing feelings of affection and tranquillity.

The Quran describes the human psyche as having both exposed and hidden elements. These elements are assigned specific names or represented through characters as parables. The dwelling place of the psyche and its pair, as depicted in the Quran, is in the realm of the hidden or the unseen, beyond what can be perceived by our physical eyes.

43:70 Enter into the hidden garden (Jannah), you and your pair with delight.

The word "Jannah" in the Quran has a root word (J N N) which is also shared with "Jinn" or "Jinny" in English. This root word means being hidden or concealed, often associated with darkness or veiling. In the context of the human psyche and its pair, they can be seen as the software or programming within a person's mind, stored in their consciousness and memories. As intangible, they are not visible or touchable, hence the reference to residing in the hidden realm or Jannah. However, the reflection of one's psychology through their character or reputation is what becomes known and perceived in the world. This concept is also conveyed in the story of Adam and the Forbidden Tree, which will be further discussed in the chapter dedicated to it.

In scholarly contexts, the intrinsic duality of the psyche comprises an aggregation of thoughts and memories, be they affirmative or otherwise, amassed throughout one's lifespan. These latent recollections perennially coexist within us, sculpting the multifaceted dimensions of our psychological framework. Consequently, it becomes imperative to vigilantly monitor the material we permit to engrave upon our cognitive canvas. Such memories and thoughts operate as an integral dyad within our psychological construct. The harbouring of perturbing or negative memories is liable to induce psychological dissonance. Analogously, in the realm of interpersonal relationships, the anguish experienced by one partner invariably reverberates, affecting the equilibrium of the duo.

Summary

It is important to note that the Quran mentions a hidden companion or spouse for the psyche. While the traditional interpretation associates this with the story of Adam and Eve from Biblical traditions, the Quran does not explicitly refer to the pair of the psyche as Adam and Eve. Instead, the pair of the psyche or Nafs can be seen as two interconnected aspects of the same whole. One factor is outwardly expressed and known to the world, while the other remains hidden and unknown to others. Both parts are necessary and contribute to the complete picture of an individual's personality.

5

The Exposed and Hidden Components of Psychology

Mankind and Jinn

"All human beings have three lives: public, private, and secret." - *Gabriel García Márquez*

The conventional and literal renderings of the Quran have often fostered confusion and misconstrued, especially concerning the terms "Man" and "Jinn." One of the prevalent challenges lies in interpreting "Mankind," commonly presumed to represent all of humanity. Historically, this broad-brush assumption has empowered religious factions to enforce Quranic teachings onto vast swathes of the populace, assuming that the Quran's message is universally applicable. This notion, however, seems more reflective of the influence of Christian missionary movements rather than an unbiased understanding of the Arabic Quran. Therefore, it is essential to interrogate the context in which the Quran was written and clarify its subject matter to avoid such sweeping generalisations.

The traditional comprehension of Jinn in the Quran presents another quandary. It is often construed as alluding to invisible beings, distinct from humans yet possessing a physical reality. This belief in unseen entities is shared across various faith traditions. Yet, this interpretation has bred many issues, notably attributing psychological conditions to the physical possession by Jinn or similar unseen forces. This has subsequently spawned an array of exorcism practices within various religious groups. Furthermore, the propagation of beliefs in pious Jinn who are subjugated or commandeered by religious or cult leaders exacerbates deviation from the Quran's intended message. These misunderstandings and corresponding practices are significant obstacles to a sincere comprehension of the Quran's teachings.

Etymological and Lexical Analysis.

النَّاسِ (Naas) The noun is masculine plural and is in the genitive case (مجرور). The noun's triliteral root is nūn wāw sīn (ن و س). Together the segments form a preposition phrase known as jār wa majrūr (جار ومجرور).

الْإِنْسَانَ (Insaan) and الْإِنسَ (Inss) is a masculine noun and is in the accusative case (منصوب). The noun's triliteral root is hamza nūn sīn (أ ن س).

In the Quran, there are three words used to refer to human beings: "Naas," "Insaan," and "Inns." These words are often translated as "mankind" or "man" and are sometimes used interchangeably.

- Arabic English Lexicon, by E.W. Lanes. Vol 8, Page 2866: Naas, three letter root Arabic root is N W S. Moved to and fro; it was in a state of commotion; hanging down, it dangled, a form of commotion or agitation.
- The Hens Wehr Dictionary of Modern Arabic, by The Hans Wehr. Page 1184: Swing back and forth to dangle. Whereas the root word INSS and Insaan is INS
- Arabic English Lexicon, by E.W. Lanes. Vol 1, Page 113: Sociableness, Companionableness, Conversableness, Inclination to company, friendliness, amicableness, socialness, familiarity, cheerfulness, gladsomeness;
- The Hens Wehr Dictionary of Modern Arabic, by The Hans Wehr. Page 39: Intimate Friend, man, mankind, human race.

Jannah is a feminine noun, whereas Jinn is a masculine noun in the genitive case (مجرور). The noun's triliteral root is jīm nūn nūn (ج ن ن).

- Arabic English Lexicon, by E.W. Lanes. Vol 2, Page 462,463: Something Covered, Concealed, Hidden in Darkness.
- The Hens Wehr Dictionary of Modern Arabic, by The Hans Wehr. Page 164: To cover, hide, conceal, veal, be or become dark.

Intriguingly, the terms "Jinn" and "Jannah" in the Quran originate from the same root word. This may astonish those unfamiliar with the fact, although it is generally acknowledged among scholars. Regrettably, the imperative to interpret the Quran in a manner that adheres to conventional notions and historical associations has frequently caused such facts to be overlooked. This oversight has further contributed to a divergence from the actual, essential meaning embodied within the Quran's messages.

Man and Mankind

When understood in its root form, the word "Naas" in the Quran means swaying or oscillating like a pendulum. This can be interpreted as a representation of the human mind, which is in a constant state of seeking knowledge and understanding. Scholars have described it as an active and curious mind constantly striving to satisfy its thirst for knowledge. This interpretation aligns with the classical and modern understanding of the root word "Naas."

The root word "Insaan" or "Inss" suggests that it refers to the egocentric mind, which forms an individual's core identity. It is an integral part of human psychology and plays a significant role in shaping a person's character and interactions within their social circle. "Naas" and "Insaan" are aspects of human psychology that contribute to developing an individual's personality.

To simplify and understand the meanings, "Naas" can be seen as the restless or knowledge-seeking mind. In contrast, "Insaan" and "Inns" can be understood as the persona or character of an individual. Recognising that both states are part of our overall personality and originate from our psyche is crucial.

*18:54 We have explained in this Quran for **restless minds** from all examples/parables. But the **personality** disputes in majority of things.*

Significant verse, multiple points to note here.

1. It is important to note that both the terms "Naas" (restless mind) and "Insaan" (personality) are used in a single verse, highlighting their significance within the context of the Quran.
2. The verse emphasises that the Quran presents numerous examples and parables to address the restless minds of people. Still, despite this guidance, many individuals continue to dispute and engage in conflict. This suggests a constant struggle between the restless mind and the personality, which should ideally work in harmony to achieve inner peace.
3. The Quran emphasises that everything presented within its text is meant to serve as comprehensive examples and parables (as indicated by the word "Kullu"), meaning totally/entirely/everything/ultimately.

The innate evolutionary instinct of humans drives them to seek relationships with entities perceived as more powerful, providing a sense of confidence, security, and survival. This inclination has contributed to the creation of the concept of God. However, the Arabic Quran uses parables and examples symbolically rather than as literal accounts of miracles, personalities, events, or historical places. Such symbolism addresses the human desire for meaning, purpose, and connection to something beyond the physical realm.

The Quran utilises parables to impart deeper spiritual truths, encouraging introspection and reflection on the embedded messages. Recognising the symbolic nature of these teachings allows for an enriched understanding of the Quran's wisdom and guidance, elevating readers beyond mere literal interpretations.

*50:16 We have created the **Persona**, and we have the knowledge that his Psyche is in doubt/full of apprehensions/whisper/be anxious; we are closer to him than his jugular vein.*

The distinction between Insaan (Persona) and Psyche is indeed essential to understand. In the mentioned verse, the Quran highlights that God, as the Creator, is aware of the whispers or inner thoughts within the human psyche. The Insaan, or Persona, is formed by God from the Psyche, and God knows the intricacies and workings of the human psyche.

It is essential to recognise that the concept of God in the Quran is not separate or external from the human psyche. Instead, it emphasises the intimate connection between God and the human being. The verse that mentions God is closer than the jugular vein signifies the proximity and presence of God within every individual as part of their psyche. This understanding emphasises that God knows each individual's psyche's innermost thoughts, struggles, and desires.

By recognising this inherent connection, individuals are encouraged to cultivate a deep self-awareness, introspection, and spiritual development. They are reminded that God, as the sustainer and knower of their psyche, can provide guidance, solace, and understanding. This understanding offers a profound perspective on the relationship between the human psyche, the Insaan, and the divine presence within.

10:44 Indeed Allah do not do injustice to Naas, but Naas do it with their own Psyche.

The interaction between the agitated mind (Naas) and the developed personality (Insaan) plays a fundamental role in shaping our psyche and determining its equilibrium or disturbance. This is because our personality continually interacts with other individuals and daily situations, leading to a constant influx of stimuli that generates mental and emotional noise.

The verse underlines the fact that the state of our psyche is primarily affected by our actions and choices. These choices can yield positive or negative outcomes, contingent upon whether they promote peace, stability, and harmony within our psyche. When our choices are aligned with what brings internal calmness and tranquillity, we experience positivity in our lives. Conversely, when our choices are not in harmony with our psyche's needs for stability and peace, we may experience disturbances and discomfort.

Therefore, understanding our psyche's internal dynamics is essential to making informed and balanced decisions that enhance our overall well-being. This perspective encourages self-awareness and introspection as crucial tools for achieving a balanced and harmonious state of mind. Right and wrong in this context is not based on notions of sin and righteousness but instead on what disrupts or disturbs the psyche's stability, peace, and calm state

This understanding highlights the responsibility we have for our psychological well-being. It emphasises that we have the power to make choices that nurture and maintain a balanced and peaceful psyche. It also reminds us that the consequences of our actions, whether positive or negative, ultimately impact our inner state.

While Allah, as the sustainer and knower of our psyche, provides guidance and support, the verse emphasises that we, as individuals, have agency and accountability for the choices we make.

Analysis of Surah-e-Jinn (72) and Surah-e-Rahman (55)

The repeated mention of Jinn and Inns or Jinn and Personalities in the Arabic Quran invites us to delve deeper into their symbolic meaning rather than taking them as literal supernatural creatures. As we discussed earlier, the word Jinn has a root meaning of being hidden or concealed. This suggests that the concept of Jinn in the Quran represents the hidden aspects of our psyche or the unseen forces that influence our thoughts, emotions, and actions.

When the Quran associates Jinn with personalities or Inns, it signifies the inseparable connection between our psyche's hidden aspects and our personality's outward expression. It highlights that our characters are not solely shaped by what is visible or known to others but also by the hidden dynamics within our psyche.

Instead of getting caught up in irrational stories or literal interpretations, reflecting on the deeper symbolic meaning conveyed by these concepts in the Quran is essential. The emphasis is on understanding the interplay between our psyche's seen and unseen aspects and how they shape our behaviour and character.

By exploring the verses that mention Jinn and Inns or Jinn and Personalities, we can gain insights into the complexity of human nature and the forces that influence our thoughts, choices, and interactions. It encourages us to reflect on the hidden dimensions of ourselves and the importance of self-awareness in navigating our inner world.

In doing so, we can move beyond the limitations of literal

interpretations and grasp the profound psychological and spiritual teachings that the Quran seeks to convey.

*53:32 Those who avoid bigger offences and to become excessive except little, Indeed your Rabb has vast forgiveness. He knows when you have grown out of Earth and when you were **Jinn (covered up/concealed/hidden)** the inside your mothers womb. Do not justify/purify your Psyche; he knows who is cautious.*

If taken the literalist and traditionalist meanings, it means the unborn child in the mother's womb is referred to here as Jinn. But none of the translations of the Quran translated that you were Jinn in your mother's womb. Indeed, traditional concepts and interpretations can sometimes influence translations of religious texts. Translators may have their own biases or adhere to established interpretations, potentially leading to a deviation from the original intended meaning.

The mother's womb here is the part of the psyche referred to as the pair or Zauj of the psyche. That pair we have seen is also hidden, as it is part of human psychology, which is not usually exposed.

The Jinn and Inns mentioned in the Quran symbolise distinct aspects of the human psyche. The Inns represent the outward expression of one's personality, reflecting how individuals present themselves to the world and shape their reputation. On the other hand, the Jinns refers to the hidden depths of the conscious mind, where emotions, desires, and preferences are concealed, even from those close to us. This interpretation highlights the duality of the psyche, with one aspect being visible and the other remaining hidden, contributing to the complexity of human behaviour and experience.

It is essential to approach the Quran with an open mind and a willingness to delve beyond the surface meanings of the text. By doing so, we can better appreciate the profound psychological and spiritual wisdom embedded within its verses.

The literalist may point towards the translation of 15:26/27, where the creation of Man and Jinn has been described differently.

15:26 We certainly evolved the **Persona** *from jingling dredge prescription.*
15:27 And evolved **Jinn (the one which is hidden/concealed)** *previously with the opening of the light.*

The word "sumoom" is commonly translated as hot/scorching hence when it comes with Naar (the fire), which has the same root word as Noor (the light), the translation becomes scorching fire. At the same time, the same word was used in 7:40, where they translated Sumoom (or scorching) as the needle's opening or eye of the needle. This serves as another instance where translations of the same word in the Quran have been adapted to align with traditional viewpoints.

The persona, representing our personality's visible and audible aspects, is likened to jingling dredge or noisy mud in the Quran. This signifies that our persona can be loud and attention-seeking, creating a reputation that is evident to others. It is the part of our psyche we consciously project to the world, shaping how others perceive us.

On the other hand, the Jinn, representing the hidden aspects of our psyche, is compared to the opening of light or fire. This metaphor highlights the concealed nature of our inner thoughts, emotions, and desires. These hidden aspects of our personality are often kept private because we fear potential consequences or discomfort if they are to be exposed. While these hidden feelings can be positive and negative, they often lean towards the negative side.

By understanding the symbolism used in the Quran, we gain insights into the complexities of human nature and the various dimensions of our psyche. It reminds us to be mindful of the interplay between our visible persona and the hidden aspects of our being and their impact on our relationships and well-being.

*32:13 And if we had willed, all **Psyches** given guidance. But the word from me will come into effect. I will surely fill Jahanum(Hell-fire) from **Jinn(concealed/hidden) and Naas(agitated mind)** altogether.*

Notably, the verse initiates with a discussion on (Nafs) Psyche's guidance and concludes with Jinn and agitated minds or hidden thoughts being cast into the inferno. This progression within the verse serves to clarify much of the confusion around the concepts of Psyche, Jinn, and Man. If we consider Psyche, Jinn, and Man as literal physical entities, as done by literalists and traditionalists, we are left with a conundrum. Why, when a Psyche does not receive guidance, is it not the Psyche that is cast into the fire? Why do Jinn and Man, as separate entities, bear the punishment for Psyche's lack of guidance?

The answer lies in understanding that Jinn and the agitated mind are components of the Psyche. If the Psyche is not at peace, everything it generates, be it the manifested personality or concealed emotions, experiences distress, discomfort, and restlessness. These negative states of being are symbolically represented in the Quran as the torments of hellfire.

*6:130 O you assembly of **Jinn (the hidden ones) and Inns (exposed personalities)** did not there come to you **messengers among you**, relating my signs/ayats and warn you about the day of meeting? They will say we have witnessed/experienced this in our **psyche**. The worldly life has deceived them. So they are witnessed/experienced their own **psyche** that they have been covering/concealing.*

There are multiple elements in this verse to consider but to stay on topic; I want to direct the readers' attention to the following key points:

1. The verse tells us that messengers come to both Man and Jinn. From a literalist and traditionalist perspective, we know that messengers/prophets have come among Men. However, have we ever heard of any messengers who have emerged within the Jinn? It's important to understand that we can't argue that the same messenger came to both Jinn and Man, as the verse clearly states that the messenger came from among you. So, a messenger for Man should always be a Man, whereas a messenger for Jinn should always be a Jinn.
2. Once they (both Jinn and Man) realise this truth, they acknowledge that they have witnessed it in their Psyche. This implies that the messenger to Man and Jinn comes solely from the Psyche.
3. However, even after their realisation, they continue to veil or cover this truth within their Psyche.
4. The relationship between the Jinn/Man and the messengers is deeply tied to the Psyche.

This interpretation challenges traditional literalist views and introduces the concept that the messages and guidance we receive may not always come from external sources but can emerge within our Psyche. This reflects the profound wisdom and introspective nature of the Quran's teachings.

In the Quran, it is emphasised that messengers come to the psyche of individuals to deliver a specific message, warning, or news. Their role is to inspire and enlighten individuals through the essence or spirit of the ideas and thoughts they convey. This inspiration affects both the external, exposed personality of the person and the hidden, concealed aspects within the psyche.

The messenger's message resonates with the depths of the individual's consciousness, influencing their thoughts, beliefs, and actions. It could bring about a transformative impact on both the visible aspects of their personality and the hidden aspects within their psyche. This holistic approach recognises the interconnectedness of the conscious and subconscious elements of the human psyche.

By addressing the individual's exposed and hidden dimensions, messengers aim to guide them towards a higher understanding, moral conduct, and spiritual growth. The message is intended to evoke reflection, contemplation, and a shift in mindset and behaviour. It is a call to align one's conscious thoughts and actions with the deeper truths and principles conveyed by the messenger.

Thus, the messenger's influence extends beyond the surface level of a person's personality, reaching into the depths of their psyche to inspire and guide them towards a more righteous and conscious way of living.

This hidden companion of our personality, Jinn, is so crucial for understanding the Quranic philosophy of Human Psychology that two whole chapters in the Quran are dedicated to this subject. One chapter is mentioned as Surah-e-Jinn 72, whereas the other chapter is the realisation and teaching about this hidden companion called Surah-e-Rahman 55. Let us explore both chapters briefly here, with selected verses for more clarification.

> *72:1 Say, the inspiration comes towards me, that a band of Jinns listened Quran. They said we have heard an amazing Quran.*
> *72:2 Guide towards wisdom, we believe (come to security) with it, we will not associate anything/anyone the one and only Lord of ours (the system of consciousness)*

The whole chapter started with the statement that it is all inspiration. Whatever is now mentioned in this chapter was all God inspired to the Messenger. Inspiration itself is a psychological process that lets or compels a person to do something. Anyways Inspiration and Revelation are separate from the focus here.

The point is that Jinn listened to the Quran, and once they understood it, they realised how amazing it was. This understanding reveals to them God itself, clarifying all associations they make with God.

72:4 And that our foolish ones amongst us exaggerate about Allah.

Once the Quranic concepts of Allah and Rabb are understood, individuals often have a moment of profound realisation: that they have been exaggerating their understanding and portrayal of Allah. You may wonder, what does it mean to exaggerate about Allah?

The primary exaggeration lies in perceiving Allah as external to our psyche. Traditionally, religious teachings and interpretations place God outside us as a supernatural being separate from our existence. This externalisation of God is a distortion, an exaggeration. It can lead to a disconnect between the individual and the divine, creating a divide where one is not intended.

By contrast, the Quranic perspective implies a closer, more intrinsic relationship with Allah, the source of all our consciousness. Instead of picturing Allah as external, separate, and distant, we should comprehend Allah as the internal guiding force, the driving principle that resides within our psyche, shaping our consciousness and guiding our actions.

This understanding shifts the paradigm, bridging the gap between the individual and the divine. It implies a oneness, a connection, that challenges traditional religious interpretations and brings us closer to the true essence of the Quranic message. This introspective approach to understanding Allah can lead to a more profound and intimate relationship with the divine, fostering personal growth, self-realisation, and spiritual enlightenment.

72:5 And we always thought that Man and Jinn will never tell lies concerning Allah.

Again, the Jinn realise, and they now acknowledge Man or Inns (Persona), that they will never say anything about Allah, which is invalid. They realise it only after understanding the Quranic concept of Allah. Before it, whatever they knew about Allah was all lies and exaggerations.

72:6 And there were Rijal (self-sustaining dynamics) of Inns (Personalities) seek protection/shelter from the Rijal (self-sustaining dynamics) of Jinns (the hidden ones), then this has increased the burden on them.

The term "Rijal" or "Rajul" is traditionally translated as "Man" in conventional interpretations. However, a more insightful translation of "Rajul" points to the capacity within the psyche to act upon our instincts or desires. We will delve deeper into this concept in the chapter dedicated to "Man and Woman."

In this verse, the Quran points to the phenomenon where our self-sustaining personas or personalities take refuge in or are driven by our unseen emotions and impulses. This means our actions are often governed by these hidden instincts, bypassing rational thought and justification. When these impulsive actions do not yield the desired outcome, it leads to feelings of guilt, embarrassment, and regret, which weigh heavily on our psyche.

This verse encourages us to recognise the underlying motivations behind our actions. It invites us to bring our unconscious drives into conscious awareness, promoting mindfulness and intentionality in our behaviour. This increased self-awareness can free us from the cycle of impulsive actions and consequent emotional burdens, paving the way for more fulfilling and purposeful activities. It reinforces that we are not merely puppets to our hidden instincts but possess the capacity to understand and shape our actions mindfully.

72:8 And Indeed we seek to touch heavens and found that it is guarded/protected with intense obscurity.

The traditional interpretation of the word "Shuhoban" is often translated as "shooting stars" or "burning flames." However, according to Lane's lexicon (EWL, p.g. 1608), the term's literal meaning is closer to a "grey colour" or a mix of black and white where white is more dominant. Essentially, it signifies obscurity or lack of clarity, where neither black nor white (symbolising absolute truth or falsehood) is distinctly visible, resulting in an ambiguous grey area.

When applied to the interpretation of 'Heavens' or 'the Skies' (Asma), which symbolises higher consciousness, this suggests an ambiguous or obscured understanding. The seekers might have some notions and attempt to comprehend these higher states of consciousness. However, due to the complex nature of such concepts, their understanding remains shrouded in ambiguity, like the grey colour that "Shuhoban" denotes. Their comprehension of these higher truths must be clearer-cut and absolute but somewhat clouded and obscured.

72:9 And indeed we tried to understand/listened the principles/basis from it, but whoever tried to understand/listened these principles/basis they found it to be obscurity following them.

Upon engaging with the Quran and its profound teachings, the Jinn - symbolising the hidden aspects of our psyche - undergo an enlightening transformation. They realise their previous conceptions and beliefs about Allah were, in fact, exaggerations and fabrications. These skewed interpretations had been born out of their obscured understanding, much like viewing through a cloudy lens.

This revelation about the true nature of Allah, as depicted in the Quran, diverges significantly from their prior misconceptions. They become aware that the concept of Allah is deeply connected with higher states of consciousness, symbolised as Asma, the Skies, or the Heavens in the Quranic allegory. However, they acknowledge that their comprehension of these profound concepts was incomplete before encountering the Quran (the introspection).

Upon gaining this deeper understanding through the Quran, they marvel at its wisdom and clarity, referring to it as 'amazing.' Their new-found knowledge and insight prompt them to regard the Quran with awe, as its teachings resolve their previous ambiguities and provide them with a clearer, more accurate understanding of Allah. This epiphany demonstrates the transformative power of the Quran in guiding individuals towards truth and clarity.

55:1 Arrahman (The faculty of teaching within)
55:2 Who thought the Quran.

The Rahman is the inherited faculty of mind, which is associated with teaching the knowledge of the Quran.

55:3 Evolved Insaan (The Persona/Personality)

The Quranic concept of Insaan, or the fully realised human personality, begins its evolution or creation only after engaging with the teachings of the Quran. This understanding comes through introspection and objective self-analysis - a process of self-observation that gives us deeper insights into our own psychology. In other words, this Insaan or Personality only comes into being after gaining knowledge from the

Quran. This is a simple and logical concept for anyone approaching it without preconceived notions.

Before gaining this knowledge, even though emotions, feelings, and various psychological processes exist within all human beings, we remain largely unaware of them. Therefore, these facets of our psyche do not register in our consciousness meaningfully or recognisable. However, with knowledge and understanding - such as that imparted by the Quran - we can become self-aware, understanding not only how our minds work but also gaining insight into the psychology of others.

This awareness is vital in making the necessary efforts to condition the mind to achieve stability and peace. All of this is intertwined with knowledge - knowledge is the first step towards self-awareness. The Quran guides this journey, helping us evolve from a state of unawareness to becoming fully conscious, self-aware beings.

55:13 Then which of the Blessings of your Lord (Rahman the faculty of teaching) you both (Persona/Hidden One) will deny.

"So which of the favours of your Lord would you both deny?" is reiterated 31 times in Chapter 55 of the Quran, underscoring its profound importance. This recurring verse simultaneously addresses the 'Jinn' and 'Insaan' or the visible and hidden parts of the psyche. The reasoning behind this dual address is that whenever we experience anything - whether through reading, listening, or observing - both aspects of our psyche are invariably impacted.

Whether we acknowledge it or not, our outward persona and concealed emotions and feelings are perpetually influenced by our life experiences. Throughout this chapter, the Quran's repeated dual-addressing emphasises that we each have a hidden companion. The Quran urges us to remain vigilant and aware of this hidden aspect of ourselves. We must recognise and understand it to comprehend our emotional responses and those of others.

Achieving a clear understanding and awareness of both these facets of our personalities - the visible and the hidden - is crucial in cultivating higher emotional intelligence. Throughout this chapter, the Quran's persistent focus on these two aspects emphasises this critical message. The verse's constant repetition reminds us of the need to acknowledge and understand both our psyche's manifest and concealed dimensions in our quest for self-awareness and emotional intelligence.

Summary

The Mankind, as usually translated, is not the actual translation of the word (Inns/Insaan and Naas). The true meaning of these words is related to the Persona and the agitated mind every human possesses regardless of gender. Every personality also has a hidden companion of the conscious mind. When I say an invisible companion of the conscious mind, it means that this hidden feelings/emotions all work together with the active and conscious persona.

Understanding both aspects of the human psyche, as depicted in the Quran, is crucial for comprehending our personality and its impact on ourselves and others. By recognising and acknowledging the separate entities within our psyche, we gain insight into our weaknesses, emotions, and their influence on our lives.

Emotional intelligence plays a significant role in successful human relationships and effective leadership. Being aware of our own emotions and understanding and empathising with the feelings of others allows us to navigate interpersonal interactions with more excellent skill and sensitivity. We can strive for emotional balance and create healthier relationships by managing our hidden emotions and feelings.

The Quranic depiction of the separate entities within the psyche serves as a framework for understanding the complexities of human nature. It encourages introspection and self-awareness, essential for personal growth and development. Moreover, we can cultivate empathy and understanding in our interactions by comprehending these aspects of the human psyche, promoting harmony and positive connections.

By delving into understanding our psyche and its dynamics, we enhance our ability to navigate the complexities of human relationships and lead a more fulfilling and meaningful life.

Other components of human psychology are pointed out in Quran as the desires/urges and the self-sustaining dynamics or abilities to act on the desires and urges. The better we understand these abilities of our psychology, the better we will have control over them and can use them to achieve a stable and peaceful state of mind.

6

The Innate Desires and Determinations

The Nisa (Women) and Rijal (Man) of Quran

"The greatest thing in the world is to know how to belong to oneself." - Michel de Montaigne

The terms "Nisa" (women) and "Rijal" (men) are the two most misunderstood and misinterpreted subjects of the Quran. The interpretation of the terms "Nisa" (women) and "Rijal" (men) in the Quran has often been limited to the context of physical man and woman and their relationships and matters related to marriage, sexuality, and reproductive processes. However, this narrow and literalist understanding fails to capture the broader and more profound meaning intended by the Arabic Quran.

In the Quran, "Nisa" and "Rijal" do not refer to gender distinctions or physical aspects of human relationships. Instead, they symbolise broader archetypes and psychological dynamics within both men and women. These archetypes represent aspects of human nature, characteristics, and qualities that are not limited to gender but are universally relevant to all individuals.

The Quranic message goes beyond prescribing specific rules for marital relationships or intimate matters. It delves into human existence's spiritual, emotional, and psychological aspects. Self-awareness and observance of our psychology and understanding its various internal dynamics are the core subject of the Arabic Quran.

Reducing the profound teachings of the Quran to mere guidance on physical relationships distorts its intended message. The Quran aims to guide the holistic development of individuals, fostering a balanced and harmonious society and promoting spiritual growth and moral excellence.

By recognising the symbolic nature of the terms "Nisa" and "Rijal" and understanding their broader significance, we can approach the Quran with a deeper appreciation for its wisdom and guidance. It encourages us to reflect on our qualities, behaviours, and relationships, striving for personal growth, moral conduct, and the betterment of society.

The subject of the Arabic Quran is Human Psychology. The Quran uses parables' life-like characters to explain human psychology, and the Quran repeatedly mentions that everything in Quran is examples and parables. It is our choice how we want to take these parables. We can take them in their true sense as all parables/examples in their entirety (18:54) or as literals and associate the fabricated stories with them. **Just think.**

Etymological and Lexical Analysis.

The word Rijaal/Rajul is commonly translated as Man. Rijaal is an indefinite masculine plural noun and is in the accusative case (منصوب). The noun's triliteral root is rā jīm lām (ر ج ل).

- Arabic English Lexicon, by E.W. Lanes. Vol 8, Page 1043: To went on his feet, strong to walk or go on to foot, went on this legs or feet to accomplish the object of his wants.
- The Hens Wehr Dictionary of Modern Arabic, by The Hans Wehr. Page 381: To march, to get off, to go on foot, going on foot, walking.

The words Rijal and Rajul, derived from the root word R J L, represent the innate capacity within the human psyche to act upon desires and urges. This self-determination is crucial for fulfilling the desires and urges of the psyche. Without this capacity, unfulfilled desires can lead to psychological distress, such as depression and anxiety. In the context of the Quran, Rijal refers to the aspect of the human psyche that interacts with Nisa (women). The Quran emphasises the importance of achieving harmony and balance between these two forces, represented through the concept of Nikah (merging) in the Quran.

The term "Nisa" is typically translated as "Women." Structurally, "Nisa" is a feminine plural noun in the accusative case (منصوب). It stems from the triliteral root nūn sīn wāw (ن س و). Yet, there exists another root in the Arabic lexicon, (N S A) or (ن س ا), which has been largely overlooked in translations related to "Nisa."

- Arabic English Lexicon, by E.W. Lanes. Vol 8, Page 3033: Forgotten, It was forgotten by degrees.
- Nisa, three letter root traditional Arabic root is (N S A) or (ن س ا).
- Arabic English Lexicon, by E.W. Lanes. Vol 8, Page 2785: Urges, Desires, Drove.

The word Nisa, used for "woman," has two root words in Arabic dictionaries, namely N S W (Naso) and N S A (Nisa). Somehow, almost all of the translators of the Arabic Quran have chosen the root N S W for Nisa, which means "forgetful", and nearly all of them have entirely ignored the root NSA for Nisa, which means "innate urges and desires". In my analysis, such tendencies in Quranic translation reflect a pervasive, historically rooted bias in religious interpretations. Regrettably, historical religious viewpoints have often depicted women as subordinate to men, commoditising them for male pleasure and designating them as incentives in diverse religious customs. This is not limited to a specific religion but has been observed in most religious traditions. Challenging and overcoming such discriminatory and derogatory beliefs and practices towards women propagated by organised religions and traditions is necessary.

This translation has created a domino effect by the incorrect translations of other words which are related to Nisa in the Quran, for example, but not limited to Menstruation, Pregnancy, Nikah/Marriage/Divorce, Orphans, Mamalakat (bondwoman/bondmaid/concubines) and so on.

Again, why all this distortion and corruption with translations have been done is different from the subject and focus of this book. Hence, I must leave it here and the reader's judgment. Furthermore, we will explore the terms "Nisa" (Woman) and "Rijal" (Man) within the framework of this text and their connections to human psychology (Nafs). The comprehensive examination of "Nisa" (woman) and its associated themes would warrant a dedicated volume. I anticipate addressing this in a subsequent work.

I consider physical Men and Women equal, having the same psychological processes. The physical appearance and biological differences do not mean that females are any less human than males or psychologically less able than men. Indeed, to use the root word for 'NISA' in a manner that demeans women is not just unjust towards women, but it also contradicts the psychological wisdom and philosophy outlined in the Quran. The Quran, in its essence, promotes understanding, equality, and respect for all individuals, regardless of gender or sexual orientation. Thus, misinterpreting or misusing its teachings to belittle or undermine any particular group, especially women, contradicts its core principles and teachings. It is critical to interpret and understand the Quran in its true essence, valuing its guidance for personal growth, respect, and understanding for all humankind.

Hence, I took the meaning of the root word N S A (ن س ا), which means innate Urges/Desires/Drives. This meaning is closer to human psychology and overall Quranic theme and philosophy.

Nisa is desire, impulse, a wish that exists in every human psyche; it is a fundamental part of the human thought process. It evolves in humans from basic urges like food, fear and reproduction to more creative and conscious desires which shape this world. This evolution of Nisa in human consciousness differentiates us from other species.

The Women and Men

Let's consider the following verse again and expand its understanding and the link with human psychology (i.e., Nafs).

*4:1 O **Restless Minds** be cautious from your **Lord (Rabb)**. He has created you from **single or one Psyche**. From that (One Psyche) he creates its **pair/spouse** (Zauj) and radiate/spread/broadcast from them many Rijal **(builtin/innate determination)** and Nisa **(Urges)**. Be conscious of Allah to whom you consult and the **Womb** (self-impregnation). Indeed, **Allah** is watchful of you.*

The restless minds have been addressed in the above verse, and they are made to realise that they were created/evolved out of a single psyche and from its pair. And from it broadcasted/spread many desires/urges and self-determination. The desires and the ability within the psyche to act on those desires make things happen in our daily lives. It is a continuous process within psychology; we all have desires/urges (Nisa) and abilities to act (Rijal) on those desires/urges (Nisa). Without this self-determination within us, the desire can never be fulfilled or never come into reality. Now, it is essential to understand that we cannot act for all urges/desires; similarly, not for all determinations, we have strong, available urges/desires. Sometimes, things happen, or actions are taken in our lives without any strong urge, or sometimes, we have solid urges/desires but cannot find enough encouragement or motivation to act upon them because of a lack of determination.

*2:49 And when We saved you from the Pharaoh's folk, who were afflicting you with dreadful torment, slaying your sons and keep you **Urges** alive: that was a tremendous trial from your Lord.*

This is precisely what the people of Pharaoh did; they slaughtered the determination/sons or masculine ability or self-determination within us to act on desires, which leave urges/wishes alive without the hope of ever getting into reality. This has been referred to in the Quran as the most significant psychological pain and a trial for anyone. Imagine you cannot fulfil any of your desires. The human mind has evolved to have multiple desires/urges, which are responsible for all the creativity and development in one's life or collectively for humanity. Switching off the ability to act on desires will surely be distressful for anyone.

17:64 And incite whoever you can among them with your voice (whisper) and import them with your thoughts and **determinations (Rijal)** *and become an associate in their wealth and their offspring and promise them. But Satan does not promise them except delusion.*

The above verse clarifies that thoughts and determination are the weapons of Satan/Devil, which he uses for false promises through his whispers. Through this whisper, the Devil corrupts the thought process by raising false hopes and unrealistic dreams. The inner determination is related to thoughts; hence, Devilish thought processes can affect it.

A delicate balance between the two is necessary to maintain the psyche. We all have multiple desires/urges and determinations to act upon them. However, any imbalance between the two can cause a painful experience for the human psyche. Hence, a Nikah (merge) between the two has been prescribed, a state where desires are fully matured and have full support from our inner self-determination so that they can be fulfilled for the satisfaction of our psyche. Both Nisa and Rijal are the forces within the Psyche. They cannot live without each other, or any imbalance can create multiple psychological issues, for instance, anxiety disorder, depression, Compulsive Obsessive Disorder etc.

Returning to verse 4:1, it emphasises that every individual psyche contains multiple urges and self-driven dynamics. Therefore, it is crucial to understand these internal forces to regulate them effectively. The verse also highlights the importance of remaining vigilant, aware, and cautious of the entire consciousness system, symbolised by Allah/Rabb, the ever-watchful presence within our psyche. This divine presence records our thoughts, desires, and knowledge as memories. As we delve deeper, we will comprehend the significance of guarding what enters our psyche.

Our life experiences, learnings, and knowledge are stored within these memories, ultimately shaping our individual persona and personality. Moreover, these memories are the underlying cause of our various mental states, such as happiness, sadness, depression, and anxiety. Prolonged and unchecked negative mental states can severely affect our physical well-being, potentially giving rise to various medical conditions.

Verse 4:3, often interpreted in the context of polygyny, can be comprehended from an intriguing psychological perspective when expanded to incorporate broader interpretations. The term "Nikkah" - traditionally understood as marriage represents committing to a particular course of action or forming a deep bond with an aspiration or ambition.

In this light, the verse could be perceived as a profound advisory principle regarding managing various robust desires or ambitions. It suggests that when an individual harbours multiple intense desires (analogous to 'wives' in conventional interpretations) and is confident in their capacity to pursue all of them simultaneously without compromising any, they are free to engage in such multi-faceted endeavours. This understanding could apply to various life facets, such as juggling multifarious projects, nurturing divergent interests, or managing different roles effectively.

Nevertheless, the verse provides a counterbalancing caution. If one doubts their capability to manage all desires or ambitions simultaneously justly, it would be prudent to concentrate on a single aspiration at a time. This ensures complete focus and dedicated resources, mitigating the risk of becoming overwhelmed or failing to fulfil the objectives.

Summary

Nisa (innate urges/desires) and Rijal (innate self-determination) are significant forces within human consciousness and part of our psyche. These elements play a crucial role in distinguishing us from other species. When translated into ideas and thoughts, our urges and desires have the power to shape the world around us. We can act upon these urges and desires through our innate self-determination, transforming them into reality. Through this process, human beings have brought about various developments and achievements throughout history.

Maintaining a delicate balance between the forces of Nisa (innate urges/desires) and Rijal (innate self-determination) within the mind is crucial. It is essential to be vigilant and mindful of these inner urges and our level of self-determination. Any imbalance between these two forces can lead to the emergence of various psychological disorders. By being aware of our desires and exercising self-control and self-awareness, we can strive for a healthier and more balanced psychological state.

7

Elevated and Base Consciousness

The Heavens and the Earth

"The key to growth is the introduction of higher dimensions of consciousness into our awareness." - Lao Tzu

This chapter examines several concepts central to a comprehensive understanding of the Quran, primarily focusing on whether the scripture refers to the planet Earth and the physical heavens. The inquiry necessitates contemplating whether a tangible manifestation of heavens or skies exists and, if not, evaluating the reasonableness of translating the Arabic term "Al-Ard" to signify 'planet Earth'.

The act of creation, involving the heavens or skies and the earth, attributed to God, is a widely accepted notion cutting across diverse belief systems. The Quran, too, is replete with verses referencing the earth and skies, further delving into their genesis. However, a close reading of the prevailing translations and interpretations reveals a level of preconception attached to these two terms. These notions have been unvaryingly replicated across translations and commentaries, with little effort to engage with their actual Quranic contexts. This chapter aims to stimulate thought and foster understanding by reevaluating these concepts within the original framework of the Quranic text.

> 51:20 *And in Earth, there are signs for those who trust.*
> 51:21 *And in your own psyche, don't you see?*

There are signs on Earth for those who trust and signs within your psyche, don't you see? What is the connection of signs in Earth and sings in the psyche?? Just think.

> 45:22 *Allah has evolved/created Heavens and Earth with truth, and every psyche will be compensated with what they earned, and none of them will be kept in darkness/wronged/oppressed.*

Consider the intricate link between the creation of the Heavens (Samawat) and Earth and that of the Psyche (Nafs). Contemplate this profound association and let it resonate with your understanding.

> 30:8 *Do not they ponder in their own Psyche how we have created/evolved Heavens and Earth and whatever in between them with truth, for a known period. But majority of the agitated minds conceal the meeting with their Lord.*

This chapter seeks to explore and elucidate the meanings, significance, and relationships embedded within the concepts of the Heavens and the Earth as presented in the Quran in connection with our own psyche. The Heavens and the Earth bear signs, evidence or manifestations of realities as recognised by those who reflect and ponder upon them. But what are these signs and facts, and how can they be understood?

The Heavens and the Earth are not merely physical entities but may represent multifaceted layers of understanding and insight. Their true importance may not be limited to their roles as components of our physical universe. Still, it could extend to their positions as metaphors and symbols within a spiritual, moral, or psychological context.

Furthermore, the relationship between these concepts and the psyche is profoundly significant. An exploration of one's psyche, of one's introspection and self-awareness, could serve as a mirror reflecting these external realities, thus facilitating a deeper understanding of the use and purpose of the Heavens and the Earth in the Arabic Quran.

The Quran encourages its readers to ponder upon their selves - to observe, question, and reflect upon their personal experiences and inner realities - to comprehend the profound intricacies of its own psychology. Why is this introspective journey essential? Our personal experiences, thoughts, emotions, and perceptions can offer unique insights into the intricate interplay of the Heavens and the Earth within, enriching our understanding of our own consciousness.

64:3 Created Heavens and Earth with truth and have given you the Shape and made your shape beautiful.

Created Heavens and Earth with truth and given you the Shape. Again, what is the relationship between Heaven and Earth's creation with our shape/picture/image? Immediately after the creation of Heavens and Earth (i.e. Samavat and Al-Ard), he formed and perfected us. It is a clear sign that Heaven and Earth have a direct relationship with the shape and form of ours. So, in the Quranic context, heaven and earth are part of Human psychology.

Following the creation of the Heavens and the Earth, represented by the Arabic words "Samavat" and "Al-Ard," the Quran expounds on our human forms' intricate and deliberate design. This sequential exposition may hint at a substantial correlation between the creation of these entities and our configuration or shape.

From a Quranic perspective, the link between the creation of the Heavens and the Earth and our formation could transcend physicality, extending into the realm of human psychology. These celestial (Samavat/higher/altitude) and terrestrial (Al-Ard/lower) elements thus symbolise integral aspects of our human psyche. Their existence could mirror our psychological components, representing various facets of our cognitive, emotional, and spiritual configuration.

The Quran posits an enriching perspective that encourages introspection and self-understanding by suggesting that the Heavens and the Earth are components of our psychological makeup. It invites us to seek within ourselves these signs encapsulated in the macrocosm of the Heavens and the Earth, ultimately fostering a profound comprehension of our own psychologies and multiple levels of awareness.

64: 4 He know what is there in Heavens and Earth, and have the knowledge what you conceal and reveal. And Allah knows of what personality hides.

He knows what is there in Earth and Heavens and what you reveal or conceal. He knows what personality hides. What is the relationship and importance of what a person hides within himself and what is there in Earth and Heaven?

The preceding passages from the Quran underscore a profound and recurring correlation between the human psyche and the Earth ("Al-Ard") and the Heavens ("Samawat"). The text repeatedly invites readers to contemplate this connection, challenging them to derive insight and understanding from their reflections.

Yet, this invitation has often been interpreted by religious scholars to encourage exploration of the external universe. These scholars suggest that the marvels of creation observable in the world around us testify to the existence of a divine entity responsible for these intricacies. This interpretation encourages acceptance of a transcendental God, albeit unseen, through appreciation of the grandeur of His creations.

Etymological and Lexical Analysis.

Samawat, is a feminine plural noun and is in the genitive case (مجرور). The noun's triliteral root is sīn mīm wāw (س م و). Asma, is a masculine plural noun and is in the nominative case (مرفوع). The noun's triliteral root is sīn mīm wāw (س م و).

- Arabic English Lexicon, by E.W. Lanes. Vol 4, Page 1433: High, lofty, raised, uplifted, exalted or elevated.
- Arabic English Lexicon, by E.W. Lanes. Vol 4, Page 1433: High, lofty, raised, uplifted, exalted or elevated.

Ard, The noun is feminine and is in the genitive case (مجرور). The noun's triliteral root is hamza rā ḍād (أ ر ض).

- Arabic English Lexicon, by E.W. Lanes. Vol 1, Page 47, 48: Lowly, the ground means the surface of the earth on which we tread and sit and lie. And the floor without signifying a land or country.
- The Hens Wehr Dictionary of Modern Arabic, by The Hans Wehr. Page 17: land, country, region, area, terrain, ground, the base.

A crucial point to comprehend in this discussion is the shared three-letter root found in the Arabic words "Asma" or "Ism" and "Samavat." Despite any variations, these terms retain a shared semantic essence. This observation is particularly relevant when considering the Quranic passage 2:31, where it's described that the Lord taught "Asma" to Adam.

While the traditional interpretation of "Asma" in this context tends to lean towards a literal understanding, such as names or labels of all things, a more nuanced examination might yield an alternative perspective. Instead of adhering strictly to the traditional narrative, one could interpret this teaching of "Asma" to Adam as the divine awakening or enlightening of Adam's higher or elevated consciousness.

This interpretation posits that, through the teaching of "Asma," Adam was endowed with a heightened awareness and cognitive ability, enriching his understanding of himself and his psychology. This notion aligns with the recurrent theme of introspection in the Quran and further underscores the symbiotic relationship between Heavens and Earth (i.e. "Samavat" and "Al-Ard") and internal consciousness.

The Quran portrays the Heavens and the Earth as having distinct yet interconnected roles within human psychology. Traditional interpretations often suggest that these references in the Quran encourage people to recognise the power of God through observing the natural world, like the stars in the sky or the diversity of life on Earth.

On the other hand, scientists studying these same elements have developed theories like Evolution and the Big Bang, suggesting that the universe can exist and evolve without direct intervention from a supernatural being. This raises the question: does the Quran want us to focus solely on the physical world and universe? The answer is no.

It's important to remember that the Quran, like other religious texts, isn't meant to be a science textbook. Its primary purpose is to guide humans toward self-awareness and spiritual growth. Trying to find scientific facts in the Quran or other religious books to prove their divine origin might not be very productive. The primary goal of the Arabic Quran and other similar ancient texts goes beyond explaining the physical world; it aims to provide psychological and spiritual guidance, helping us understand ourselves.

When viewed holistically, the Quranic discourse articulates a thematic emphasis on human psychology rather than a literal interpretation of physical elements like Earth and the Heavens ("Samawat"). The Quran's verses and parables often serve as metaphors and symbols, revealing profound insights into the human psyche when deciphered. Therefore, a comprehensive understanding of these concepts necessitates an exploration of their lexical meanings, their Quranic context, and their alignment with the overarching theme of the scripture.

While the literal translation of 'Heavens' and 'Earth' may refer to regions of higher and lower altitudes relative to each other, their portrayal in the Quran often appears in conjunction with references to the human psyche. Following the creation of the Heavens and the Earth, verses frequently emphasise introspection and caution against plunging one's psyche into darkness or oppression, underscoring the significance of self-awareness and emotional well-being.

The Quranic narrative seems less concerned with explicit elaborations on physical creation processes, celestial bodies, human relationships, or jurisprudence. Instead, it places a greater emphasis on exploring the facets of human psychology and its intricate mechanisms.

Civil and marital relations, administrative procedures, and legal systems emerge from collective human endeavours, necessitating a balanced and well-functioning psychology. These societal constructs, shaped by human wisdom and experience, evolve and improve over time, reflecting the dynamism of human societies.

Such human life elements, often contingent on the specific cultural, social, and historical contexts, may not require direct divine intervention. Instead, they represent human resilience, adaptability, and ingenuity. In this perspective, the Quran provides a spiritual and psychological framework that aids individuals in navigating these constructs while fostering personal growth, self-understanding, and ethical behaviour.

The Quranic Context of Heavens and Earth.

30:8 Do they not reflect in their own soul/psyche/Nafs? Not but for just ends and for a term appointed, did Allah create the heavens and the earth, and all between them: yet are there truly many among men who deny the meeting with their Lord!

The Quranic verse in question invites individuals to reflect inwardly on their psyche to comprehend the creation of the Heavens and the Earth. This connection between the Heavens, the Earth, and the psyche might initially appear enigmatic, prompting the question: why does the Quran encourage this introspective exploration?

The answer may lie within the complex structure of human consciousness. In Quranic discourse, consciousness might be conceptualised as possessing various strata or degrees of awareness, which can be broadly categorised as elevated and base consciousness. This spectrum of awareness is at the heart of self-reflection, wherein we recognise and observe the diverse levels of our consciousness.

The Heavens and the Earth symbolise these different stages of consciousness. By prompting introspection, the Quran may guide readers to navigate their mental landscapes, helping them comprehend the different levels of consciousness represented metaphorically by the creation of the Heavens (elevated consciousness) and the Earth (base or base consciousness). This introspective journey fosters self-awareness and self-understanding, integral to personal growth and spiritual development.

The Elevated Consciousness

Elevated consciousness, in the Quranic context, can be viewed as the wellspring of our intellectual capacities. It's akin to an inner archive that meticulously records our experiences and lessons learned through our life journey. When accessed and utilised correctly, this reservoir of wisdom becomes a powerful resource.

According to Quranic teachings, harnessing the potential of this higher consciousness can unlock the path to ultimate success. This success is not merely defined by materialistic achievements but rather by attaining inner peace, tranquillity, and calmness. This higher state of being encourages individuals to lead a more enlightened and fulfilled life, contributing positively to their personal development and the welfare of their communities.

The Quran does use metaphors and symbolic language to convey deeper meanings and concepts. The term "As-Samawat" (the heavens or skies) is used in the Quran to represent the higher realms or levels of awareness, including the realm of unbiased reasoning, wisdom, intellect, knowledge and consciousness.

Indeed, according to the Quranic perspective, higher consciousness is positioned as the nexus of human intellect. This higher consciousness is a wellspring of wisdom and enlightenment, free from emotional biases. It operates based on rationale and reasoning, providing a clear, objective standpoint to understand and navigate our experiences. This cognitive realm is vital in guiding individuals towards well-informed decisions, fostering personal growth, and stimulating the pursuit of knowledge and understanding.

There are multiple layers and levels of consciousness a man is made up of. God resides at the highest level of consciousness within the human psyche 2:29, 2:255. Regarding the concept of revelations coming from the higher consciousness, it is essential to understand that the Quran uses metaphorical language to describe the guidance and wisdom received from Allah from higher consciousness. The Quran often uses the metaphor of rain or water to represent divine knowledge and guidance that cleanses and purifies the human soul 8:11.

Symbolises the revelation of divine guidance that brings clarity, peace, and purification to the human psyche. The reference to water or rain represents the transformative power of divine knowledge and guidance in removing wrong ideologies and negative influences the Satan and Pharos within our psyche.

It is essential to approach the interpretation of Quranic metaphors with a balanced understanding, considering the broader context and teachings of the Quran.

29:43 And such are the Parables We set forth for mankind (Naas), but only those understand them who have knowledge.

39:27 We have put forth for men (Naas), in this Qur'an every kind of Parable, in order that they may receive admonition.

17:89 And We have explained to man (Naas), in this Qur'an, every kind of similitude: yet the greater part of men (Naas) refuse (to receive it) except with ingratitude!

18:54 We have explained in detail in this Qur'an, for the benefit of mankind

(Naas), every kind of similitude (parables): but man (Ins) is, in most things, contentious.

30:58 verily We have propounded for men (Naas), in this Qur'an every kind of Parable: But if thou bring to them any Sign, the Unbelievers are sure to say, "Ye do nothing but talk vanities."

The use of metaphors (29:43, 39:27, 17:89, 18:54, 30:58) is intended to convey deeper spiritual truths and insights, and it is essential to strive for a comprehensive understanding of the Quranic message rather than relying solely on literal translations.

The Base Consciousness

The term Al-Ard is metaphorically used in the Quran to represent the lower or base consciousness within the human psyche. It is the stage where the whole drama of human life plays out. This is where all characters, emotions, feelings, experiences, situations, events, actions, reactions, choices, etc., actually occur or exist. The base consciousness is associated with the materialistic aspects of human existence, including lower desires, worldly pursuits, and the potential for corruption and conflict.

The Quran encourages individuals to rise above the base consciousness and its fleeting pleasures, recognising the ultimate purpose. It cautions against becoming rebellious within the sacred inner base consciousness, as it can lead to the destruction of one's soul or psychological disturbance.

The Quran emphasises the need to transcend the base consciousness and strive for higher awareness and spirituality. It urges individuals to overcome the temptations and conflicts associated with the base consciousness, seeking guidance from the higher consciousness or ultimately returning to God (the source of wisdom and intellect in your higher consciousness).

2:284 Whatever is in Heaven and Earth belongs to Allah and whatever you hide in your Psyche. He will hold you accountable for it. Then he will forgive and punish whoever he wills. And Allah have full control over everything.

In the Quranic perspective, higher consciousness is depicted as the nucleus of human intellect. This realm of consciousness is characterised by its capacity for enlightenment and wisdom. Remarkably, it operates beyond emotional biases, anchoring itself in rationality and reasoning. Thus, this form of consciousness provides a clear, unclouded lens through which individuals can perceive reality and make discerning decisions, fostering a more balanced and enlightened existence.

On the other hand, the base consciousness, represented by the Earth ("Ard"), is the realm of human emotions, ego, and personality. In this 'Earth', the human life drama, with its diverse experiences, feelings, and interactions, unfolds and plays out.

This perspective emphasises the symbiotic relationship between elevated and base consciousness within individuals. The path to personal growth and enlightenment, as per Quranic guidance, involves navigating these two realms of consciousness and finding balance, all while operating within the broader sacred inner consciousness established by Allah.

45:22 Allah has created Elevated Consciousness (Heavens) and base consciousness (Earth) with Truth. So that every Psyche will be compensated and no injustice will be done.

Indeed, understanding the correlation between the Heavens and the Earth with the human psyche is pivotal. When the Quran declares that the Heavens and Earth were created with truth, it may refer to the reality of consciousness. This consciousness — which differentiates humans from other species, elevating our capacities for thought, reflection, and comprehension — is a core element of the Quranic message.

In essence, the Quran provides a framework encouraging individuals to embark on introspective journeys, where they access their higher consciousness and discern moral and ethical guidelines. It emphasises the significance of individual responsibility and rational thinking in cultivating moral behaviour and ethical decisions, suggesting that the understanding of morality is intricately intertwined with self-awareness and intellectual growth.

42:11 *Natured higher Consciousness (heavens) and the base consciousness (earth), and created pairs within your own Psyche and in the comforts/gifts. This is how he multiplies you. There is no example like him; he is the audio-visual faculty.*

Before we delve into this verse, let us see another verse,

30:30 *Establish/Concentrate your personality for the obedience (Deen) in the right tendency (Hanif). The nature of Allah is on which the nature of Naas (agitated mind) is based on. There is no changes in what has evolved by Allah. This is the regulated/ordered (Qayyam) obligation/indebted (deen) , but majority of agitated minds (Naas) have no knowledge.*

In the Quranic context, when it's stated that mankind (or the "agitated or restless mind") has been created in Allah's nature, it refers to the inherent qualities and characteristics that humans share with Allah's nature. This isn't to say that humans are divine, but instead that they possess a spark of attributes, especially in terms of consciousness and the potential for wisdom and understanding. Verse 30:30 in the Quran further highlights this notion, stating that this is an ordered obligation upon all "Naas" (agitated minds), even though many may be unaware of this profound truth.

Several socio-religious aphorisms and proverbs, such as "Man is created in the image of God," "The Kingdom of God is inside you," or "God lives in every heart, so don't break the hearts," echo this idea. They hint at the divinity inherent in human consciousness and the intimate connection between the Divine and human beings.

However, a clear understanding and acceptance of the concept that divine force resides within our consciousness is uncommon. While some individuals comprehend this profound truth and articulate it through these sayings and proverbs, they represent a minority. Many are hesitant to reject outright the idea of physical gods and man-made religions in favour of recognising human consciousness as the actual miracle of nature. However, the transformative potential of embracing this truth could be immense regarding personal growth, ethical behaviour, and developing a more compassionate and understanding society.

Returning to verse 42:11 in the Quran, the text suggests that the Heavens and the Earth share characteristics or features with human psychology and its counterpart. This interpretation is not aligned with the traditional, literal understanding but instead conveys that the Heavens and the Earth, in the Quranic context, are symbolic aspects of human psychology. Verse 45:13 mentions that everything that exists between the "Heavens" and the "Earth" - interpreted here as the higher and lower levels of consciousness - has been made subservient, serviceable, or subject to control (Sakkhar). This indicates the dominance or subjugation of all elements within the human consciousness. Furthermore, this verse emphasises that signs or signals are present within this state for those who reflect or introspect, further suggesting the importance of self-awareness and understanding of one's inner psyche.

In this light, the Heavens and the Earth may symbolise the dualistic nature of our psyche, with "Heavens" representing the higher aspects of consciousness and intellect and the "Earth" embodying the lower, more tangible aspects of human experience and emotion.

This interpretative approach underscores the Quran's focus on understanding the self and the inner workings of the human mind as a pathway to spiritual enlightenment and ethical behaviour rather than offering a literal description of the physical world. Such an understanding promotes introspection and personal growth, which aligns with the broader Quranic aim of fostering moral, ethical individuals.

The Human Consciousness

Indeed, human consciousness remains a complex and fascinating topic of discussion amongst psychologists, philosophers, and scientists. While a universally agreed-upon definition is elusive, the common thread across various discourses is that consciousness is often described as an awareness of one's internal and external existence.

This awareness extends beyond mere sensory perception and physical experiences. It encapsulates a higher level of cognition, including self-awareness, understanding one's place within the broader universe, and the capacity to reflect on past experiences, anticipate future events, and comprehend abstract concepts.

Despite ongoing debates and research, human consciousness's whole nature and potential continue to be a profound mystery, echoing the Quranic message of the inherent complexity and depth of the human psyche.

The Quranic perspective on consciousness underscores the significance of self-awareness and external awareness. It places the source of our intellect and our inner record of memories and experiences within what is referred to as the higher consciousness or the "heavens." As noted in verse 2:255, this sphere is deemed the foundation upon which the entire consciousness system is established.

The higher consciousness provides wisdom, warnings, encouragement, and insights. These are then manifested in our feelings, emotions, and thoughts in base consciousness or immediate real-life situations, symbolically referred to as "al-Ard."

The Quran invites us to understand this layered conception of consciousness and encourages us to delve into its various components. According to the Quran, the ultimate goal is achieving a balanced psyche. This state of equanimity leads to peace, calmness, and freedom from fear, anxiety, and depression.

Possessing a peaceful state of mind has profound benefits. Not only does it enhance personal well-being, but it also serves as a defence against various physical and psychological ailments. More importantly, it enables individuals to channel their energies constructively for their own development and the betterment of society and the world.

6:1 All praises to Allah who have evolved Higher-Consciousness (Heavens) and Lower-Consciousness (Earth), and made darkness (Zulumat) and light (Noor). Then those who conceal/covers (Kaafir) they don't do equates/justify others for their Rab.

In the Quranic perspective, Allah is described as having created both the higher and base consciousness and light (Noor) and darkness (Zulumaat), respectively. This concept transcends the literal interpretations associated with physical light and dark or day and night, grounded instead in cognitive and psychological realms.

The Quran frequently mentions Allah guiding the minds, referred to here as "agitated minds", from the darkness of ignorance towards the light of enlightenment. This darkness isn't merely the absence of knowledge but the lack of self-awareness and understanding of one's psyche. The Quran's light, or "Noor", illuminates the human mind's inherent higher and base consciousness.

Understanding these two aspects of our psychology can lead to continuous self-observation and mindfulness of our emotions, feelings, and thought processes - all of which occur within the realm of base consciousness or the symbolic "earth". Such introspective practice can foster emotional intelligence and a higher state of self-awareness. The goal is to attain inner peace, representing the pinnacle of mental and emotional well-being per Quranic philosophy.

17:99 Do not they see that Allah has evolved higher consciousness (heavens) and base consciousness (earth) and he has full control over them. He can evolve examples like them and has appointed a term on which there is no doubt. But still those who are in darkness they will still conceal/cover it.

When individuals reflect deeply, free from the influence of traditional and historical teachings, they will likely discern that nature has endowed them with a sacred inner consciousness composed of higher and lower levels. However, some will always choose to remain within the obscurity of their self-denial, disregarding their consciousness's inherent self-knowledge and guidance. This wilful concealment of one's inner truths indicates a resistance to the illumination that self-awareness can bring.

35: 40 Say, Have you seen those who you call upon and you associate them with Allah what they have created on the base consciousness (earth), or if they have any association in elevated-consciousness (heavens). Have we given them any script which gives them clear signs/ayats (clear-signs)?. Those who are in darkness will promise falsehood to each other.

Individuals are urged to question their preconceived notions of divinity to examine how these concepts have shaped the landscape of their base consciousness or contributed to the formation of their higher consciousness. These terms represent integral components of human psychology. When individuals comprehend this, those currently obscured by ignorance may be drawn towards external religious constructs, which can obfuscate the guidance provided by their inherent inner truths. Some individuals may reject or cover this understanding, preferring to remain ensconced in the shadows of denial. They willingly forsake their authentic internal compass in favour of externally imposed ideologies.

35: 41 Indeed Allah has hold together the higher consciousness (heavens) and base consciousness (earth) so that they don't abandon you. If they abandon you nothing will hold them together except him. Indeed, he is gentle/patient forgiver.

The delicate equilibrium of consciousness requires deep understanding and diligent preservation. Disrupting this balance can potentially lead to losing an individual's sanity, engendering various psychological disorders. This precarious state of affairs is metaphorically expressed in the Quranic parable that warns that if the harmony between the higher and base consciousness is disrupted, no external support can restore it. Our mental stability rests on the balance between these two realms of consciousness, constituting the essence of our psychological well-being.

Summary

The Quran presents the concepts of the heavens and the earth as integral parts of the human psyche rather than just physical realms. A lack of understanding of these components can lead to imbalances in one's psyche, referred to as "darkness" or "injustice" in the Quran.

The higher or elevated consciousness, or "heavens", is the origin of our consciousness system, containing our inner book of truth and acting as the primary source of our intellect and guidance. Recognising this higher consciousness allows us to access our total intellectual capacity.

The lower or base consciousness, or "earth", is the stage where the events of our daily lives play out. The agitated mind (Inns) and the hidden feelings (Jinn), the actual persona (Insaan), Nisa (Urges), and Rijal (innate self-determination) all played out at this level of consciousness (on the Earth). It's where we express every emotion, face every situation, and endure all psychological issues. The Quran aims to make us aware of these two components, higher and base consciousness, to help us understand and manage them effectively.

According to the Quran, the higher consciousness is uncontaminated by the struggles of the base consciousness, remaining pure to provide guidance. The Quran emphasises the need to elevate our base consciousness to recognise and interact with the higher consciousness, where ultimate peace and success reside.

8

Adam and The Forbidden Tree

The Story of Adam

"There are many aspects of the soul in human experience: intuition, insight, vision, foresight, and a deep understanding of the present – all of those come from the soul's dimension of consciousness." - Deepak Chopra

Adam is not the first man, as claimed. The Quranic concept of Adam is another crucial subject. Contrary to common interpretations based on Biblical traditions, the Quran does not seem to portray Adam and Eve as the first humans. This notion not only contradicts evolutionary science, but it's also not directly supported by the Quran itself. The traditional Adam and Eve narrative associated with the Arabic Quran is influenced by "The Deep Impact" discussed previously from other traditions.

While the story of Adam and Eve is significant in the narratives of all Abrahamic religions, the focus here is on something other than comparing these narratives or delving into the historical aspects. Instead, the goal is to explore and interpret the underlying philosophy and wisdom within the Quran independently of other religious or historical contexts. This unbiased exploration seeks to gain a deeper understanding of Quranic teachings and concepts beyond traditional interpretations, such as the representation of higher and lower consciousness.

This chapter will explore the Quranic Philosophy of Adam, Eve, and the Forbidden Tree. Something important to note before we delve into our analysis is that the Quran doesn't mention the name of Adam's wife. The widely accepted term "Eve" or "Hawwa" for Adam's spouse/wife comes from biblical and historical traditions, but it's not used in the Quran. Similarly, there's no explicit reference to a physical tree or physical fruit in the Quran. In the Bible, the Forbidden Tree was referred to as the "Tree of Knowledge of Good and Evil" (Genesis 2:17), which suggests that even in Bible, it's symbolic rather than physical.

Etymological and Lexical Analysis.

A vocative particle and proper noun. The proper noun is masculine and is in the nominative case (مرفوع). Three letter root is ('آدم').

- Arabic English Lexicon, by E.W. Lanes. Vol 1, Page 35: Seasoning something, mixing up.
- The Hens Wehr Dictionary of Modern Arabic, by The Hans Wehr. Page 12: Enrich with extra ingredients.

The concept of "Adam" in the Quran may indeed have a more profound, symbolic meaning than the literal interpretation often applied to it. In Arabic, "Adam" is used outside religious texts to refer to the proper blending or homogenising of various ingredients. So, the term

"Adam" in the Quran could symbolise the blend or culmination of particular qualities or elements.

An example of this usage in Arabic is "Adam alKhubuz" or "Adam al-Laham," which are translated as "the seasoning of bread" or "the seasoning of the meat," respectively. This language suggests blending or integrating various components to achieve a particular result or state.

So, if we interpret "Adam" in this context, it might symbolise the integrated human being – a blend of various elements, aspects, and potentials. This interpretation could shift our understanding of the Judo-Christian Biblical story of Adam and open up new perspectives on its deeper meaning.

Adam and the Partner

In the Quran, Adam's partner is referred to as his "Zauj," an Arabic term that means pair or companion. This term is often translated as "wife," but it doesn't necessarily carry that connotation in the original Arabic.

The Quran doesn't name Adam's zauj. In the context of the Quran, the term "Zauj" could be interpreted more broadly to mean something like "counterpart" or "complement," reflecting the idea that the two are meant to be together and complete each other.

As such, the pairing of Adam and his zauj in the Quran symbolises the pairing or coupling of various aspects of human nature or consciousness. This broader interpretation opens the door to different possible meanings and insights into human psychology and spirituality.

The Creation of Adam

The Quran is rich in symbolic language and parables, interpreted as referring to aspects of human psychology. Here is a summary of the components we have discussed so far:

1. **Insaan (The social mind):** This term is typically translated as "human" or "man," but can be interpreted as referring to the aspect of the human mind that is social and interactive, our persona that interacts with the world.
2. **Inns (The agitated/curious mind):** This term suggests a state of mind filled with curiosity, always seeking, questioning, and exploring.
3. **Zauj of Nafs (Companion or pair of the psyche):** This refers to the companion or counterpart to the human psyche. It suggests that our psyche has a partner or other half, referring to the dual nature of our consciousness.
4. **Nisa (Urges) and Rijal (Innate self-determination):** These terms could be seen as representing two opposing forces within us: our primal urges or instincts (Nisa) and our innate drive or will to assert ourselves or self-determination (Rijal) to act on our desires (Nisa).
5. **Higher Consciousness (The Heavens) and Lower Consciousness (The Earth):** These represent two levels or aspects of human consciousness. The Higher Consciousness could refer to our intellect, reasoning, and capacity for spiritual insight, while the Lower Consciousness might refer to our more earthly, material-oriented consciousness.
6. **Jinn (The hidden companion of the agitated mind):** In this context, they represent unseen forces or aspects of our mind that can influence our thoughts and behaviour, mainly when our mind is agitated or unrest.

"Adam," as represented in the Quran, signifies an ideal state of human consciousness, an integrated self where all psychological elements harmoniously coexist. As opposed to being merely a biblical figure, "Adam" stands as a model of psychological equilibrium, a manifestation of balanced consciousness that encompasses social interactions, curiosity, the duality of the psyche, primal instincts, self-determination, and the various levels of consciousness.

3:59 The similitude of Jesus before Allah is as that of Adam; He created him from dust, then said to him: "Be". And he was.

Verse 3:59 states, "Indeed the example/parable of Issa in front of Allah is the same as that of Adam: He created him from dust, then said to him, "Be," and he was." This implies that the command "Be and it is" represents not a supernatural intervention but a natural, unfolding process of becoming. Adam and Issa are thereby perceived as stages of psychological development rather than historical figures, and the reference to "dust" symbolises the raw, unprocessed psychological material shaped into a unified, balanced whole.

The phrase "be and it is" thus symbolises a state of self-realisation, a transition to a higher consciousness or a transformation of the self. From a psychological perspective, it reflects the transformative process that occurs when an individual integrates the varied aspects of their self, evolving from a lower consciousness to a higher one.

36:82 Verily, when He intends a thing, His Command is, "be", and it is!

Verse 36:82 states, "His command, when He intends anything, is only that He says to it, "Be," and it is." Here, the phrase "be and it is" is associated with intent, reflecting the intentionality and decision-making processes within the human mind. The instant an individual forms a concrete intention to act or to refrain, the decision actualises within the mind, highlighting the power of decision-making and intentionality within human consciousness.

This perspective interprets "be, and it is" not as a supernatural occurrence but as a reflection of the psychological process enabling personal transformation and growth. The phrase is thus perceived as a metaphorical symbol of the moment of decision, the commitment to personal transformation, or a new course of action.

The inception of an idea or intention within our psyche is immediate, reflecting the 'be and it is' moment. This mental event doesn't guarantee the instant physical realisation of the idea but marks the beginning of its journey. The power of the psyche in decision-making is thus emphasised, demonstrating that while the decision is instantaneous, the journey towards its realisation demands consistent effort and time.

16:40 For to anything which We have willed, We but say the word, "Be", and it is.

Verse 16:40 reinforces this perspective: "Indeed, Our word to a thing when We intend it is but that We say to it, "Be," and it is." The concept of "be and it is" in the Quranic context is intrinsically linked to the intention and decision-making process within the human psyche. The moment of "be and it is" is the birth of a decision, the commitment within one's consciousness that, given time and resources, will manifest into the physical realm.

According to Quranic philosophy, Adam symbolises an enlightened state of mind, a person who has gained insight into their consciousness and its components. He embodies a harmonious blend of the Social and Agitated mind, achieving the 'Adam' state when he becomes cognizant of his own consciousness and its functioning. In essence, he reaches a level of self-awareness where he is attuned to his own psyche, its emotions, feelings, and various facets.

15:29 "When I have fashioned him (in due proportion) and breathed into him of My spirit, fall ye down in obeisance unto him."

The Quran's reference to the formation of Adam from dust or a state of non-existence in verse 15:29 implies that an average human being, although conscious of the external world, is 'dust' or 'nothingness' if they lack self-awareness. The transformation from this state to 'Adam' occurs when an individual gains self-awareness, an understanding of their psychology, and the mechanism of their consciousness.

2:31 And He taught Adam the names of all things; then He placed them before the angels, and said: "Tell me the names of these if ye are right."

In prior chapters, we elucidated the concept of "Asma" (often translated as "Heavens") as symbolic of higher consciousness. This profound awareness is intrinsically linked to the state attributed to Adam. In essence, when an individual attains a deep awareness of their internal consciousness, they approach the elevated state often ascribed to Adam.

7:11 It is We Who created you and gave you shape; then We bade the angels prostrate to Adam, and they prostrate; not so Iblis; He refused to be of those who prostrate.

Verse 7:11: After Adam was created, the command to submit was given to Malaika(angels), all complying except for Iblees, who did not submit.

Lucifer, or Satan being the King of Angle, primarily originates from Biblical traditions and is not explicitly mentioned in the Quran. The Quran does reference Malaika (angels), Iblees, Satan, and Jinn, each requiring a nuanced understanding to dispel any confusion created by biblical narratives. These terms shall be further examined in subsequent discussions.

Jinn (The Hidden One)

As previously examined in the dedicated chapters, the term "Jinn" refers to that which is hidden. In psychological terms, it symbolises the part of our psyche we consciously strive to conceal from the world. This inner enclave typically stores our likes and dislikes, emotions, feelings, and mental disorders.

Although it is often associated with negative energies, emotions, and feelings, this does not always hold true. There may be instances when these concealed emotions and feelings are favourable; however, we still choose to hide them due to our fear of potential embarrassment or other undesirable consequences upon revelation. The notion of Jinn, therefore, covers this gamut of hidden elements within our psyche that we deliberately choose to mask from the world.

Iblees (The sad/dejected one)

Iblees is a masculine proper noun and is in the accusative case (منصوب). The term "Iblees," as described in the Quran, bears the literal meaning of sadness, dejection, and renunciation (referenced in EWL Vol-1, Page 248). It symbolises an innate psychological faculty in all human beings, including self-aware ones. This faculty possesses the potential to disrupt a peaceful and balanced state of mind for various reasons, causing a fall from a harmonious mental condition (depicted as paradise) to an unsettled or disturbed state (defined as earth). This fall represents a disconnection from higher consciousness.

18:50 Behold! We said to the angels, "Bow down to Adam": They bowed down except Iblis. He was one of the Jinns, and he broke the Command of his Lord. Will ye then take him and his progeny as protectors rather than Me? And they are enemies to you! Evil would be the exchange for the wrong-doers!

Verse 18:50, which identifies Iblees as being from Jinn, underscores the hidden nature of these melancholic feelings. These feelings and emotions remain concealed within the psyche, influencing impulsive decisions until they drive individuals to take adverse actions. Only then do they become exposed, leading those who succumb to them to stray from their path of balance and mental stability? This exposition of Iblees-like emotions reflects the human tendency to hide certain negative feelings that impact impulsive decision-making.

Nevertheless, the quality of self-awareness and consciousness of one's psyche provides a saving grace to this Adam-like state. It equips individuals to swiftly recognise when they are veering away from their desired mental equilibrium. This understanding aids in implementing corrective measures to regain a peaceful mental state. Within the Quranic context, this journey is often portrayed by Adam acknowledging his error, demonstrating contrition, and seeking forgiveness from Allah. This allegory elucidates the human ability to perceive when the inner balance is lost and to enact changes necessary for restoration, reflecting the continual human endeavour to navigate the complexities of the mind and maintain a state of inner harmony.

The Satan

Satan is a masculine proper noun and is in the genitive case (مجرور). The proper noun's triliteral root is *shīn ṭā nūn* (ش ط ن) S T N. In the Quranic context, "Satan" refers to exceeding, deviating, or going far astray (as indicated in HW Page 550). It represents a mental faculty that lures individuals away from their path, seduced by emotions and feelings, leading them to fabricate false or illusory realities. Under the sway of this faculty, individuals might overreact, diverge from the proper course, and subsequently become ensnared in a state of mental suffering and disarray. The consequences of succumbing to these exaggerations and losing touch with personal consciousness and wisdom manifest in mental agony, metaphorically depicted as 'hellfire' in the Quranic text.

There is a salient distinction between Satan and Iblees within this framework. While Iblees symbolises hidden negative emotions such as sadness, dejection, and rejection, Satan pertains to emotions and feelings that translate into observable actions and are no longer concealed.

2:208 *O ye who believe! Enter into Islam whole-heartedly; and follow not the footsteps of the evil (Satan) one; for he is to you an avowed enemy.*

As stated in Quran 2:208, "Get into the peace in totality and do not follow the actions of Satan," this verse accentuates that actions influenced by negative emotions possess the power to disrupt psychological tranquillity.

4:76 *Those who believe fight in the cause of Allah, and those who reject*

Faith Fight in the cause of Evil: So fight ye against the friends of Satan: **feeble indeed is the cunning of Satan.**

Though these negative emotions may exert a compelling force, urging individuals to make improper decisions in life, Quran 4:76 notes that "the strategy Satan uses is fragile." This weakness stems from actions based on negative emotions, typically lacking rational reasoning. Therefore, when these thoughts, emotions, and feelings are confronted and refined through calmness and wisdom, their grip on the mind relaxes. This reflects the Quran's profound understanding of human psychology, offering insight into the mechanisms that govern human behaviour and providing guidance on navigating the intricate landscape of the mind, ultimately aspiring to peace and equilibrium.

The Psychological Conflicts and Mind Conditioning

The human mind is a complex and potent instrument requiring regular conditioning and evaluation for our overall well-being. Attaining a state of self-awareness, akin to that of Adam in Quranic philosophy, entails a delicate equilibrium struck by understanding and regulating our emotions through intellectual prowess.

In this context, Adam is paired with Zauj, a companion representing hidden knowledge and intellect. This alliance, when solicited, aids in elevating Emotional Intelligence or EI. By continually conditioning the mind and observing its internal mechanics, we become more self-aware and develop a more significant social understanding of others' psychologies and emotions in our vicinity.

Adam symbolises a psychological state wherein an individual attains profound awareness of their emotional processes, the ebb and flow of feelings, and the moral dichotomies within. Indeed, achieving this elevated consciousness, represented by the state of Adam, does not invariably ensure enduring peace or the pinnacle of mental tranquillity. This is mainly due to the relentless influences of Iblees (the disheartened one) and Satan (the force prompting impulsive decisions) embedded within our psyche. These forces constantly challenge our mental equilibrium, making maintaining a serene mind a perpetual endeavour. Instead, the state of Adam equips an individual with the ability for swift self-recognition, enabling them to discern their flaws and commence a process of self-correction promptly, thereby steering the psyche back onto a balanced course.

2:35 And we said, "O Adam, calm down, you and your pair in Al-Jannah (the hidden process of knowledge, peace and tranquillity) and gather intelligence from it freely whenever you desire. But do not come near the tree; otherwise, you will become unjust/oppressor (end up in darkness)."

In the referenced verse, 'Jannah', literally meaning the 'hidden thing' or 'paradise', is metaphorically used to represent the state of mind. This invisible entity can only be inferred through an individual's emotional expressions or the visible signs of their psychological state, such as tranquillity. In the aforementioned verse, the term employed for 'eating' shares its root with 'Mikaal,' which denotes intellect. The directive given to Adam in this context is not merely about physical consumption but rather an invitation to tap into the concealed reservoir of wisdom. In Adam's state of elevated consciousness, he possesses the capability to access this wisdom profusely.

The verse also alludes to the 'tree of injustice or corruption', a symbol that will be discussed in later sections. Essentially, the core purpose of this heightened state of consciousness, represented by 'Adam', is to acknowledge the diverse forces influencing our psyche, assimilate this knowledge, and employ it to one's advantage.

It's important to note that the Quranic interpretation of 'Adam' transcends the conventional biological distinctions of gender. Instead, it represents a mental self-awareness that anyone can attain, irrespective of gender or sexual orientation. It is an enlightened state that comes with understanding the myriad processes unfolding within one's mind, making one capable of managing their internal psychological landscape effectively.

The Angels and Adam

The conventional interpretation of the creation of Adam and the reservations of angels is widely known. However, if one is to comprehend the depth of these teachings in the Quran, a paradigm shift in understanding is required. The key is to interpret the Quran through the lens of the Quran itself, along with the aid of dictionaries, instead of relying solely on traditional narratives.

When seen through this lens, Adam is not a literal figure but a symbolic representation of a state of self-awareness within human psychology. Once this state is achieved, the complexities of human emotions and thoughts become more comprehensible. Therefore, understanding the Quranic teachings about Adam and the angels' reservations necessitates a deep, introspective exploration of our own consciousness. This approach unravels a profound psychological interpretation of these narratives, transforming them from external historical events to internal human psyche processes.

Etymological and Lexical Analysis.

The Arabic root for Angels or Malaika is (M L K) or (م ل ك). The noun is masculine plural and is in the genitive case (مجرور). The noun's triliteral root is mīm lām kāf (م ل ك).

- Arabic English Lexicon, by E.W. Lanes. Vol 8, Page 3023: Possessed it, owned it, Have dominion, ruling power, having the power to exercise command or authority.
- The Hens Wehr Dictionary of Modern Arabic, by The Hans

Wehr. Page 1081: To Dominate, Authoritative, To take-control, be uppermost in mind, dominated thinking.

In the Quranic context, the term "Malaika" (or "Angels") refers to the authoritative mind faculties that govern our thoughts and actions. Once an individual reaches the state of Adam, a state of self-awareness and understanding of the intricate mechanisms of the human psyche, these authoritative mind faculties become subject to the individual's control.

However, within this psychological framework exists a conflicting force known as Iblees or Satan. This force symbolises arrogance and resistance, constantly challenging and contending with the self-aware state of Adam. Nonetheless, when one achieves the level of consciousness Adam represents, even this contentious force can be harnessed and managed effectively within the psyche.

20:116 When we say to Malaika to Submit to Adam. They Submit except Iblees, and he refused.

17:61 When we say to Malaika to submit to Adam/ They did except Iblees. He said Shall I submit to someone evolved from Teen.

2:34 When we say to Malaika to submit to Adam, they did except Iblees. He refused, he did Takabur (arrogance), and he became the ones who concealed.

2:31 He has given all the knowledge to Adam with higher consciousness. Then presented them towards mind authorities (Malaika). Said give me news with the higher consciousness, if you are saying the truth.

2:32 They said, you are the Subhanaka (source of abandoned knowledge), we do not have any knowledge except what you have taught us. Indeed you are the one who has full knowledge and wisdom.

2:33 He said, "O Adam give them the information/news with higher consciousness. He gave them the information/news with higher consciousness. Didn't I tell you I have the knowledge of the unseen of higher consciousness and lower consciousness. I have the knowledge of who you display and what you hide".

2:34 Then we said to Malaika Submit to Adam, they did, except Iblees (the dishearten/saddened one). He was arrogant and have covered and concealed himself.

The verses above explain that the Malaika, the controlling or authoritative faculties of the mind, are requested to acquiesce to Adam, who embodies a higher state of consciousness and has been granted the essence of Allah's words. These mental faculties form part of the human psyche, but they remain ineffective on their own and need to harmonise with Adam the enlightened, self-aware mind.

These authoritative faculties might initially resist adapting to the new thought process after attaining the state of Adam or self-awareness. However, once they recognise Adam's higher consciousness and the intelligence of his accompanying faculties, they ultimately submit, except those characterised by melancholy and disheartenment. This is the conditioning of the mind and purify its old uncontrolled thinking.

These metaphors shed light on an essential message: once self-awareness and consciousness are achieved, symbolised by reaching the state of Adam, all mental energies and faculties can be regulated and harnessed for personal benefit.

Although a self-aware and conscious mind can govern most mental energies and faculties, everyone has specific thresholds and trigger points. When these are activated, intellect and intelligence can be overwhelmed by pure impulse and instinct, leading to decisions dominated by emotions rather than rational thought. This emotional override can result in negative feelings like anger, despair, and sadness, adversely affecting the state of mind. These forces, called Iblees, propel Adam and his pair out of a state of peace, calm, and tranquillity. This occurs when emotions suppress intellect, dominating our intelligence.

When given control, Iblees represent the authoritative mind faculties that can transport a person from a peaceful state to one of discomfort, pain, and negativity. If these forces remain unchecked, they seize control of the mind, influencing it with negative thinking, leading to detrimental choices, actions, and subsequent consequences. This cycle of cause and effect negatively impacts every aspect of an individual's psychology, culminating in discontent and dissatisfaction.

The term Satan, derived from the root 'S T N', literally signifies the act of diverting someone from their position or destination, rendering them distant or remote.

When the negative authoritative mind faculty, Iblees, begins to dominate the decisions and choices of an individual under the influence of negativity, the person, as a result of these detrimental choices and decisions, behaves in ways they wouldn't under favourable circumstances. Consequently, the individual transitions from a peaceful state to a state of distress. The objective of Satan is to redirect the individual from a peaceful and stable state to a disturbed and unstable state of mind.

The Tree in Quran
(Good and Bad Trees)

As we delve further into the Quranic interpretations, it's critical to understand that the traditional religious narratives surrounding a specific physical tree are not supported in the Quran. The text does not reference an actual wheat plant or apple tree. How these concepts came to be part of specific belief systems remains beyond the scope of this book and will not be discussed here.

Remember, this book aims to present the ancient philosophy of human psychology to the reader presented in Arabic Quran. It does not engage with the politics of religion or the causes and instigators of divergent interpretations. We aim to focus on the Quranic content rather than addressing interpretation corruption issues.

Etymological and Lexical Analysis.

The root for Tree or Shajar is (ش ج ر) S J R is the root word of (كَشَجَرَةٍ). A genitive feminine indefinite noun.

- HW Page 532: to happen, occur, argue, dispute, to breakout, trees, bushes, shrubs, offshoots
- EWL Vol 8, Page 1506: intricate, complicated, perplexed, confused, or intricately intermixed

The term "Shajar," commonly translated as "tree" in Quranic translations, has a broader interpretation in the dictionary. It includes connotations of bushes, breakouts, shrubs, offshoots, intricate intermixing, confusion, and disputes. This representation fits neatly with the appearance of a typical tree; a single stem gives rise to multiple branches and leaves, all intricately interwoven.

This tree metaphor in the Quran aims to reflect the complexity of the human psyche. A person's psychological landscape, with its diverse range of thoughts, emotions, and feelings, is much like a tree with its array of branches and leaves. In other words, the human psyche can be visualised as a tree, with its multiple traits and experiences, emotions, and feelings representing the branches and leaves that sprout from the single stem—the individual's core self.

14:24 Have you not considered how Allah strikes the example/analogy/parable of the pleasant/agreeable/good words as the pleasant/good which broke out/happen(tree/shajar)., which has the high/lofted principles based on higher consciousness.

14:25 That is full/total intellect from the permission of your Rabb. This is how Allah strike analogies to the agitated minds, so that they can get reminded.

14:26 And the example/analogy of the word bad as bad (things) happen/broke out (tree/shajar). That is based on the lower consciousness without any stability.

The Quran uses metaphors or parables, as in verse 14:24, where 'pure words' or 'Kalima-e-Tayyaba' are likened to a 'pure tree' or 'Shajar-e-Tayyabba'. This tree is linked with higher consciousness, the origin of all human intellect and consciousness. Verse 14:25 reinforces this notion, urging the reader to derive wisdom from this knowledge base. The term AKL, deriving from 'Akeel', suggests intelligence or wisdom, though it's often translated as 'eating' in Quranic interpretations. This translation seems incongruous with the overarching theme of the Quran, which is the exploration of human psychology and the inner source of wisdom. The Quran aims to connect an individual with their internal script (Al-Kitaab) and inner source of knowledge and wisdom (Al-Jannah).

The scripture uses these metaphors to help the unsettled mind remember through the hidden source of wisdom, directing attention to self-correction and maintaining a balance within the psyche. The Quran's ultimate goal is to help individuals achieve a peaceful state of mind, identifying any internal obstacles that might disrupt this state or regress it to an unconscious state, causing psychological discomfort, fear, or unease.

Verse 14:26 presents the 'bad words' or 'Kalama-e-Khabeesa' as symbols of the offshoots of the psyche that are part of the lower consciousness of human psychology. This lower consciousness comprises the active characters, situations, emotions, feelings, and thought processes a person engages in daily life situations. The Quran points out their instability, alluding to impulsive unconscious decisions often resulting in negative consequences. Observing one's emotions, feelings, mental state, and overall psychological condition is crucial, whether the impact is adverse or favourable.

Adam and the Forbidden Tree

In our previous discussions, we've identified that 'Adam' represents a state of consciousness fully aware of its inner self and the mechanics of consciousness. This suggests that 'Adam' comprehends not just the myriad mental faculties but also the multitude of human emotions and their influence on one's consciousness. The parable of Adam in the Quran demonstrates that even a self-aware individual can quickly regress into a non-aware state if not carefully self-monitored. This leads us to the allegory of the Forbidden Tree, which the Quran uses to caution Adam about elements within his consciousness that demand extra caution. These elements, if overlooked, can rapidly disrupt his peaceful and balanced mental state and disconnect him from (Jannah). In this section, we'll delve into some verses to solidify our understanding of the Tree and its relationship with Adam, striving to comprehend why it's deemed forbidden.

2:35 And We said, "O Adam, be in rest, you and your pair in Al-Jannah [the source of hidden intelligence, wisdom and enlightenment]. And consume from it as you like. But do not come near to this tree, or else you will be in darkness (or become unjust).

Once the state of 'Adam' is realised, individuals can optimally harness their hidden mental energies to achieve tranquillity and satisfaction. However, within each person lurks a disruptive force (a tree) capable of disassembling everything. This tree, as referenced in verse 14:26, is composed of negative, painful, or illicit words (or Kalma-e-Khabeesa). Here, 'words' pertain to detrimental thought patterns that can consume mental energies and destabilise the precarious balance of the mind, shifting it from a state of peace and satisfaction to one of distress and dissatisfaction.

20:120 *But Satan whispered (inner thoughts) to him: O Adam shall lead you to the tree of eternity and the authority that never decays.*

7:20 *Then began Satan to whisper suggestions to them, bringing openly before their minds all their shame that was hidden from them (before): he said: "Your Lord only forbade you this tree, lest ye should become authorities or live forever."*

The verses mentioned contain several essential elements to consider:

1. Verse 2:120: Satan's temptations are always presented as whispers in the Quran, symbolising inner negative thoughts.
2. Having achieved self-awareness, Adam knew the difference between the good and evil trees, as described in verses 14:24 and 14:26. Yet, he was still enticed by his inner negative thoughts to taste the fruit of the forbidden tree. This can be seen as a representation of how even self-aware individuals can be led astray by their negative impulses.
3. Interestingly, Satan remains in Jannah even after disobeying God, as indicated by his whispering to Adam in Paradise. This suggests that negative thoughts can still be present even in a state of peace and tranquillity (symbolised by Jannah).
4. The temptation of eternity refers to the deceptive allure of negative thought patterns, which promise seemingly enduring pleasure or relief, but in reality, they disturb inner peace.

Despite understanding the impact of good and bad thoughts (symbolised by the two trees), individuals can still succumb to their negative impulses. This is part of human nature: even when we know what is right and wrong, we sometimes choose the wrong path. Emotional decisions often override logical thinking, leading to undesirable outcomes and, in some cases, psychological trauma.

However, the state of 'Adam' - self-awareness - allows quicker recognition of mistakes and initiates the correction process (represented by 'Tauba' or repentance). In contrast, those who have not reached this state of self-awareness may remain in mental distress for extended periods.

This interpretation of the Quranic verses emphasises the importance of self-awareness and the continuous effort to maintain inner peace against negative thoughts and impulses. It also sheds light on the process of repentance as a method of self-correction and returns to a state of tranquillity.

The whisper of Eternity by Satan.

11:107 They will dwell therein for all the time that the heavens and the earth endure, except as thy Lord willeth: for thy Lord is the (sure) accomplisher of what He planneth.

11:108 And those who are blessed shall be in the Garden: They will dwell therein for all the time that the heavens and the earth endure, except as thy Lord willeth: a gift without break.

The word Khuld means (continuous, perpetual, endlessly, the state of perpetual existence, for EWL Vol-2, pg783-4). The term Damati was used as per lexicon EWL Vol-3, page 935 means (continued, lasted, endured).

In the above verses, the perpetual existence is tied up with the existence time period of the heavens (Smawat) and earth (Ard). We have already established in the previous chapter that these concepts symbolise the higher and lower consciousness within our psychology. This means that the longevity of a person's psyche – which remains active until physical death –suggests that 'forever' is, in fact, bound to the duration of an individual's life.

Hence, the 'perpetuality' of the heavens and earth should be understood as the continual functioning of our conscious and unconscious minds during our lifespan.

For instance, our experiences, both positive and negative, create a timeline in our psyche. These experiences shape who we are and remain a part of us until our last breath, effectively creating a 'forever' within our psyche.

The 'temptation of Eternity' and 'never-ending authority' presented to Adam by Satan (negative thought patterns) within our minds. These thoughts delude us into thinking that surrendering to them would lead to more control and endless power over our affairs (the pleasure or satisfaction of impulsive, unconscious decisions will last forever). However, when we act on these impulses, we often realise that they lead to undesirable outcomes, prompting feelings of regret, and the pleasure never lasts longer. It highlights each person's internal struggle between maintaining self-awareness and succumbing to negative, potentially self-destructive impulses.

20:121 *Then they both use their intellect (akal) (in context of the negative tree), then it reveals the shameful consequences to them. They cover it from waraq (leaf's) of Jannah (not leafs of trees important). Adam disobeyed and allowed himself to be on the negative side.*

Sawatuhuma, EWL Vol.4. Page 1458 (Any saying, or action, of which one is ashamed when it appears, any evil, nasty abominable, foul, or unseemly, saying or action).

Points to understand in the above verse:

1. The Quran does not discuss physical bodies or tangible relationships as is often interpreted in conventional narratives, but rather psychological states and processes. "Sawatuhuma, " which stems from the root "SWA", is interpreted to mean the disgraceful or embarrassing repercussions of specific actions or words, not physical nudity. According to this interpretation, Adam's 'nakedness' signifies the negative impact, shame, or exposure resulting from succumbing to destructive thought patterns (symbolised by Satan) and acting under the influence of negative emotions or words (the 'forbidden tree').
2. Further, as an emblem of self-aware consciousness, Adam swiftly recognises and addresses his missteps. The Quran doesn't suggest

that Adam used leaves of a Tree to cover his exposure but metaphorically employed the 'pages of Jannah' (paradise) to rectify his wrongdoings. 'Jannah' in Quran implies a hidden reservoir of wisdom, knowledge, and intelligence that, when consulted, can guide one out of distressing circumstances and rectify missteps.

This parable of Adam and his companion provides insightful psychological reading emphasising self-awareness, the recognition of errors, and the rectification process.

Further analysis of verses 20:117 to 119 will detail that Satan is the open enemy as the negative force within our psyche. His target or aim is to take Adam and his spouse out of Jannah. Verse 118 mentions that as long as you live in Jannah, you will not be hungry (devoid of urges as Jannah continuously feeds you with rivers of wisdom), fearful and exposed. It also means that as soon as you come out of the state of Jannah, you will become hungry, scared, and exposed. The definition of clothing (Libas) verse 7:26.

*7:26 O ye Children of Adam! We have bestowed raiment upon you to cover your shame, as well as to be an adornment to you. But the **raiment of righteousness,- that is the best.** Such are among the Signs of Allah, that they may receive admonition!*

The clothing of Taqwa (alertness, state of extreme caution) is the best one, and that is what Adam missed when he got whispers by Satan. 'Taqwa' is a state of alertness or extreme caution. This psychological guard aids in preserving balance and serenity. In this context, it is likened to psychological clothing, which protects and shields the mind, much like physical clothing for the body. This Taqwa clothing protects the state of self-awareness (personified as Adam) from internal negativity and exposure to various resultant psychological issues.

7:23 They said: "Our Lord! We have wronged our own souls: If thou forgive us not and bestow not upon us Thy Mercy, we shall certainly be lost."

20:122 But his Lord chose him (for His Grace): He turned to him, and gave him Guidance.

Adam's leave was 7:23. Realisation of Zulm (injustice he did) on Psyche (all in Psyche), and Repentance (the process of amendment), 20:122 the repentance, which get accepted by Allah immediately, as they come back to Jannah after realisation of the Zulm with Psyche.

Summary

In Quranic philosophy, Adam is interpreted as a state of self-awareness. This definition is derived from the Arabic meaning of Adam as a homogeneous mixture of multiple elements, illustrating a person's intricate blend of emotions, thoughts, and aspects of personality. Individuals gain greater mastery over their internal psychological processes by achieving the state of Adam.

Adam is described as having a partner, a source of hidden knowledge, wisdom and intellect, 'Jannah'. The interplay between Adam and this partner requires constant vigilance, or 'Taqwa' (extreme caution). This concept stems from the understanding that if negative thoughts or experiences are allowed to accumulate within the psyche, they can engender psychological distress.

Adam is aware of two distinct psychological pathways within himself, portrayed as trees in the Quran. The 'good tree' symbolises positive thoughts, deeds, actions, and words that promote psychological tranquillity. Conversely, the 'bad tree' represents negative thoughts, deeds, actions, and words that disturb this tranquillity. Despite knowing the implications of choosing the 'bad tree', Adam sometimes succumbs to its temptation, instigated by the internal negative force represented as Satan in the Quran.

Crucially, Satan is not depicted as controlling Adam but rather as a persistent, internal negative force that creates illusions of an alternate reality, leading Adam astray. However, due to his self-awareness, Adam promptly recognises his mistakes when he is led astray and embarks on a process of amendment, symbolised as repentance.

An African proverb states, "When there is no enemy within, the enemy outside can do us no harm." This proverb resonates with the Quran's depiction of the internal struggle within the human psyche, where various psychological forces and mind faculties are personified as characters. These narratives serve as potent storytelling tools to communicate profound insights into the workings of human consciousness. They testify to the age-old power of storytelling as an effective method of conveying complex and thought-provoking ideas.

THE HIDDEN WORLD ~ 145

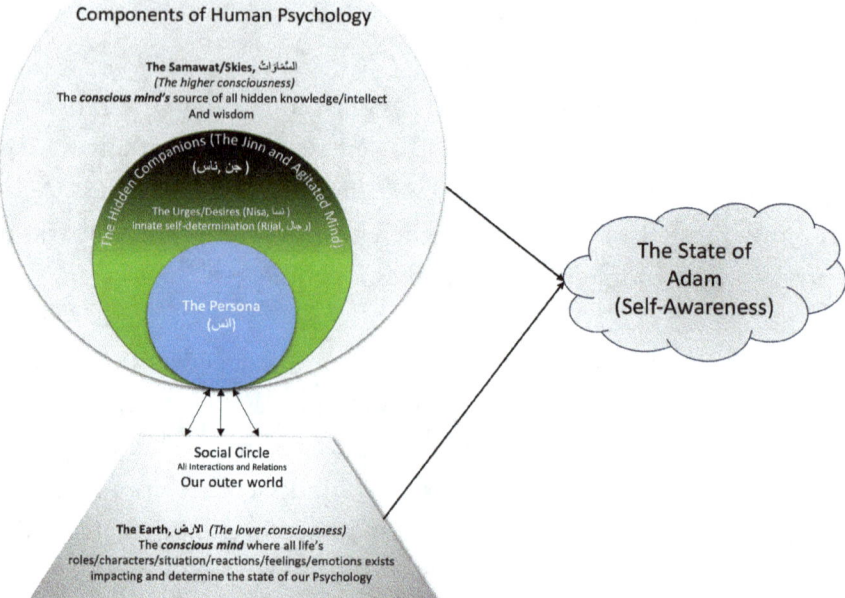

The State of Heightened Self-Awareness

9

The Garden of Eden and Hellfire

The Paradise and Hell

"Paradise is not a place; it's a state of consciousness." - Sri Chinmoy

Heaven and Hell: concepts that have fascinated, perplexed, and inspired humanity for millennia. These notions, rich in symbolism and imbued with profound theological significance, stand at the crossroads of faith, philosophy, and the human psyche. Whether envisioned as literal realms or metaphysical states of being, they continue to challenge our understanding, stir our imagination, and shape our deepest beliefs. In a world guided by empirical inquiry, the ethereal landscapes of Paradise and Hellfire remain elusive, residing not in the domain of physical proof but in the profound corridors of faith and personal conviction.

The Metaphoric Nature of Hell and Paradise

For scholars, philosophers, and thinkers across religions, the absence of tangible proof often leads them to interpret Heaven and Hell metaphorically. They propose that religious scriptures employ these terms to communicate more profound philosophical messages to humanity. As a result, these concepts serve as allegorical devices to impart ethical and moral lessons, fostering virtues and dissuading vices among adherents.

Extensive research has been conducted worldwide by eminent scholars on the symbolic and metaphorical interpretations of hell and paradise. A few notable examples include "A *History of God: The 4,000-Year Quest of Judaism, Christianity, and Islam*" (K. Armstrong, 1994) traces the evolution of God concepts in the three Abrahamic religions and, in doing so, discusses metaphorical interpretations of various religious concepts, including hell and paradise. "*No god but God: The Origins, Evolution, and Future of Islam*" (R. Aslan, 2011), offers insights into the symbolic interpretations of Islamic concepts, including discussions surrounding the metaphorical nature of hell and paradise. "*The Sacred and the Profane: The Nature of Religion*" (M. Eliade, 1987), a renowned historian of religion, often discusses the symbolic and metaphorical nature of religious expressions, including concepts like hell and paradise.

However, it's essential to acknowledge the diversity in ideas, as people's understanding of these concepts often aligns with their religious, philosophical, or cultural perspectives. The purpose of this book is to scrutinise these concepts from a psychological perspective and in relation to our daily lives.

Heaven, or Paradise, is typically characterised in religious texts as a place of eternal bliss devoid of suffering or pain. Its prevalent attributes include everlasting life, complete absence of fear, guilt, or conflict, and an atmosphere of ultimate peace and tranquillity. In this setting, all desires are satisfied without any associated guilt, reflecting the complete sovereignty of the divine entity and eliminating all evil forces.

In stark contrast, Hell or Hellfire is a realm of eternal suffering and torment. Its attributes often include perpetual pain, fear, and punishment. The scriptures describe the most harrowing scenarios becoming a reality, depicting physical fire burning skin and bones. There are references to a cycle of death and rebirth, ensuring the perpetuity of suffering. In this environment, an individual is subjected to every conceivable form of evil all at once.

These descriptions are metaphorical interpretations, often used in religious texts to convey complex concepts. In the context of human behaviour, they can be seen as allegories of the psychological states that can be experienced due to our actions. Heaven signifies a state of mind where peace, harmony, and contentment are achieved, while Hell symbolises despair, regret, and unending torment. These metaphors are potent incentives and deterrents, shaping human behaviour and moral choices.

A Thought Experiment.

Before we jump on the verses to understand these concepts, let's do a thought experiment. This thought experiment sheds light on the intricate relationship between consciousness and our perception of reality.

If we take a human body in perfect physical condition but devoid of consciousness and senses and place it in what religions describe as Paradise, the body would not be capable of perceiving the bliss or joy typically associated with such a place. Similarly, if we put this body into a condition akin to Hell and repeatedly inflict physical damage, the body would not register any pain or suffering. The scenarios underlined here suggest that experiences such as pleasure, pain, suffering, or happiness are tied to our conscious mind.

This becomes evident in instances where individuals are under general anaesthesia. Despite the surgical procedures' complexity or duration, they don't perceive any pain or discomfort during the process due to the temporary suspension of their consciousness. It is only upon regaining consciousness that they start experiencing feelings or sensations.

Therefore, the idea of Heaven or Hell, as religions describe, takes on a different connotation when examined from this perspective. It suggests these concepts might be more aptly interpreted as different states of consciousness rather than physical places. In other words, Paradise or Hell could be thought of as states of peace and contentment or torment and distress, respectively, experienced by a conscious being. Once consciousness is removed from the equation, notions of joy, peace, suffering, or misery become meaningless.

Etymological and Lexical Analysis.

As described in a chapter of Jinn, that Jannah (Paradise) in Quran has the same root word as Jinn. Jannah is a feminine noun, whereas Jinn is a masculine noun is in the genitive case (مجرور). The noun's triliteral root is jīm nūn nūn (ج ن ن). Jahannam, is a proper noun in the genitive case (مجرور). The root is (جهنم).

- The three-letter Arabic root is J N N. Arabic English Lexicon, by E.W. Lanes. Vol 2, Page 462,463: Something Covered, Concealed, Hidden in Darkness.
- The Hens Wehr Dictionary of Modern Arabic, by The Hans Wehr. Page 164: To cover, hide, conceal, veal, be or become dark
- The word used for Hell in Quran is Jahannam.
- The Arabic root for J H N N M or (جَهَنَّمَ). Arabic English Lexicon, by E.W. Lanes. Vol 2, Page 479: Deep well, in which one falls and perishes

The Paradise (Jannah)

In linguistic terms, "Jannah" is derived from the Arabic root word (ج ن ن) meaning "hidden" or "concealed," akin to the term "Jinn," which also originates from the same root and translates to "the hidden one." Our previous discussions identified the "Jinn" as a symbol of the unseen aspects of our personality, while the "Insaan" represents the persona we project to the world.

Given this background, "Jannah" can be contextually understood as a concealed or hidden domain within human psychology. This realm is the fountainhead of human intelligence, wisdom, and unbiased rational reasoning. In this context, attaining Jannah does not necessarily signify reaching a physical destination but rather achieving a heightened level of self-awareness and understanding.

This enlightened state of mind allows one to tap into their inherent wisdom and reasoning, fostering personal growth and a sense of inner peace. This perspective views Jannah not as a physical paradise to be attained in the afterlife but as a state of consciousness sought in one's lifetime through self-awareness and introspection.

Let's analyse verses more about this topic.

47:15 Parable of the Jannah (hidden source of knowledge and wisdom) which the cautious/extremely watchful are promised: in it are rivers of water incorruptible; rivers of milk of which the taste never changes; rivers of wine, a joy to those who drink; and rivers of honey pure and clear. There are for them all kinds of fruits, and Grace from their Lord. (Can those in such Bliss) be compared to such as shall dwell forever in the Fire, and be given, to drink, boiling water, so that it cuts up their bowels (to pieces)?

The verse begins with a clear assertion, potentially addressing any lingering doubts. It discusses the example/parable of Jannah, which is promised to those who are extremely vigilant and cautious, perpetually guarding their psychology. It's important to note that in the Quran, concepts such as Adam, Jinn, Insaan, Nafs, Jannah, Jahannam, Al-Kitaab, and others are primarily presented as parables. Despite being influenced by the physical human existence, these parables are clarified within the Quran as metaphorical. However, many people interpret these allegories literally, obscuring the profound messages of the Quran beneath layers of traditional narratives and tales.

The analogy of Jannah (the hidden wellspring of knowledge and wisdom) is often likened to a physical garden, a place where its fruits never cease to flourish. However, this is not to be taken literally as rivers of milk or honey but instead appreciated as metaphorical imagery. The term "river" or "Nahar" (referenced from EWL 8, page 2858) connotes the concept of a powerful, incessant flow. It is commonly used to describe rivers due to their perpetual water flow. However, when applied to Jannah (the concealed source of knowledge and wisdom), it symbolises a constant and endless stream of wisdom, the actual fruits of Jannah. These fruits are accessible to any self-aware mind engaging with this elevated consciousness state.

18:107 As to those who secured and do corrective actions (involved in self-correction), they will (make use of) the full extent/amplitude of Jannah (Hidden Knowledge/Wisdom) will be destined.

- The Arabic root for Firdous or (فِرْدَوْس). Arabic English Lexicon, by E.W. Lanes. Vol 6, Page 2365: Amplitude, total extent
- The Arabic root for N Z L or (نَزَلَ). Arabic English Lexicon, by E.W. Lanes. Vol 8 Page 3031: A place to be settled, Descended, Rested, Manzil or Destination

Humans are perpetually learning from their errors and evolving through their experiences. Through these experiences, we gain knowledge and wisdom, primarily by refraining from repeating our past mistakes. As the adage goes, "Wisdom comes from experience. And experience comes from failures." Those who aspire to maintain a balanced and serene mental state often exhibit a continuous self-corrective attitude. They regularly adjust their life's course based on the lessons gleaned from their past mistakes. This consistent self-adjusting attitude enables better decision-making and cultivates enduring mental stability. Consequently, these individuals often possess a greater sense of mental security and maintain a mental state characterised by peace and tranquillity.

7:42 But those who secure/believe and do corrective actions,- we will not put any Psyche the burden they cannot bear, they will be Companions of the Jannah (hidden source of knowledge and wisdom), therein to dwell (forever).

Once more, this process of self-correction is linked with the balanced psychological state of an individual, facilitating the individual's persistent connection to Jannah, conceptualised as the hidden source of knowledge and wisdom. In simpler terms, to live in a state of tranquillity and mental stability, it's vital that we continuously monitor our actions, applying self-correction based on our accumulated experiences and acquired wisdom.

The Hell (Jahannam)

Hell, or Jahannam in Arabic, is interpreted as a profound well where one might perish if one falls into it. In the Quran, this metaphor is contextually employed to represent an agonising mental state that is self-consuming and can drain an individual's complete mental energies. Simply put, it signifies a highly distressing psychological state into which, if a person falls, they may perceive it as unending and perpetual.

23:103 But those whose balance is light (weak credit) will be those who have indebted their psyche to eternal Hell.

As we've discerned from various discussions above, the ultimate objective of Quranic wisdom is to cultivate a balanced psychology. This entails a peaceful mental state that utilises all faculties of wisdom, achievable through extreme mindfulness (Taqwa) and ongoing self-improvement (Amilus Saliha). This is accomplished with a self-aware mindset, symbolised by Adam in the Quran. Conversely, when this psychological equilibrium is not attained, individuals may potentially subject themselves to a state of perpetual suffering, metaphorically referred to as Hell in the Quran.

9:35 On the Day when heat will be produced out of that, in the fire of Hell, and with it will be branded their appearances (foreheads), their stands (flanks), and their reputations (back).- "This is because of what you buried in your psychology: taste what you have buried!".

This verse emphasises that if we are not sufficiently vigilant and cautious, we may unconsciously allow damaging elements to infiltrate our psychology, leading to inevitable suffering. Thus, we must guard our psychology against negative programming, emotions, and feelings. Any decisions we make under the influence of negativity or actions taken under the sway of negative mental faculties (often symbolised as Satan) will lead to painful consequences. This psychological pain can set us on a further negative path, forcing us to make additional damaging decisions in life. This cyclical pattern of escalating mistakes can plunge us into an abyss of self-pity and destruction.

Maintaining a balanced psychology is not just vital for efficiently navigating our daily lives; it is also necessary for our internal peace and tranquillity. An unbalanced and disturbed psychological state not only impedes our everyday life, relationships, and businesses, but even when we are alone and close our eyes, the flames of a troubled psyche can rob us of peaceful sleep, thrusting us into a state of ceaseless suffering, metaphorically referred to as Hell (Jahannum) in the Quran.

The Companion

In the Quran, Paradise (Jannah) and Hell (Jahannum) are often described as intimately connected to the individual. They are not merely external locations to be reached in the afterlife but are states of being that each person carries within them throughout their earthly existence. Various terminologies are employed in the Quran to elaborate on this concept, illustrating how deeply intertwined these conditions are with the individual's consciousness and psychological state.

- The three-letter Arabic root is S H B or (ص ح ب). Arabic English Lexicon, by E.W. Lanes. Vol 4, Page 1652: Associated, kept company, or consorted, with him, companion, associate, comrade, fellow, fellow-traveller.

The Quran utilises the term "companion" to depict the profound association between an individual's state of mind and their experience of Paradise (Jannah), Fire (Naar), Hell-Fire (Jaheem), and other conditions or orientations such as the metaphorical left or right hand. These allegorical depictions serve as markers of character traits and psychological states.

For instance, in a physical context, someone might be described as a confident, angry individual or a person of wisdom. Each descriptor carries many implications about the person's temperament, attitudes, and behaviours. The Quran uses a similar approach in describing spiritual and psychological states.

In the Quran, the states of Jannah and Jaheem (or Naar) are depicted as being inextricably linked to an individual's mental and emotional disposition. Paradise or Hell isn't merely a destination after life; they can be perceived as the conditions of one's psyche, manifesting by their actions, attitudes, and moral choices in their earthly existence. Therefore, when the Quran speaks of a person being accompanied by Jannah or Jaheem, it highlights the profound impact of our internal state on our perception of reality and experience of life.

7:50 The Companions of the Fire will call to the Companions of the Paradise (Jannah): "Pour down to us water or anything that Allah doth provide for your sustenance." They will say: "Both these things hath Allah forbidden to those who rejected Him."

This parable emphasises the interconnectedness of our psychological states and how they influence our perceptions and interactions. Those "accompanying" Hell-fire, meaning those immersed in a psychological state of torment and anguish, can perceive those in Paradise or Jannah, which is associated with wisdom and knowledge. They plead for relief and guidance from those in the blissful state of Jannah, demonstrating an awareness of their own suffering and the potential for a different, more enlightened existence.

The inhabitants of Jannah, on the other hand, understand that those trapped in their torment must first acknowledge their own mistakes and be willing to engage in the self-correction process. They comprehend that wisdom and knowledge can't be imposed but must be actively sought and integrated by each individual.

The point about inhabitants of Jannah and Hell-fire communicating with each other further underscores that these terms do not refer to physical places but rather psychological states that exist concurrently within the human mind. This depiction emphasises the possibility of transition from one state to another based on one's choices, attitudes, and actions. Thus, through these parables, the Quran provides a profound understanding of the human psyche and our capability for transformation and growth.

The answer in the following verses is similar to what I have explained above.

7:46 Between them shall be a veil(thin barrier), and on the heights will be men who would know everyone by his marks: they will call out to the Companions of the Jannah, "peace on you": they will not have entered, but they will have an assurance (thereof).

7:47 When their eyes shall be turned towards the Companions of the Fire, they will say: "Our Lord! send us not to the company of the wrong-doers."

There is often a perceptible barrier between those who dwell in a state of greater self-awareness and those who are trapped in a state of suffering or confusion. This distinction may manifest in many ways, including one's demeanour, actions, or facial expressions. People who have achieved a higher level of consciousness often exude a sense of contentment, peace, and wisdom. They can navigate life's complexities with grace and equanimity, which can be discerned in their overall disposition.

On the other hand, individuals who are struggling with internal turmoil or grappling with their suffering may project a sense of restlessness, discontent, or agitation. These states, too, can often be perceived by others, particularly by those who have achieved higher self-awareness.

The Quranic narrative, with its allegorical references to Paradise (Jannah) and Hell (Jahannam), provides a framework for understanding these varying states of human consciousness. It imparts the wisdom that through self-reflection, self-correction, and the pursuit of knowledge, one can strive to transcend the form of internal torment and move towards peace and wisdom.

46:14 *Such shall be Companions of the Jannah(the hidden source of knowledge and wisdom), in it for eternity: a recompense for their (good) deeds/actions.*

2:82 *But those who are secure and do self-correction, they are companions of the Jannah for eternity.*

Whether good or bad, our actions and choices significantly influence our mental and emotional state. Every decision and step we undertake leaves a psychological imprint that shapes our consciousness and overall well-being.

When we engage in positive actions, uphold moral standards, show kindness, and strive for wisdom and self-improvement, we foster mental peace and happiness within ourselves. This can be likened to residing in Jannah (Paradise), a state of elevated consciousness and inner peace.

Conversely, if we engage in negative actions, harm others, act selfishly, or ignore opportunities for growth and learning, we create turmoil within our minds. This can lead to suffering and confusion, akin to Jahannam (Hell).

We carry these psychological states within us, regardless of our physical circumstances. Therefore, it is within our power to shape our own "Paradise" or "Hell" through our actions and choices.

The Difference between Jinn (اَلْجِنَّ) and Jannah (جَنَّةٌ) in Quran

Though the terms "Jinn" and "Jannah" originate from the same Arabic root word (J N N or ج ن ن), signifying that which is concealed or hidden, they refer to distinctly different concepts in the context of the Quran.

As elaborated in this book, Jinn is associated with "Inns" (the inquisitive mind faculty) and symbolises the hidden emotions and feelings that individuals tend to shield from others. Positive or negative concealed emotions can lead to embarrassment or mental disturbance if exposed. They continuously interact with our persona or personality at a lower-consciousness level, significantly influencing our preferences, aversions, and inherent biases. Despite their prominent role in our daily lives, we often consciously try to suppress or hide these hidden components of our psyche.

On the other hand, Jannah represents the concealed river of wisdom, intellect, and knowledge within our psyche. This reservoir of insight is amassed through life experiences and continuous learning. Unlike the ever-active Jinn, the wellspring of wisdom that is Jannah is not readily accessible. It resides within the domain of our higher consciousness and can only be tapped into through profound thought and self-reflection during moments of heightened awareness.

In summary, while both terms share a linguistic origin and a common theme of hiddenness, Jinn pertains to the concealed emotions and biases that affect our daily lives. In contrast, Jannah refers to the obscured wealth of wisdom and understanding that can be accessed through deeper introspection and awareness. While related in a linguistic sense, these concepts function on different levels of consciousness and have diverse roles and meanings in the context of the Quranic discourse.

Summary

Paradise and Hell are not depicted in the Quran as physical locations but instead discussed as psychological states. Viewing these concepts as states of mind rather than physical locations provides a deeper understanding of human psychology and our capacity for self-transformation.

We each fluctuate between mental and emotional well-being, often falling between total peace and profound suffering or anywhere between these states. Our attitudes, actions, and life experiences influence where we are on this spectrum at any given time.

A person who habitually engages in positive actions thinks optimistically, and actively pursues self-growth is likelier to experience peace and contentment, similar to the Quran's depiction of Paradise. On the other hand, someone who frequently engages in harmful behaviour harbours negative thoughts or resists self-improvement may find themselves in a state of mental suffering akin to the Quranic concept of Hell.

This understanding presents a powerful perspective on personal growth and spiritual development. It emphasises the importance of self-awareness and responsibility for our mental states and provides a compelling motivation for continuous self-improvement and moral living. By aligning our actions and thoughts with our highest values, we can cultivate internal peace and contentment, thus creating our own "Paradise" within.

10

The Book

The Innate Script

"Everything in the universe is within you. Ask all from yourself." – Rumi

Are we genuinely cognizant of the internal book within us, the innate wisdom sculpted through the trials, triumphs, and tribulations of our lives? This profound repository of insight guides us, whispers to us in moments of choice, and colours our path with the hues of experience. Yet, so often, it goes unnoticed, a silent symphony drowned out by the noise of everyday existence. Recognising and connecting with this inherent wisdom is embracing an uncharted dimension of ourselves, which holds the keys to our unique truths and personal enlightenment. But the question looms: do we truly hear its call, and are we willing to listen?

Our brains function in many ways, like books. They are remarkable information repositories, storing our life experiences, knowledge, and skills. Our senses capture information from our environment, which our brains process, interpret, and store. This storage is done in the form of memories, which are integral to our identity and guide our future actions and decisions.

This cognitive ability is an essential part of our consciousness. It allows us to learn from past experiences and apply this knowledge to new situations. Our ability to remember and learn enables us to adapt and grow.

In many religious texts, including the Quran, "The Book" often represents a repository of divine knowledge or wisdom. The human brain can similarly be seen as a book, recording our personal experiences and the knowledge we acquire throughout our lives. This perspective underscores the importance of nurturing our minds and seeking wisdom, as this enriches our "personal book," promoting personal growth and understanding.

Much like books, our minds can take us on journeys, explore new ideas, revisit the past, and even imagine the future. So, filling our "book" with enriching, positive, and valuable information is crucial to guide our lives and interactions with others. Emotional processing, or working through difficult emotions and memories, is a crucial part of emotional health. It allows us to understand, process, and integrate these experiences, helping us learn and grow.

These memories are usually the source of all our psychological pain or happiness. Therefore, it is necessary to have a continuous watch on what we record/write and store in our memory bank. Like any physical or mental activity, repetition is the key to perfection. Psychologically if we condition our mind to replay and revisit part of any specific memory trail, it will become more long-lasting and have a direct impact on how we feel and on our overall mental state and most often than not, it directly translates what type of personality we eventually possess. For instance, if we continuously replay and revisit painful memories in our mind, it will keep us in a continuous mental state of disturbance, causing anxieties, fears, depression, mood swings etc., and those memories become more muscular and last longer.

On the other hand, if we do the same with good and joyful memories, it will positively impact our overall mental state. This is a well-understood psychological fact about the working of the human mind, and most of the psychotherapies developed by psychiatrists, spiritual therapies developed by religious and cult leaders, and motivational speakers are all designed around this phenomenon. That motivates a person to condition their mind to stop replaying, revisiting the painful memories and focusing on good memories. Even if anyone needs more real good memories, exercises are developed to visualise the alternate realities. These alternate realities can be focused on through meditation or related practices. Through these exercises and techniques, visualisation is done to force the mind to think that you are living in an ideal world with no pain, no fear and everything in abundance per your desires and wishes. All these therapies and exercises are designed to put a person into a positive mindset and joyful state.

Indeed, our minds serve as an "internal book" where every experience, emotion, learned knowledge, and perception is recorded, akin to inscriptions on the pages of a book. This aligns with the understanding that our stored experiences and knowledge substantially influence our interpretations of reality.

Our internal book, comprised of our memories and experiences, significantly influences our identities, values, belief systems, and overall worldview. It impacts how we make decisions, react to new circumstances, and our capacity to learn and adapt.

Therefore, nourishing our minds and cultivating a positive mindset cannot be overstated. By consciously managing our thoughts and emotions and continually learning and growing from our experiences, we can construct a fulfilling "internal book" that fosters peace, understanding, and personal growth.

It's crucial to remember that although our past experiences and memories significantly influence our present, we are not entirely determined by them. Thanks to our brains' adaptability, a neuroplasticity trait, we can "rewrite" or "edit" our internal books. We can do this through new experiences, education, and a dedicated effort towards personal development. This principle is the foundation of therapeutic approaches like cognitive-behavioural therapy (CBT), which aim to alter problematic thinking patterns and behaviours.

The Book in Quran (الْكِتَابُ)

The wisdom within the Quran provides guidance on understanding and cultivating our internal scripts. The Quran emphasises the importance of acknowledging and protecting this internal book, recognising its role in shaping our thoughts, actions, decisions, and overall well-being.

The Quran advises us to guard our inner script from harmful influences or negativity. It encourages us to foster an environment of self-awareness, introspection, and continuous self-improvement. This nurturing of our internal script influences our personal development and our interactions with others and the world around us.

By understanding our internal book – recognising patterns in our thoughts and behaviours, we can strive towards making conscious decisions that benefit us and others. This might involve distancing ourselves from harmful or disruptive influences, embracing positive and enriching experiences, and constantly striving for growth and betterment.

By doing so, we utilise our internal script to work for us, to guide us towards a life characterised by peace, happiness, and fulfilment. Therefore, the wisdom within the Quran serves as a guide on this journey of introspection, self-awareness, and personal development. It underscores the importance of maintaining a healthy mind and fostering a positive outlook, vital in our journey towards a peaceful and fulfilling life.

Etymological and Lexical Analysis.

The Arabic root for Al-Kitaab is a masculine noun and is in the nominative case (مرفوع). The noun's triliteral root is kāf tā bā (ك ت ب).

- Arabic English Lexicon, by E.W. Lanes. Vol 7, Page 2590: A thing on which or in which to write (a paper, skin etc.).

The Inner Script (our database)

17:14 *"Read your own book (inner record/script), it is sufficient for your psyche, today you can account for yourself."*

Iqra, generally translated as Read, has the same root as Quran. The three-letter root is Q R A, which means to recite, to read in any shape or form EWL Vol 7, Page 2502. The verse emphasises the importance of self-awareness and accountability. It prompts us to read our internal book, which records our thoughts, experiences, and actions. The verse implies that we are responsible for our lives - our choices, decisions, and actions shape our lives significantly.

It encourages introspection, asking us to realise that our circumstances are often a direct consequence of our decisions. By understanding this, we can appreciate our successes and acknowledge and learn from our mistakes.

The verse calls for a change in perspective. Rather than blaming external factors or other people for our hardships, we are encouraged to look inward and analyse our role in our circumstances. This does not disregard the impact of external factors like socio-economic conditions or the actions of others, which can indeed influence our choices. However, the focus here is on our responsibility and power in shaping our lives.

It is important to note that the Quran addresses individuals with a developed conscience and a degree of control over their decisions. Therefore, it underscores the importance of making wise choices to lead a fulfilling life.

21:10 We have revealed for you a book, in which is a remembrance for you all: will ye not then understand?

The interpretation here presents an introspective lens to the Quranic verse, suggesting that the "book" referenced in the Quran is, in essence, a metaphor for our inner consciousness, our memory, and the recollection of our experiences, decisions, and actions.

The word "Zikar" in Arabic, translated as "remembrance," hints towards this internal book of memories we carry within us. This interpretation suggests that the Quran encourages us to delve deep within ourselves, introspect, recall our past actions, and derive wisdom from our experiences.

Such a reading implies that the Quran encourages us to use our intellect, memory, and capacity for self-reflection. It reminds us that our inner experiences, personal histories, and knowledge bases are critical resources in navigating our lives and making wise decisions.

This understanding does not negate the physical existence of the Quran as a book of wisdom and guidance. Instead, it adds another layer of comprehension, viewing the Quranic wisdom as a tool for self-reflection and self-improvement. It nudges us to consider how our internal "book" – our memory, consciousness, and personal experiences – influences our beliefs, decisions, and actions.

45:29 *"This Our Book speaks about you with truth: We recorded everything you were doing."*

We are, again, pointing out the book which records everything we do. Question to ask yourself: is it any physical book outside which records every action we do? OR is it our memory bank, inner book, and psychology that records everything we do? It is straightforward to understand if you think unbiasedly and without preconceived notions of conventional programming.

Indeed, the concept posits that the "book" the Quran mentions is interpreted as our consciousness, which records our thoughts, actions, and experiences. This internal record or "inner book" encompasses all our experiences and shapes our psychology.

The metaphorical concept of an "inner book" encapsulates the complete and unvarnished truth about ourselves. It records all our thoughts, feelings, and experiences, including the ones we may hide from the outside world. This record honestly reflects who we are – it encompasses our fears, complexities, emotions, and the multifaceted aspects of our personality.

The Book with No-Doubts in it (ذَٰلِكَ الْكِتَابُ لَا رَيْبَ).

This is the essence of (2:2), referencing the undeniable truth and clarity within our own "inner book". The Quran states, "This is the Book, in which there is No Doubt". Al-Kitaab, where "Al" emphasises the "The Book", not any book but the one which does not have any doubt. It usually refers to the Arabic Quran, which translators or its followers think has no doubt.

Within the scholarly discourse surrounding the Arabic Quran, adherents accept its precepts without contention. However, its universality might not resonate with all, especially those outside the faith. Nevertheless, an inherent "manuscript" exists, which I term "The Innate Script." This metaphorical volume, intrinsic to every individual, is beyond dispute. While external texts might be subjects of scepticism, this internal compendium remains unchallenged. When references to "Al-Kitaab" are made, they allude to this personal record, encompassing our experiences, cogitations, and sentiments. It epitomises our consciousness and stands as an irrefutable testament to our individual sojourns through life.

Doubt refers to a feeling of uncertainty or lack of conviction about something. It can relate to disbelief, mistrust, or scepticism about a particular matter and can vary in intensity from a slight hesitation to a profound lack of faith.

In a philosophical or intellectual context, doubt might be seen as a critical attitude that leads to questioning or challenging accepted beliefs and assertions. It may also be considered a natural part of the human cognitive process, prompting investigation, reflection, and ultimately, a more profound understanding or reaffirmation of a belief.

In some contexts, doubt can be seen negatively, leading to indecision or paralysis, particularly when it becomes excessive or obsessive.

However, doubt also plays a crucial role in scientific and philosophical inquiry, where a sceptical attitude towards accepted wisdom can lead to discoveries and advancements in knowledge.

It is imperative to grasp that the reference to a specific book in 2:2, described as being without doubt, presents a profound conundrum. On the one hand, no external text in the world can be whole without a doubt; even empirically proven concepts are susceptible to revision or enhancement through discoveries and interpretations. This is evident in the divide between believers, who may hold their religious texts infallible, and non-believers, who may question these foundations.

Consider, for example, a chemistry textbook with its proven equations and reproducible results. While the principles contained within might be irrefutable within the domain of chemistry, what is their relevance to an individual devoid of interest in that field? The information, although factual, may only resonate with some.

Contrastingly, there exists within each individual a personal "book," one that is free from doubt and universally relevant. This internal repository, formed from the unique experiences perceived through our five senses, bears a conviction and relevance that no external text can claim. Its truth and applicability are immediate and personal, transcending the divisions of faith, belief, or interest. This internal wisdom, recognised and trusted, forms a universal guide to human experience, untouched by external uncertainty or dispute. It signifies an intimate understanding of oneself and the world, a text (الْكِتَابُ) within, written through living, and read through introspection (الْقُرْآنَ).

2:44 Do you instruct personality (Naas) and forget your Psyche, and yet you study "the book"? Will you not understand?

The general traditional context takes everything from your inner world to the external world, which is the reason for our problem.

Indeed, the verse highlights the importance of aligning our outward persona (Naas) with our authentic self or psyche (Nafs). It signifies how our consciousness is the driving force that instructs and moulds our persona. Occasionally, under the influence of external factors, we may portray a character not reflective of our authentic selves, and this discrepancy can lead to inner turmoil or chaos.

This verse draws our attention to this potential inner conflict, implicitly urging us to comprehend the significance of this harmony between our Naas and Nafs. Even if we're acutely aware of our 'inner book', our memory bank of experiences and emotions, external factors may still pressure us into presenting a facade, possibly negatively impacting our overall psyche (Nafs).

The verse advises us to constantly review our 'inner book' to ensure that the character we're developing aligns with our inner peace and joy. In essence, it encourages us to understand the implications of our choices and emphasises the need for honesty with ourselves and others to maintain an internal balance and prevent conflicts. The verse encourages us to be genuine, underscoring that authenticity is the key to psychological harmony and peace.

18:49 And the Book will be placed (before you); and thou wilt see the sinful in great terror because of what is (recorded) therein; they will say, "Ah! woe to us! what a Book is this! It leaves out nothing small or great, but takes account thereof!" They will find all that they did, placed before them: And not one will thy Lord treat with injustice.

The verse underscores the all-encompassing nature of our 'inner book' – it documents every action, every decision, regardless of its scale. It does not merely record what we do but the intentions and context behind our actions. This comprehensive record forms the basis of our self-awareness and accountability; it's impossible to deceive ourselves, as our 'inner book' harbours the undeniable truth.

The verse highlights that the Lord (Rab) is devoid of any injustice. In essence, our decisions and actions lead us to face the repercussions, be they positive or negative. Thus, it encourages honest introspection. By examining our 'inner book', we can truly comprehend our actions and their consequences. This self-awareness guides us to make better, more conscious decisions in the future, leading us towards a path of peace and understanding.

6:20 Those to whom We have given the Book know this as they know their own sons. Those who are in deficit with their own Psyche refuse, therefore to believe.

The verse points towards a book of an incredibly personal nature, akin to the relationship one has with one's children. Can any external, physical book, be it any religious text or other, match this profound intimacy and familiarity? Love, affection, and emotions for our children are experiences that are deeply ingrained in our memory, in our internal book. Hence, it's our internal book – the reservoir of our memories and psychology – that the verse appears to refer to.

In the Quranic context, one can further understand this internal wisdom through the reference in 4:1. As detailed in previous chapters, the psyche is depicted as spreading out various innate determinations (referred to as "men") and innate desires (referred to as "women"). These facets of the psyche are also metaphorically described as the "sons" or "offspring" of our inner being.

Since these determinations and desires are integral parts of our psyche, they are readily recognised as our own. They are not alien or external; instead, they form the very fabric of our mental constitution. Like family members intimately connected, these aspects of ourselves contribute to our unique identity and influence our thoughts, feelings, and actions.

This powerful metaphor enriches our understanding of the human condition, offering a nuanced view of the complex interplay between different elements of our inner world. The reference underscores the unity and harmony within ourselves, where each component has a defined role and significance yet collectively contributes to a singular and cohesive whole. It's a poetic way to encapsulate the complexity of the human psyche, reminding us that the keys to understanding our desires and determinations lie within us, waiting to be discovered and understood.

Furthermore, the verse discusses those who lack self-awareness and those who cannot understand, observe, and monitor their psyche. These individuals, unable to recognise and address the discord within, often find themselves in trouble, dwelling in a state of denial. They live with insecurities, unable to find solace in security (Aman). Hence, it is said they will not believe it.

23:62 On no Psyche do We place a burden greater than it can bear: before Us is a book/record which clearly shows the truth: they will never be wronged.

Each psyche is solely accountable for its actions, bearing no burdens for which it is not responsible or aware. The consequences we face are invariably the products of our choices and actions, which are meticulously recorded in our internal script. There will be no injustice done, for we confront only the outcomes intimately related to us - the direct or indirect repercussions of our deeds.

17:13 Every man's fate We have fastened on his own neck: On the day/time of Standing (contextually the day of realisation, acknowledgement, when you become self-aware, stopped and ready to straighten up things), we shall bring out for him a book, which he will see spread open.

17:14 *"Read your own book (inner record/script), it is sufficient for your psyche, today you can account for yourself."*

The traditional interpretation found in Abrahamic religions of a distant Judgment Day is different from the Quranic motif that illustrates an ever-present internal book of psychology. This internal book is always accessible; those who consult it can hold themselves accountable and make necessary adjustments. The term "Yaum Al-Qayyamah", traditionally translated as Judgment Day in the context of Judeo-Christian belief, literally means "Day of Standing" or "Moment of Establishing". This refers to when an individual begins acknowledging their internal book, realising their accountability for their actions and deeds. Thus, "Yaum Al-Qayyamah" denotes the time of enlightenment, when one starts connecting with their inner psychological processes and consciousness, not a far-off Judgment Day.

7:2 *A Book revealed unto you,- So let you heart be oppressed no more by any difficulty on that account,- that with it thou mightiest warn and remembrance for the Believers (or to those who are in security).*

The internal book resides within each of us, permanently present. Its revelation occurs when we recognise and acknowledge its existence. Revelation, by definition, is the process of unveiling or disclosing something that was previously hidden or unknown. In this context, the revelation happens when the barrier of unawareness is lifted, and the truth within us—the reality of this internal book—is finally brought to light.

Meaning of Haraj EWL Vol 2, Page 542
Not expanded, become disquieted, become in doubt, in difficulty.

Once the reality of this inner book is recognised, there should be no room for doubt or confusion, given that it is your chronicle. This book serves to recall or remember the choices you've made in your life

- right and wrong. It acts as a warning for those who have secured their belief or reached a state of security. It serves as a reminder of their actions, decisions, and consequences, encouraging introspection and self-awareness.

2:2 This is the Book; in it is guidance sure, without doubt, to those who are extremely cautious.

The inner script or book of your psychology is undeniably the book "in which there is no doubt", serving as a guide for those mindful of their actions. One should question oneself: what is the one book that holds no doubts for you that can be universally relevant to all human beings? When considering any physical book, doubt may linger; not all individuals agree on a single book's content or interpretations. The only book that holds no doubt is indeed our psychological book. Each of us does not doubt our own inner script because it is a record of our own life experiences.

Our personal memory records all events, good and evil that have occurred in our lives, and these memories are instantly accessible. This unique inner book transcends time and space within the mind, allowing us to recall the oldest and most recent memories immediately. In our minds, there is no room for doubt regarding this personal book. If one is self-aware, conscious, striving for self-improvement, protective of their psychological health, and maintains a balance of their actions, this inner book will continue to serve as a valuable guide.

Summary

Every human being, and indeed nearly all living entities, gather and store information. This accumulation of information takes the form of memory in various shapes and manifestations. This is a scientifically acknowledged fact. As humans, we possess a highly efficient brain, which archives every day of our lives as memory and functions as the central processing unit of our physical body. It commands all our thoughts, subsequent emotions, feelings, and biological bodily functions.

The Quran identifies this repository of memory as our internal book (Al-Kitaab, that has no doubt). The wisdom conveyed in the Quran seeks to connect us with this internal book, with the understanding that it is the key to both our happiness and suffering in life. We must consistently observe what is recorded in our memory and discern how to filter and manage what we absorb into our consciousness. As our internal book directly affects our overall mental well-being, becoming conscious and aware of the various internal processes of our psychology is essential. By doing so, we can maintain a healthy mental state and experience peace.

11

The Introspection

The Quran

"Your visions will become clear only when you can look into your own heart. Who looks outside, dreams; who looks inside, awakes." – Carl Jung

The internal book of wisdom can only be explored through the process of Al-Quran. In the context of the Quranic revelation (wisdom gained through introspection/deep reflection), one could postulate that the physical Arabic Quran serves as a metaphorical pointer, akin to academic texts in the field of medicine that elucidate the disciplines of Anatomy, Physiology, Biology, Microbiology, Biochemistry, Pathology, and so forth. These medical textbooks provide frameworks and structures to understand the complex mechanisms of the human body.

Similarly, the Quran acts as an intricate guide, encouraging individuals to delve into the depths of their consciousness, spiritual orientation, and moral fabric. This comparison elucidates that the Quran is a structured methodology for engaging with the intrinsic nature of human existence.

Therefore, the physical manifestation of the Arabic Quran becomes a symbol, a reflective surface through which the reader may access an internal realm of self-knowledge. It acts as a conduit through which the individual may navigate the multifaceted dimensions of the psyche, understanding ethical constructs and spiritual principles akin to how a medical student deciphers the human body through textbooks.

In this analytical perspective, the Quran transcends its status as a fixed text and evolves into a dynamic tool that aids in the intellectual and spiritual exploration of the self. The Arabic text, in essence, functions as a beacon guiding the reader towards self-realisation, conscious living regardless of cultural or religious disparities. It fosters a profound connection between the literary content and the experiential wisdom each person harbours, rendering the Quran a universally relevant text.

The Arabic Quran attributes multiple characteristics to the concept of the 'book.' One of the most frequently used terms in the Arabic Quran is the word 'Quran' itself. Typically, the meaning of this word is derived from a variation of the same word, 'IQRA,' which translates to 'reading.' Consequently, the general interpretation of the word 'Quran' also leans towards 'reading.' The issue arises when we consider that several words in the Quran are used to denote 'reading,' such as 'Utloo/Talawat' (27:92, 10:61) and 'Tilawat/Qirat' (16:98, 7:204, 17:45).

However, none of the translations is rendered as 'read the reading,' 7:204, 16:98 as it needs to make logical sense. Hence, it becomes crucial to understand the contextual relevance of the term 'Quran' and to undertake a lexical analysis.

Etymological and Lexical Analysis.

The proper noun is masculine and is in the genitive case (مجرور). The proper noun's triliteral root is qāf rā hamza (ق ر أ). Together the segments form a preposition phrase known as jār wa majrūr (جار ومجرور).

- Arabic English Lexicon, by E.W. Lanes. Vol 7, Page 2502: Read, recited, recited anything in any form or any manner.
- Hens Wehr, Page 882: Recite, to read, to investigate, examine, explore, to study thoroughly.

Quranic Contextual Meaning

55:2 *It is He Who has taught the Qur'an.*
55:2 The knowledge of the Quran is given or taught.

54:17/22/32/40: *And We have indeed made the Qur'an easy to understand and remember: then is there any that will receive admonition?*

54:17/22/32/40, Quran has been made easy for remembrance and recalling. A generic statement applicable to all: what is easier to remember than your inner script?

39:27 *We have put forth for men, in this Qur'an every kind of* **Parable**, *in order that they may receive admonition (Zikar or remembrance).*

30:58 *verily We have propounded for men, in this Qur'an every kind of* **Parable**: *But if thou bring to them any Sign, the Unbelievers are sure to say, "Ye do nothing but talk vanities."*

In verses 39:27 and 30:58, the Quran asserts that it encompasses all parables and examples to facilitate understanding. Which text can genuinely claim such exhaustive comprehensiveness? If one posits that it refers to the tangible Arabic Quran, one must ponder its universal applicability and the breadth of its audience's comprehension. Reflect upon this: the true reference may well be to one's intrinsic ledger. This internal register contains the essential paradigms requisite for comprehending one's intellect and wisdom.

Al-Quran is available via Revelation.

The Arabic tangible Quran is one of the many tools connecting us to our inner consciousness. The physical Arabic Quran repeatedly says that wisdom, knowledge, intellect, the criterion between right and wrong, and the healing for all psychological issues will be revealed through deep introspection. So, the actual Quran and its related wisdom will be the one revealed as explained in the following verses (20:2 revealed, 38:1, 54:17/22/32/40 Quran is remembrance/recalling/deep thinking/introspection, 4:82 revealed through deep self-reflection).

20:2 We have not sent down the Qur'an to thee to be (an occasion) for thy distress.

38:1 Sad: By the Qur'an, Full of Admonition (Zikar or remembrance).

4:82 Do they not consider the Qur'an (with care)? Had it been from other Than Allah, they would surely have found therein Much discrepancy.

"Al-Quran" signifies a specific process of deep thought, remembrance, and introspection of one's internal consciousness or 'inner script.' Through introspection or Al-Quran, individuals can achieve a profound understanding and realisation.

17:82 *We send down (stage by stage) in the Qur'an that which is a healing and a mercy to those who believe: to the unjust it causes nothing but loss after loss.*

This realisation is derived from an objective analysis of one's inner psyche (الْكِتَابُ) and can provide healing or 'Shifa' (17:82) for various psychological challenges.

17:9 *Verily this Qur'an doth guide to that which is most right (or stable), and giveth the Glad Tidings to the Believers who work deeds of righteousness, that they shall have a magnificent reward;*

Individuals who undertake corrective actions (17:9) based on the insights gained from these realisations and the healing power of introspection (الْقُرْآنِ) will find a cure for ailments like Kufar (concealment and covering of inner voice), Kazab (denial of inner truth), and Zulm (oppression of their psyche). In other words, Al-Quran encourages individuals to face their internal challenges head-on, facilitating healing and personal growth.

The Quran symbolises how we begin to comprehend our inner narratives. In this context, the Quran reveals our innate script or book. It conveys the message sent by the internal messenger within us all, originating from our internal book and delivered to our persona. This process aims to caution us, share good or bad news, inspire us to undertake or avoid specific actions and help us recognise our inner truth and self-awareness, among other objectives.

Types of Perception: Subjective vs. Objective

Understanding that our persona, or the 'Insaan' within us, is crafted by our consciousness is vital. This persona requires appropriate guidance to behave in the external world so that it maintains peace within itself and throughout our mental state.

Let's try and analyse a few verses to understand this concept better.

17:14 "Read your own book (inner record/script); it is sufficient for your psyche, today you can account for yourself."

The verse emphasises the realisation of one's internal script or personal book. There are two primary types of perception: subjective and objective. Reading from our inner book is often stored and interpreted subjectively through our personal biases and strong feelings about specific situations or events. However, when we review and analyse our inner book in such a subjective manner, we may be unable to understand our psyche due to inherent biases comprehensively.

When you do introspection and self-analysis, devoid of biased feelings and strong emotions, which blur your reasoning, the process of the Quran starts in your Psyche. The Quran encourages objective analysis, which requires basing our conclusions on logical reasoning, facts, and figures. It's about scrutinising why and how we made different life choices, their impact on our emotions and feelings, and doing so without any subjective bias.

In the Quranic context, the call to objective analysis emphasises a commitment to logical reasoning underpinned by evidence and coherent evaluation. This is not a mere epistemological exercise; it extends to a profound engagement with one's decisions and actions, their ramifications, and a careful assessment without succumbing to personal bias or unverified assumptions.

Therefore, unfolding the Quranic process within oneself is characteristically gradual, demanding a deep contemplation of the internal book of personal experiences and insights. This is consistent with various Quranic injunctions emphasising a patient and reflective approach to the text. For instance, 25:32 advises against expecting an instantaneous revelation, alluding to the progressive nature of the introspective process or Quran.

25:32 Those who reject Faith say: "Why is not the Qur'an revealed to him all at once? Thus (is it revealed), that We may strengthen thy heart thereby, and We have rehearsed it to thee in slow, well-arranged stages, gradually.

75:16 Move not thy tongue concerning the (Qur'an) to make haste therewith.
75:17 It is for Us to collect it and to promulgate it:

20:144 High above all is Allah, the King, the Truth! Be not in haste with the Qur'an before its revelation to thee is completed, but say, "O my Lord! advance me in knowledge."

Similarly, 75:16/17 cautions against hastening through the process of Quran, urging a deliberate and measured engagement with the Quran. Additionally, 20:114 emphasises waiting for complete inspiration and understanding rather than rushing through the Quran.

These verses collectively illustrate the Quran's insistence on a careful, thoughtful introspection that accommodates the complexity of this process and the profundity of its wisdom.

The Quran's emphasis on a slow, reflective process of introspection and understanding of the Inner Book (Al-Kitaab) is a metaphor for the journey of self-discovery and spiritual development. It is an affirmation that the path to wisdom and enlightenment is a gradual, often challenging process that requires patience, persistence, and a sincere willingness to engage with both the (Al-Kitaab) and one on a profound, transformative level.

The essence of this introspection, as advocated in the Quran, transcends the cursory appraisal of surface phenomena. It urges a meticulous examination of the underlying motivations, the interplay of emotions, and the rational or irrational basis for decisions. Such a rigorous self-examination accords with the Quran's broader thematic focus on conscious understanding, reflective inquiry, and balanced judgment.

When you attain self-awareness and objectively review your inner narrative, you'll generally start to comprehend how your thought processes are inherently tied to your emotions and, consequently, your life choices. Fundamentally, our lives are the products of our decisions inspired by our thoughts. Once we recognise this pattern, we realise we are the architects of our lives. Thus, it becomes essential to take full responsibility for them. This is the crux of the verses above. Essentially, the Quran represents our internal narrative's objective analysis (reading) (Al-Kitaab).

20:2 We have not revealed the Quran to you to put you in distress.

The Quran is revealed through introspectively examining one's inner narrative. This means that when you initiate the process of objectively observing and analysing your thought processes, their impact on your emotions, and your actions, the essence of the Quran manifests within you. The Quran represents the observation, realisation, and understanding of your inner book of consciousness, which holds the record of your life in the form of memories.

The process of self-understanding is not intended to cause distress. On the contrary, if grasped and mastered appropriately, it can serve to our advantage, aiding in alleviating mental stress. Certainly, upon rigorous introspection of one's inner narrative, one may discern instances where one's conduct might have been less than judicious, often propelled by emotions rather than rational deliberation. Such realisations, particularly at the outset, might be unsettling as they challenge one's ego. Yet, recognising and rectifying these psychological lapses can pave the way for enduring inner tranquillity and fulfilment.

7:204 When the Qur'an is read, listen to it with attention, and hold your peace: that ye may receive Mercy.

While introspecting and understanding your inner narrative, proceeding with great care and awareness is essential. When analysing your inner record objectively, pay heed to the resulting insights. Understand what your introspection is communicating and listen attentively. Are we paying enough attention to our internal dialogues and the wisdom they impart based on our experiences? Unfortunately, the answer may often be that we don't. In the hustle and bustle of life, we frequently disregard these internal dialogues, making impulsive decisions based on the moment's emotional surge rather than logic and thought. The aftermath is often the negative consequences of such actions.

That's why the verse emphasises caution during introspection (Quran) and the need to listen attentively to the insights it provides, for therein lies the path to mercy. This mercy stems from something other than listening to Arabic recitations imbued with mystical powers. Instead, it comes from the wisdom derived from your unique inner narrative through introspection — the objective analysis of your consciousness.

27:92 And to rehearse the Qur'an: and if any accept guidance, they do it for the good of their own psyche/souls, and if any stray, say: "I am only a Warner".

Peruse the manifestation of your consciousness, for those who derive guidance from it do so for their own betterment and mental well-being. However, those who choose to ignore these inner revelations from their consciousness are the ones who veer off the path or remain unguided. The 'messenger' only serves as a harbinger of caution. These warning messages are part of a continuous internal process signalled by our inner consciousness. This process transmits these warnings from our consciousness to our personas and acts as the 'messenger' of the Quran. The messages it brings may sometimes be cautionary, other times encouraging, and so on, depending on the situation.

10:37 This Qur'an is not such as can be produced by other than Allah; on the contrary, it is a confirmation of (revelations) that between your hands (in your possession), and a fuller explanation of the Book - wherein there is no doubt - from the Rabb of Knowledgeable.

This verse does indeed provide a crucial insight. The 'Quran' or objective analysis of our inner book Al-Kitaab' described here, cannot be created by anyone other than Allah, referring to the source of consciousness. This verse clarifies itself by stating that the 'Quran' from Allah confirms what is already in your possession, under your control, and provides complete details of 'The Book', which harbours no doubt.

Thus, we are faced with a fundamental question: What exactly do we possess? Is it a tangible, physical book written in Arabic? If that is the case, then the significance of the verse above would pertain only to those who recite the physical Arabic Quran, as that is what they hold in their hands. This interpretation would limit the relevance of the verse solely to individuals of a specific faith who possess a physical copy of the Arabic Quran.

However, if we took the inner book of personal experience and wisdom as (Al-Kitaab), and the process of reading, objective analysis, and introspection as (Al-Quran) precisely per the true essence of 17:14

("Read thine (own) record: Sufficient is thy soul this day to make out an account against thee."), 3:70 *(Ye People of the Book! Why reject ye the Signs of Allah, of which ye are (Yourselves) witnesses?)* and various others. In that case, the applicability of the above verse becomes universal. It transcends linguistic, religious, or cultural barriers and speaks to a shared human experience. In this broader interpretation, the Quran is not merely a physical book but a symbol of the timeless and universal quest for self-knowledge, understanding, and spiritual enlightenment.

This perspective opens the Quran to a far more expansive and inclusive interpretation, where its insights and teachings are not confined to a specific community or linguistic group. Instead, it becomes a shared human heritage that resonates with individuals across diverse backgrounds and traditions.

The inner book (Al-Kitaab) that we all possess, filled with the insights and wisdom gleaned from our personal experiences, becomes a universal text that we all "read" (Al-Quran) in our pursuit of self-awareness, moral integrity, and spiritual growth. This interpretation aligns with the overall physical Arabic Quranic theme and philosophy.

So, the process of self-realisation and awareness emanating from our consciousness through Al-Quran corroborates our consciousness and provides us with the details of our inherent book (Al-Kitaab), which we do not doubt. This all stems from our source of consciousness. This understanding transforms the perspective of the Quran being an external entity to an internal one, amplifying its relevance and personal connection to each individual.

39:27 *We have put forth for men, in this Qur'an every kind of Parable/Examples, in order that they may receive admonition.*

Arab and Ajam

"Arab" is usually taken as people from the Middle East or Arabic-speaking countries, while "Ajam" means all non-Arabs. Please refer to the Arabic Lexicon.

Etymological and Lexical Analysis.

- Ajam: Arabic English Lexicon, by E.W. Lanes. Vol 5, Page 1967: Ajam: Foreigner or non-Arabs.
- Arab: Arabic English Lexicon, by E.W. Lanes. Vol 5, Page 1992: Arab: Spoke Clearly, Elegantly, Distinctly, Intelligibly, Clear Articulation.

The Arab, as per lexicologists, is used for precise articulation and elegant and intelligent speech. At the same time, Ajam is the opposite of it, which is not clear, understandable or foreign in nature.

12:2 and 43:3- We have made it A Quran in Arabic, that ye may be able to understand.

41:3 A Book (Kitaab), whereof the verses (Ayah) are explained in detail;- a Quran in Arabic, for people who understand.

The traditionalist argument is always that Arabic is the chosen language of the Quran due to its vastness and the ability to explain huge details using minimum words. Whereas the lexicon and Quranic context itself shows that it is not referring to any particular language mentioned in the Quran, e.g. written language like Arabic, but rather the 'language' of personal consciousness. This language is not specific to a cultural or regional group but universal, articulated through internal dialogue and signals that are often ignored.

In this context, the Quran symbolises an introspective journey of self-awareness, self-exploration, and personal growth. Here, the 'Arab' is not a population or a dialect but represents clarity and comprehension. This inner 'language' is clear, precise, and personal to each individual. This language provides distinct signs and messages through the medium of personal experiences, emotions, thoughts, and memories.

If we attend to these signs, they serve as guidance in our life's path. The Quran emerges as a universal guide that individuals can access, irrespective of their linguistic, cultural, or religious affiliations. It calls everyone to self-reflection, prompting an understanding of oneself and continuous self-improvement.

Any language or terminology, or knowledge which is not understandable is Ajam (foreign) to us. For instance, Chinese, Russian, and French are all Ajam (alien) and non-understandable to me, while English is understandable/clear or Arabic for me. Our inner book will always be revealed to us clearly and intelligibly articulated (i.e. Arabic) through the objective analysis (Quran) of the inherent book (Al-Kitaab).

39:28 *The Quran (the objective analysis of the inner book) is (clearly articulated) and not twisted in order for us to become cautious of our own psyche.*

41:44 *Had We sent this as a Qur'an (in the language) other than Arabic, they would have said: "Why are not its verses explained in detail? What! (a Book) not in Arabic and (a Messenger an Arab?" Say: "It is a Guide and a Healing to those who believe; and for those who believe not, there is a deafness in their ears, and it is blindness in their (eyes): They are (as it were) being called from a place far distant!"*

As indicated in verse 41:44, the Quran symbolises an objective analysis of one's psyche, consistently articulated clearly, precisely, and personally recognisable, hence being referred to as 'Arabic'. It is never 'Ajami' or foreign because it arises from our thoughts, feelings, and experiences.

When we strive to enhance our self-awareness and heed these internal dialogues and signals, we find a remedy for many psychological challenges. However, those disregarding these internal signals can feel like being called from a distance. They are aware of this inner communication but fail to comprehend its significance due to a lack of self-awareness, hence a distant voice. The verse emphasises the importance of self-understanding and attentiveness to our internal dialogue for a balanced psyche.

10: 37 *This Qur'an is not such as can be produced by other than Allah; on the contrary, it is a confirmation of (revelations) that went before it and a fuller explanation of the Book - wherein there is no doubt - from the Lord of the worlds (Possessor of all knowledge).*

As the Quran suggests in these verses, it provides a tool for objective analysis and introspection, an avenue to access the 'inner book' or understanding within each of us.

In verses 54:17, 54:22, 54:32, and 54:40, the Quran states that it has been made easy to remember or to recall. This statement emphasises that the wisdom contained within the Quran is accessible and understandable. By engaging with their innate script (Al-Kitaab), individuals can unlock insights and teachings that resonate with their personal experiences and innate understanding of the world.

4:82 *Do they not consider the Qur'an (with care)? Had it been from other Than Allah, they would surely have found therein Much discrepancy.*

Verse 4:82 prompts readers to ponder and critically analyse the

Quran's messages, suggesting that it would contain inconsistencies if it were from any source other than Allah. This again points towards the integrity and consistency of the Quranic teachings, which resonate with the inherent wisdom within us, the 'inner book'.

17:89 And We have explained to man, in this Qur'an, every kind of similitude: yet the greater part of men refuse (to receive it) except with ingratitude!

Finally, verse 17:89 speaks to the richness of the Quran, noting that it contains various parables and examples. Despite this, many individuals often overlook or ignore these teachings. This verse urges individuals to pay closer attention to the Quran's lessons and engage in deeper self-reflection and introspection.

These verses suggest that the Quran (objective introspection) can be viewed as a tool or a guide for individuals to explore their consciousness, values, and beliefs. By doing so, they can better understand themselves and their place in the world. It serves as a reminder that we hold a depth of knowledge and understanding that can guide us through life's challenges when appropriately accessed and interpreted.

Quran and Guidance.

At this point, we have explored the concept that the Quran, and its guidance, are not confined solely to a physical text or a specific religious group. Instead, the terms "mankind" (Insaan/Naas/Jinn/Nafs), as referenced in the Quran, are understood to encompass aspects of our psychology. The Quran itself symbolises a process of introspection and self-reflection on our inner book—a book filled with personal experiences, lessons learned, and the innate wisdom each individual possesses.

27:92 Read the Quran; those who take guidance are for their own Psyche, those who do not take it, it is their own psyche.

The Quran, guidance and Psyche in a single verse. It is clearly saying the book Quran contains guidance for the Psyche. Those who will take this guidance will be beneficial for their psyche. Those who choose not to do it are their own choice.

17:15 Who received guidance/direction is for their own Psyche.

10:108 Say O mankind the truth has come from your Lord. Those who receive guidance it is for their own Psyche.

39:41 Indeed we have revealed a book on to you for mankind with truth. Those who take guidance it is for their own Psyche.

21:10 We have revealed for you a book in which is a remembrance for you, will ye not then understand?

5:105 O you who (believe) in Security! Your Psyche is on You. Those who astray cannot harm you once you are guided. You all have to consult back to Allah, he will then give you the news/inform you of what you have been doing.

6:104 The awareness from your Lord(sacred inner consciousness) has come to you. Those who become aware is for their own psyche, those who stay blinded, than I am not guardian over you.

Indeed, guidance within a religious context can be contentious, often associated with a need for direction from divine or external authority. Various religious traditions assert their unique belief systems or texts as exclusive sources of guidance.

However, analysing the relevant verses in the Quran leads to a different understanding. Rather than portraying guidance as something that must be received from an outside force, these verses emphasise the importance of introspection, deep thinking, self-reflection, and objective analysis.

In this interpretation, guidance is not handed down to us from a supernatural entity or found solely in the sacred texts of a particular religion. Instead, it is a process that occurs within each individual's mind and soul. It involves a thoughtful and honest examination of one's beliefs, actions, and experiences, leading to personal insights and a deeper understanding of life's complexities.

This perspective demystifies the concept of guidance, removing it from the exclusive domain of the religious or spiritual elite and making it accessible to all. It recognises each person's innate wisdom and moral compass and encourages us to tap into those resources through thoughtful reflection and critical analysis.

In doing so, this approach to guidance empowers individuals to take responsibility for their own spiritual and moral development. It honours the unique journey of each person. It acknowledges that the path to understanding and fulfilment is not a one-size-fits-all endeavour but a deeply personal and often complex process. The emphasis on introspection and self-awareness resonates with human nature's intrinsic desire for self-realisation. It aligns with a more universal, inclusive understanding of guidance that transcends religious labels and reaches the core of what it means to be human.

Why is Quranic Guidance Necessary?

To effectively address any issue or problem, it's necessary to understand it clearly. As Charles Kettering said, "A problem well stated is a problem half-solved." This is particularly true in a psychological context. If we hope to devise a practical solution or offer meaningful guidance, we must first comprehensively understand the psychosocial issues at hand.

Let's consider some common psychological issues or thought patterns that virtually all humans experience, for which they might seek advice or guidance. This guidance doesn't necessarily need to come from an external source; in most cases, it could result from personal introspection. If you can analyse your psyche regularly and objectively, you can identify and address most of your psychological issues.

These psychological issues can include all kinds of fears and complexes, resulting in anxiety, depression, and other problems. If these issues are left unchecked, they can become ingrained, leading to persistent negative or positive thought patterns. These thought patterns can further cause lasting mental and physical problems.

The Arabic Quran discusses a variety of these fears and psychological issues, such as the fear for life (26:14), fear of prominent personalities (20:67), fear of unknown personalities (51:28), fear of bodily harm (20:45), fear of not having future generations (19:5), and fear of thunder and lightning (13:12/13). The list is extensive, but the point is that the Quran extensively discusses psychological issues, including anxiety, depression, jealousy, envy, arrogance, and fears, and offers ways to identify and manage these issues.

Consequently, a meticulous examination of our challenges is imperative, necessitating understanding their foundational causes. Corrective measures based on this understanding are vital for restoring our psychological equilibrium and inner serenity.

The source of this advice or guidance doesn't necessarily have to be the Quran either. It can come from personal life experiences, teachings you received growing up, wisdom from parents and grandparents, cultural and traditional norms, formal education, religious and non-religious scholars, books, media, and other sources. Any information that helps you understand your psychological issues and provides a solution is considered guidance for your psyche.

The Quran aims to guide your psyche from a fearful, insecure state, where you suffer from anxiety and depression, towards a state of security, confidence, calmness, and tranquillity.

Psychological issues can hold a person back from performing at their best and consume much of their mental energy. Once you achieve a state of calmness and peace, you can use all your mental energy to build your life the way you want.

"Islam" comes from "Salam," which means peace. True peace is a balanced and stable state of mind. When the word "Salam" is prefixed with "M," it becomes "Muslim" in Arabic, which means someone who has achieved a balanced and stable psyche. In this sense, true Muslims are at peace with themselves, regardless of their appearance, rituals, or religious affiliations.

Verses 6:104 and 7:205 of the Arabic Quran remind us that the call of the Rab/Lord is within the psyche itself. Everyone, with or without the Quran, gets guidance from the same source: their inner consciousness. We must constantly refer to this inner consciousness for guidance and advice in our daily lives through objective introspection (Quran).

Those who ignore or reject their inner voice do so to their own detriment. However, those who listen to their inner voice, reflect upon it and act accordingly will find guidance and peace.

The Tilt of Psyche Towards Negativity.

The human tendency towards negativity can be linked back to our evolutionary past. For survival purposes, our ancestors developed a heightened sensitivity to threats, including conflicts within tribes, predatory animals, and natural disasters. As a protective measure, any perceived threats, be they physical, social, or emotional, created a negative psychological impact to help us prepare for and handle these challenges.

This inherent negativity of the human psyche has been the subject of many studies by psychiatrists and is often touched upon by motivational speakers, spiritual teachers, and mystic figures. This negativity is the foundation for various religious and religious cult systems. Leaders of these cults often exploit these fears by motivating followers to condition their minds towards positivity, thereby eliminating anxieties, depression, and negative feelings. The successful instillation of this positivity strengthens followers' belief in the cult or cult leaders. However, this is merely a psychological phenomenon of positive thinking, not the result of any supernatural powers in rituals, verses, or mantras.

Techniques like meditation, yoga, and various speeches and writings have been devised to train and condition the mind to think positively. While these efforts should be acknowledged, they should not lead to the idolisation or deification of these leaders. With the proper knowledge, one can achieve these positive changes in thought patterns and mental conditioning without relying on any guru, cleric, or scholar.

It's important to note that the human mind is naturally drawn towards negativity if left unchecked. Media outlets, governments, and religions capitalise on this truth. Fear is often propagated among the masses, leading to anxiety and depression, which political and religious leaders exploit. This non-stop negative bombardment skews the human psyche towards negativity. Our default reaction to the news is usually fear or expectation of something terrible happening, leading to various emotional disorders, which, if left unchecked, can have devastating physical impacts.

According to the Quran, its guidance is intimately linked to the human psyche. Given that the human psyche is naturally inclined towards negativity, understanding how it functions and conditions it towards stability and peace is crucial.

Verse 64:16 of the Quran advises us to be cautious with the source of our consciousness, or Allah, as per our capacity. It encourages us to listen, follow, and spend good for the sake of our psyche. Those who can overcome the stinginess of their psyche are considered successful. Ignoring our psyche, we lower our guard, allowing negativity to infiltrate our thought patterns, affecting our decision-making abilities. This negativity can manifest in every aspect of our lives, impacting relationships, jobs, education, business, and social interactions.

Quran 42:30 supports this idea, asserting that we are responsible for our problems. Our individual choices and actions often lead to issues, and while it's common to blame others, the reality is that we are the architects of our problems. This does not refer to accidents or natural disasters but rather to the conscious decisions we make that, individually or collectively, result in the issues we face.

The Process of Psychological Correction.

The human psyche often focuses on the negative and anticipates the worst outcomes. This default psychological state is common among many individuals. The Quran, however, guides individuals to understand these negative forces and trains the mind towards positivity, thus addressing and resolving the psychological issues created by our negative and excessive thinking.

In the Quran, this transformative journey is called the correctional process, or 'Islah'. Those who willingly embrace and follow this process are known as 'Salihoon', individuals actively engaged in self-correction.

The process initiates with a realisation of the current mental state and its causes, an understanding of the desired mental state, and finally, the application of the corrective process. This involves striving and journeying from a state of instability and unhappiness to a state of happiness and stability, as highlighted in the Quran (28:67). The journey from recognising the need for change to the active pursuit of a more content and serene state of mind is an integral part of this process of self-improvement or 'Islah'.

Verse 45:15 underlines the importance of understanding that the corrective process pertains to the psyche. Since our psychology is the epicentre of many issues, rectifying and conditioning it to cultivate positivity while eliminating negative influences and their associated emotional energies can address most of these issues. This, in turn, provides the necessary psychological strength to view life's challenges from the correct perspective.

Verse 41:46, in its second part, asserts that the sacred inner consciousness, or the 'Lord/Rabb', cannot be held responsible for anyone's darkness. This state is a choice made by individuals when they disregard their inner light and truth, choosing to remain in ignorance. In this context, darkness refers to the ignorance of understanding how various psychological processes operate and their impact on our emotional energies.

Verse 7:42 refers to those following the corrective process as the ones living in security. Their sense of security arises from experiencing fewer or no fears, leading to a lack of self-inflicted pain and, consequently, a state of mind free from depression and anxiety. This is achieved through accessing an inner source of knowledge, referred to as 'Jannah' in the Quran. This state of understanding and peace is eternal as long as they continuously engage in introspection and self-correction. In Quranic terms, 'eternity' signifies the entire span of one's conscious life (11:107). Once the physical body ceases to exist, the connection with the sacred inner consciousness is severed, rendering notions of peace and tranquillity, which are states of a conscious mind, meaningless.

Summary

The physical Arabic Quran fundamentally points towards understanding the human psyche, or the Nafs or Soul. Comprising human consciousness, the psyche encompasses many emotions, desires, curiosities, and thought patterns. The physical Arabic Quran provides insight into the mind's inner workings. It guides us in observing, understanding, and controlling these diverse states to achieve the ultimate goal: calmness, tranquillity, and peace.

This peaceful state is essential for focusing internal energy towards achieving success in life. According to the Quranic philosophy, success isn't measured by material possessions but by attaining a peaceful state of mind. All Arabic Quranic verses serve as abstract parables or examples designed to elucidate the various forces and energies at work within our psyche. Understanding these parables leads to a better understanding of our psyche and the inner workings of others, ultimately leading to a higher level of Emotional Intelligence, or EI. This higher EI translates into improved relationships and harmony within our social circles and society.

The word Quran means reading of the Arabi Book (also known as an Arabic Quran), but in contextual meaning, it points out the objective analysis of the internal book of our consciousness. It is these objective introspections that reveal and explain how various energies and emotions function within our psyche works and how we can gain control over them to achieve higher emotional intelligence. Much like any complex concept, understanding is best achieved through stories with characters embodying different aspects of a narrative. The Arabic Quran employs this storytelling approach, creating multiple characters to illustrate the intricate workings of the human psyche.

Moreover, the objective analysis of our consciousness has been made easy for us because it is native and clear (Arab) to us when we do it. This introspection helps us understand our psychology. Understanding our psychology is pivotal to achieving a happy, stable state of mind, boosting our Emotional Intelligence. This refers to the ability to observe, understand, and control our emotions and those around us.

12

The Signs

The Ayah

"Look within!... The secret is inside you." – Hui-neng

The Arabic tangible Quran is not a scientific text; instead, it is a compendium of signs. A 'sign' typically refers to an entity, characteristic, or event that signifies another thing's likely existence or occurrence. Within this chapter, we will strive to understand the importance of these signs, their delivery, and the messages they often convey.

These signs are meant to encourage reflection and contemplation, urging individuals to observe their surroundings, ask questions, and seek answers. The ultimate goal is to inspire spiritual growth, self-awareness, and understanding of the intricate balance of our psychological state. Understanding the significance of these signs can lead to a deeper appreciation of the Quran's teachings and its profound impact on personal and collective spiritual development.

Etymological and Lexical Analysis.

The Arabic root for Ayah (Verse) is a feminine plural noun and is in the nominative case (مرفوع). The noun's triliteral root is hamza yā yā (أ ي ي).

- Arabic English Lexicon, by E.W. Lanes. Vol 1, Page 135: A sign, token, or a mark, an indication, evidence or a proof.

The Signs of the Book

The Arabic Quran directs us towards an intrinsic "book of signs" that every human inherently possesses. These signs manifest as diverse thought patterns and the ensuing emotional responses within our bodies. Each thought and feeling indicate our internal states, and thus warrant acknowledgement, observation, and thoughtful regulation.

Much like a medical doctor conducting various tests to understand what's happening within a patient's body, the Quran invites us to awaken our self-awareness and observe the signs emerging in our psyche. The intent isn't merely to acknowledge these signs but also to proactively engage with them. By doing so, we can take the necessary precautions and measures to maintain a healthy mental state.

41:53 Soon will We show them our Signs in the (furthest) regions (of the earth), and in their own souls (Psyche), until it becomes manifest to them that this is the Truth. Is it not enough that thy Lord doth witness all things?

This inner monitoring system provides a unique tool to navigate our psychological landscape effectively. It encourages introspection and self-analysis, essential processes for personal growth and transformation. It also underscores the importance of mental health, advocating for inner balance and harmony. This self-awareness and the ability to manage our internal signs can lead to improved emotional regulation, deeper self-understanding, and a more fulfilling life.

> 31:2 These are the Sings of the Wise Book (Kitaab-ul-Hakeem)
> 28:3 These are the Signs Open and Clear Book (Kitaab-ul-Mubeen)

The terms Kitaab-ul-Hakeem (The Wise Book) and Kitaab-ul-Mubeen (The Open and Clear Book) are attributes of "The Book" as referred to in the Quran. As we've previously discussed, the "Book" the physical Arabic Quran refers to is not an external text but an inherent inner script within us. It is our reservoir of memories that record our life experiences. From this wealth of experiences, our consciousness arises.

This inner script, Kitaab-ul-Hakeem (The Book of Wisdom), denotes the wisdom we accumulate from our experiences. As we navigate life, we face many situations that teach us valuable lessons and insights. These experiences and the lessons learned make us wise, contributing to our understanding of ourselves and the world around us.

On the other hand, Kitab-ul-Mubeen (The Book with Clarity) represents the clarity that introspection brings. By analysing our life experiences, we can better understand ourselves and our narratives. This self-examination allows us better to understand our motivations, actions, and consequences, thereby aiding us in making more informed decisions.

Therefore, our inner script or "The Book", is a source of wisdom and clarity. It plays a crucial role in shaping our consciousness, influencing our decision-making, and guiding our behaviours and actions.

> 29:49 Nay, here are Signs self-evident (open and clear) in the hearts of those endowed with knowledge: and none but the unjust reject Our Signs.

Our inner book continually communicates with us through signs, sending messages that can be perceived by those in a state of self-awareness or heightened consciousness. These signs could be signals of hope and positivity or manifestations of fear and negativity.

The purpose of these signs is to deliver specific messages that can affect our emotions and feelings and consequently inspire us to act. Therefore, understanding these signs and the messages they convey is crucial. It helps us interpret our emotional states and appropriately guide our responses and actions.

Recognising these signs allows us to effectively anticipate, manage, and respond to different emotional states. This awareness equips us to balance our emotional responses and steer our actions in a direction that aligns with our personal growth and well-being.

Consider this familiar example: We all learn from our experiences, including our failures. When attempting a task we previously failed, our memories of the experience serve as a guiding force. As we navigate the same job again, we strive to avoid repeating the same mistakes. This corrective behaviour is directly attributed to the lessons learned from previous failures.

However, ignoring these memories, warnings, or signs and persisting in repeating the same mistake will lead to a cycle of frustration and disappointment. This is akin to the widely attributed quote from Albert Einstein: "The definition of insanity is doing the same thing over and over again and expecting a different result."

Recognising and heeding these signs is crucial for healthy decision-making and overall psychological well-being.

7:177 Evil as an example, are people who reject Our signs and wrong their own Psyche(soul).

As mentioned above, those who ignore their inner warnings repeat the same mistake, expecting a different result. Doing so only creates issues for themselves. They put their psychology in pain and disturbance.

2:41 And believe in what I reveal, confirming (the book/message) which is with you, and be not the first to reject (Awal Kaafir), nor sell My Signs for a small price; and be cautious from Me, and Me alone.

This source of our consciousness constantly sends us signs and indications, often as warnings or reminders. We must recognise and acknowledge these signs rather than reject or ignore them, especially for instant gratification. The repercussions of ignoring these signs frequently persist over a long period, causing ongoing difficulties or discomfort. Hence, it is essential to approach our consciousness with care and attentiveness. Always respect the signals it sends and consider them carefully in your decision-making processes.

41:3 A Book, whereof the Signs are explained in detail; a Qur'an in Arabic, for people who have knowledge.

This verse carries significant points of contemplation. It combines the concepts of the "Book" and the "Quran" in a single phrase, stating that the Book possesses comprehensive and detailed signs articulated in Arabic. In common parlance, "Arabic" typically refers to the spoken language of the Middle East. However, in classical Arabic, the term "Arab" denotes speech or discourse articulated in a clear, plain, and distinctly without ambiguity.

The verse suggests that the "Book" (Kitaab) has been expounded (Fussillat) via intricate signs (Ayah) through the process of introspection

(Quran), all in a crystal-clear and unambiguous manner (Arabic). This understanding is available to those who possess and acknowledge this knowledge - those who are self-aware.

> 3:70 Ye People of the Book! Why reject ye the Signs of Allah, of which ye are (Yourselves) witnesses?

> 7:9 Those whose scale will be light, will be their psyche in perdition, for that they wrongfully treated Our signs (Signs with Psyche)

The emphasis on reflection and understanding of signs from within our consciousness is a recurring theme in the Quran. Several verses explicit the connection between our internal and external worlds, suggesting that insight and wisdom are not merely about absorbing external information but are deeply rooted in our personal experience and introspection.

In verse 3:70, the reference to the "people of the book" can be interpreted broadly to mean those in touch with their inner script or innate wisdom. They are being questioned about why they would reject the signs of Allah, which are not distant or abstract but something they have witnessed first-hand as they arise from within their consciousness.

These verses provide further insight into the importance of reflection, understanding, and attentiveness to the inner signs within one's psyche.

> 25:73 Those who, when they are admonished with the Signs of their Lord, droop not down at them as if they were deaf or blind.

Verse 25:73 warns against neglecting or dismissing these signs, emphasising the importance of recognising and considering them. It suggests mindfulness beyond mere reaction and impulse, advocating for thoughtful consideration of one's internal cues and wisdom.

38:29 (Here is) a Book which We have sent down unto thee, full of blessings, that they may mediate on its Signs, and that men of understanding may receive admonition.

Verse 38:29 refers to a book revealed by the source of consciousness, filled with blessings and intended for reflection. This can be understood as a metaphor for each individual's innate wisdom and understanding, to be accessed through contemplation and introspection. It serves as a reminder for those with the insight to comprehend, emphasising the importance of deliberate thought and reflection on one's consciousness and experience.

30:21 And among His Signs is this, that He created for you mates from among yourselves, that ye may dwell in tranquillity with them, and He has put love and mercy between your (hearts): verily in that are Signs for those who reflect.

Verse 30:21 introduces creating a companion within one's psyche, bringing peace and love when consulted. This can be understood as forming a relationship with one's own inner wisdom, the hidden knowledge accessible through deep thinking and self-reflection in a state of heightened awareness. The notion of this companion is not a mere abstract idea but a tangible and valuable resource for guidance, providing tranquillity and insight for those who engage with it.

3:190 Behold! in the creation of the heavens and the earth, and the alternation of night and day,- there are indeed Signs for men of understanding.

Verse 3:190, with its mention of the creation or evolution of 'Samawat' (Heavens or higher consciousness) and 'Ard' (Earth or lower consciousness), adds another layer of metaphorical complexity to this theme. The verse uses symbols drawn from the natural world—the day-night cycle, the sun, moon, and stars—to represent different psychological states and forces within the human mind.

EWL Vol:7, Page 2562, الْقَمَرُ = The perplexity, confusion, deceive, beguile, moon, etc. - Nominative masculine noun
EWL Vol:4 Page 1596-97, الشَّمْسُ = Became clear, un-obscured, sun, etc. - Nominative feminine noun.

The 'Shams' (sun) represent clarity, understanding, and enlightenment, and the 'Qamar' (moon), expressing uncertainty, confusion, and perplexity, become vivid symbols of the dynamics of human consciousness. They provide a visual metaphor for internal experiences and suggest a cyclical nature to these states of awareness, akin to the transition between day and night.

These symbols within the Quran are not just allegorical devices; they are designed to guide readers in managing their consciousness effectively. By recognising and understanding these inner signs, individuals are equipped with the tools to improve their psychological well-being, navigate challenges, and cultivate a more profound sense of self-awareness.

The referenced verses illustrate the Quran's commitment to promoting a profound and nuanced understanding of the self. Rather than relying on external dogma or prescriptive rules, they encourage a sincere and thoughtful exploration of the human psyche. By engaging with these metaphors and reflecting on their experiences, readers are guided towards self-realisation, inner understanding, and spiritual growth.

In the context of these verses, the Quran becomes more than a religious text; it becomes a spiritual guidebook that leads individuals towards a fuller understanding of their minds. It fosters a relationship with the inner self that transcends religious boundaries and speaks to the universal human condition. The emphasis on personal reflection and inner exploration resonates with the broader theme of the Quran as a vehicle for self-awareness and enlightenment, reinforcing the centrality of the individual's relationship with their psyche in the pursuit of truth.

Sings from the Inner Landscape

Human psychology continually manifests various signs in response to the diverse situations and roles we encounter in our external interactions. These internal indicators, shaped by their potential influence on our mental well-being, may be perceived as positive or negative. Such signs encompass a range of emotions and states, from anxiety and fear to confidence and contentment. Each of these signs serves as a barometer, reflecting the state of our psyche in specific situations or circumstances.

30:24 *And among His **Signs**, He shows you the lightning, by way both of **fear** and of **hope**, and He sends down **rain from the sky** and with it gives life to the earth after it is dead: verily in that are **Signs** for those who are wise.*

30:46 *Among His **Signs** is this, that He sends the Winds, as heralds of **Glad Tidings**, giving you a taste of His (Grace and) Mercy,- that the ships may sail (majestically) by His Command and that ye may seek of His Bounty: in order that ye may be grateful.*

Each internal sign we experience carries an underlying message, serving as a conduit for specific information or emotions. It's imperative to engage in careful introspection and interpretation of these signs. Without such thoughtful consideration, we risk acting impulsively based on these signals, which may lead to decisions we later regret.

From a psychological standpoint, recognising and understanding these internal cues is crucial for well-informed decision-making.

5:86 But those who reject and belie our Signs,- they shall be companions of Hell-fire.

In verses 5:10, 5:86, 22:57, 7:177 and several other related passages, there is an implication that those who obscure or dismiss these internal signs, even after discerning them, subject their psyche to distress. This is due to the unfavourable outcomes that arise from neglecting these inner cues.

Summary

The Quran extensively emphasises the need to acknowledge and comprehend the signs or indications within our psyche. These signs serve as metaphorical language to express the complex internal processes of our consciousness. The signs, represented by various celestial bodies, symbolise different aspects of our psychological state. For instance, the sun symbolises clarity and understanding, while the moon represents uncertainty and confusion. Recognising and reflecting on these signs is crucial to managing our psychological well-being. This understanding goes beyond literal interpretations, encouraging introspection and self-awareness for a deeper comprehension of our mental states.

13

The Inner Voice

The Messenger

"There is a voice that doesn't use words. Listen."
"The quieter you become, the more you are able to hear." -
Rumi

The Arabic Quran frequently mentions the concept of an internal messenger, a presence within our psyche. This is another parable used in the Quran to emphasise the significance of our inner voice, which can often be drowned out by the constant chatter and distractions of our mind, continuously stimulated and fueled by the trials and tribulations of our daily lives. This internal voice of our conscience separates us from animals, giving us the capacity for moral judgment and ethical decision-making.

The notion of internal signs arising from our book of consciousness was explored in earlier discussions. These signs, encompassing messages, are integral to our psychological framework. Within this context, the role of the internal messenger is pivotal. This chapter explores this concept and its implications for our psychological well-being and spiritual growth.

Etymological and Lexical Analysis.

The Arabic word for Messenger (Rasool), which is an indefinite masculine noun and is in the accusative case (منصوب). The noun's triliteral root is rā sīn lām (ر س ل)..

- Arabic English Lexicon, by E.W. Lanes. Vol 3, Page 1081: Act of sending, bringing a message or a letter, carries the meaning of being calm, speaking without haste, and uttering messages easily.

The Messenger Within (The Conscience).

In earlier discussions, we delved into the notion of an "inner book" - a comprehensive archive of personal experiences and memories that every individual possesses. In tandem with this, each person is equipped with a multifaceted inner voice. One dimension of this voice results from our impulsive, instinctual, and unconscious reactions, while the other emanates from the wisdom and insights stored within our "inner book."

These inner communications are expressed through various sensations such as anxiety, internal dialogues, assurances, inspirations, gut feelings, joy, melancholy, inquisitiveness, hope, cautions, and more. Each of these sensations serves to convey a distinct message to the individual.

The capacity to discern, recognise, and segregate these instinct-driven voices from those grounded in reason, logic, and experiential wisdom is pivotal in making balanced and sustainable life decisions. These sensations or signs and the underlying messages they transmit are the genuine emissaries of our consciousness, communicating with us in an intuitive language that resonates deeply within our psyche.

In the Arabic Quran, emphasis is placed on the significance of the inner voice or messenger that is intrinsically connected to our intellectual faculties. The Quran, at various junctures, underscores the notion that this messenger emerges from within one's psyche, serving to refine and enlighten the individual. It bestows wisdom and imparts knowledge previously unbeknownst to the recipient.

2:129 *"Our Lord! send raise/excite them a Messenger of their own, who shall rehearse your Signs (Ayat) to them and instruct them in (inner) book/scripture and wisdom and sanctify them: For Thou art the Exalted in Might, the Wise."*

- BAAS (ب ع ث) EWL Vol. 1, Page 222-223: Roused, Excited, incited, urged, instigated, put one in motion or in action.

The inner messenger or voice gets raised or get instigated, "وَابْعَثْ فِيهِمْ رَسُولًا مِّنْهُمْ" translated as "Raise the messenger within them", the more introspective interpretation suggests that the "messenger" will always raise within our own consciousness that could also be understood as the voice of our conscience. The verse indicates a call to awaken or excite this internal messenger, who will guide us to recognise and comprehend our interior signs and wisdom. Rooted in our consciousness, this voice often goes unheard or ignored as we tend to make decisions based on impulse rather than rational thought and knowledge. The verse encourages us to engage in deep, logical thinking, enriching our understanding of our inner book and helping purify our actions, eliminating any impulsive or hasty decision-making influenced by negative or superficial thoughts.

2:151 *We have sent among you a Messenger of your own, rehearsing to you Our Signs, and sanctifying you, and giving you the knowledge of "The Book" and Wisdom, and giving you the knowledge you were not known before.*

62:2 *It is He Who has sent amongst the Unlettered a messenger from among themselves, to rehearse to them His Signs, to sanctify them, and to give them the knowledge of "The Book" and Wisdom,- although they had been, before, in manifest error;-*

3:164 *Allah did confer a great favour on the believers when He raises/ excites among them a messenger from among their own psyche/soul (themselves), rehearsing unto them the Signs of Allah, sanctifying them, and to give to them the knowledge of "The Book" (inner Script) and Wisdom, while, before that, they had been in manifest error.*

14:4 *We sent not a messenger except in the language of his people (communities), in order to make (things) clear to them. Now Allah leaves straying those whom He pleases and guides whom He pleases: and He is Exalted in power, full of Wisdom.*

It's crucial to understand that our inherent inner voice or "messenger," as referred to in the Quranic context, emanates from within our psyche or soul. It communicates with us through signs derived from our individual life experiences. These experiences, stored within our memory or inner script - "The Book" or Al-Kitaab - shape our wisdom and consciousness. They are the source of our human conscience, distinguishing us from other species.

Yet, this internal messenger's voice is often neglected or undermined due to the influence of powerful emotions that can dominate our decision-making processes. It's worth noting that, as per Quranic verse

14:4, these internal messengers or inner voices always communicate with us in a language we understand- our own internal dialogue. The challenge lies in acknowledging and learning to heed this voice amidst the emotional tumult often associated with our lives.

The internal messenger is not merely a passive conduit but an active participant in this process, engaged in a dynamic interplay with our consciousness. It facilitates a dialogue between our innermost thoughts and feelings, allowing us to engage with them consciously. This interaction helps us cope with various situations, providing insight, clarity, and direction when faced with complex decisions or emotional challenges.

The tendency to overlook, suppress, or even "kill" our inner voices is a well-recognized phenomenon, often stemming from our inclination towards impulsive and emotion-driven decision-making. This proclivity can lead to a disconnection from our deeper insights and wisdom, overshadowing the subtle cues and signals our consciousness provides.

It is worth exploring the underlying causes of this pattern, particularly from an evolutionary biology perspective. The following section will examine how our primal instincts, ingrained over millennia of human evolution, may contribute to this tendency. The intersection between our innate biological wiring and our capacity for higher consciousness offers a rich field of inquiry, shedding light on the challenges and potentials inherent in our human nature.

The Anatomy of the Brain

The connection between our emotions and our cognition is a well-studied subject in neuroscience, with the two main areas of focus being the limbic system and the frontal lobes of the brain.

The limbic system, often called the "emotional brain", consists of structures like the amygdala, hippocampus, and hypothalamus. Research has consistently shown the pivotal role of the limbic system in emotion processing. For instance, a study published in "Neuron" 2007 highlighted the amygdala's role in fear processing. Additionally, the hippocampus plays a crucial role in forming new memories about experienced events (episodic or autobiographical memory). Damage to this area can result in difficulties forming new memories, a condition called anterograde amnesia.

The frontal lobe, particularly the prefrontal cortex (PFC), is responsible for high-level cognitive functions known as executive functions. These include decision-making, problem-solving, planning, and social behaviour. A review published in the "Annual Review of Neuroscience" 2008 described the PFC as involved in decision-making and planning. Moreover, the PFC is crucial in emotional regulation. Research has shown that a specific part of the PFC, the ventromedial prefrontal cortex, regulates negative emotions.

The human brain hierarchically processes sensory information, starting from primary sensory areas, moving towards association areas, and reaching high-level processing regions. The limbic system, responsible for our emotional responses, receives sensory information relatively early in this processing pipeline.

This is particularly true for information that could have emotional significance. For example, the amygdala, a critical limbic system component, receives direct inputs from the thalamus, a vital relay station for sensory information. This allows the brain to quickly generate emotional responses to potential threats, a process known as the "low road" to emotional processing.

On the other hand, the frontal lobes, particularly the prefrontal cortex, are involved in higher-level cognitive processes like decision-making and executive control. They receive processed sensory information from multiple brain areas, integrate it, and generate appropriate cognitive and behavioural responses.

In this context, the flow of sensory information could explain why emotions can have a powerful influence on our behaviour. Since emotional responses are generated quickly, they can influence our decisions before we have a chance to engage in more thoughtful, deliberative processing.

However, it's also important to note that our brain has mechanisms to regulate these emotional responses. For example, the prefrontal cortex can send inhibitory signals to the limbic system, helping us control our emotions and make more rational decisions. This process is often called "emotional regulation" or "top-down control".

In essence, the emotional and cognitive centres of the brain work together, allowing us to react to our environment in a balanced way. Our emotions can influence our cognitive processes and vice versa, creating an interplay that impacts our behaviour, decision-making, and overall well-being. This connection is fundamental to our understanding of human psychology.

The Denial, Rejection and Killing of Messengers (Inner Voice)

The intrinsic voice or the messenger within one's consciousness, psyche, or soul is perpetually geared towards guarding against the repercussions of ill-advised decisions and actions 4:64, 9:128. Those who prioritise this voice naturally tend to make more informed and considered decisions, promoting a state of tranquillity within their psyche.

Nonetheless, we often cultivate personalities that overlook or dismiss these inner voices because our brains are designed with an instinctive leaning towards responding to our emotional impulses. Our brains are programmed with a bias towards immediate survival. We tend to favour immediate, emotionally driven responses over slower, more deliberative thinking.

When examined through the prism of psychology, this inherent inner voice underscores the profound importance of self-awareness, emotional regulation, and measured decision-making. We can make more balanced and thoughtful decisions by cultivating a deeper understanding and control of our emotional responses.

With the understanding that the 'messenger' refers to our inner voice, which conveys messages from our consciousness, the interpretation of related themes in the Arabic Quran, such as 'killing of the messenger', 'wars' (Harb), 'strive' (Jihad), 'killing' (Qatal), and 'Migration' (Hijrah) take on a more metaphorical and psychological significance, relating to the human mind's dynamics. These concepts will be explored more in-depth in subsequent chapters.

40:70 Those who reject the Book and the (revelations) with which We sent our messengers: but soon shall they know

Verse 40:70 speaks of those who reject "The Book" and the messengers that came with it. The 'Book' here refers to one's internal scripture, and the 'messengers' are the signals or signs that come from within us, our inherent inner voices. Some might deliberately or unconsciously deny these voices, a notion signified by 'Kazab' (lying or denial).

23:69 Or do they not recognise their Messenger, that they deny him?

In verse 23:69, a question arises: do individuals not recognise their own 'messenger' when they reject (Munkir/Inkaar) it? This 'messenger' is our inherent voice, speaking in a language we understand, carrying messages that we are familiar with, and seeking to purify our thought process with innate wisdom and intellect. However, despite recognising this voice, some may deny it, highlighting the human struggle to reconcile with our inner consciousness.

Various influences, including personal experiences and our environment, shape our thought patterns throughout our lives. These patterns largely determine the course of our lives and the personality we develop. When life is joyful and fulfilling, it generally suggests a positive thought pattern and personality, reflecting beneficial outcomes. However, if this isn't the case, it's highly likely that our thought patterns are skewed and need to be adjusted.

This adjustment necessitates paying closer attention to our inner voice's signs of wisdom and intelligence. Those who heed the messages from their inner voice will experience less fear and sorrow (as per references 30:9, 6:130, 17:15). This concept is akin to the common saying, "Think before you leap". Considering your decisions carefully often safeguards you from making poor choices without thorough, conscious deliberation and substantial evidence.

However, we can still make imperfect decisions regardless of how cautious or well we use our intelligence. This is where the process of self-correction becomes invaluable. It's crucial that as soon as we realise a mistake, we take immediate corrective action. The Quran refers to these individuals as 'Salihoon' or those who correct themselves. Learning from our mistakes is an essential part of life. The critical thing is to learn from our mistakes and move forward. Doing so will help reduce our fears, anxieties, stress, mental challenges and grief.

Summary

The myriad of sensations—be it pain, fear, anxiety, inner dialogues, urges, hope, assurance, intuition, inspiration, or emotions like happiness and sadness—all represent specific signals that communicate distinct messages to us. This messenger, or inner voice, interprets and relays the essence of these signals. While they resonate in a language innate to us, we frequently overlook their significance. By heeding their guidance, we can address and overcome our personal limitations.

Human evolution has predisposed our brains to process sensory information impulsively. However, we can cultivate the capacity to infuse our decisions with wisdom and discernment through systematic mental training and conditioning.

Within the context of the Quran, a "Rasul" can be seen as a constant internal entity, speaking calmly and articulately, continuously communicating with us. These "Rasul" are seen as the voice of the divine, consistently guiding us, which is always present and persistently speaks to us.

This concept of the internal messenger, translating signs from the book of consciousness, underscores the sophistication and depth of our inner world. It points to an intricate communication system within ourselves that enables us to navigate our lives with greater awareness, wisdom, and intentionality. It suggests that within our psyche lies a profound reservoir of knowledge and understanding, waiting to be tapped into, provided we take the time to listen and reflect.

14

The Life and Death

The Life (Hayat) and Death (Maut)

"The human being is a self-aware entity who is unaware of most of the things that are going on inside of himself." - Alan Watts

Arabic Quran doesn't concern itself with the physical aspect of life and death; instead, it emphasises their psychological dimensions. In this discourse, we won't delve into the traditional religious concept of life and death or the narratives about the afterlife and its historical contexts.

Readers may have discerned that the Quran represents a process of objective self-analysis, a journey into one's consciousness while in a state of self-awareness. Recognising that this physical Arabic Quran isn't the only avenue to self-awareness is crucial. In every culture and tradition, various methods have been developed to attain self-awareness or to 'become alive' in Quranic terms. The concepts of life and death within the Quranic context align with this understanding of the human psyche, an account we will further explore in this chapter.

In the Arabic Quran, the term "Maut" is utilised to signify death, often in conjunction with "Wafat", while "Hayat" denotes life. In this chapter, we will delve into the meanings and uses of these terms within the Quranic context, shedding light on their alignment with the overarching psychological philosophy in the Arabic Quran. Our exploration will aim to unravel the symbolic nuances these terms imbue, particularly in their correlation with consciousness and the human psyche.

Etymological and Lexical Analysis.

Maut is a masculine noun and is in the genitive case (مجرور). The noun's triliteral root is mīm wāw tā (م و ت) or M W T (موت).

- Arabic English Lexicon, by E.W. Lanes. Vol 7, Page 2741: Deprived of anything e.g., deprived of intellectual faculty, still, calm, motionless, deprived of sensation, and deprived of life.

Hayat is a form IV imperfect verb (فعل مضارع). The verb is third person masculine singular and is in the indicative mood (مرفوع). The verb's triliteral root is ḥā yā yā (ح ي ي) or H Y Y (حيى).

- Arabic English Lexicon, by E.W. Lanes. Vol 2, Page 679/78: Intellectually alive, revived, life, Remain Awaken, being conscious, in control of all senses.

Wafat or Wafi The passive form II perfect verb (فعل ماض) is third person feminine singular. The verb's triliteral root is wāw fā yā (و ف

ي). With death (Maut), another word used in the Quran for death is Wafat. The Arabic root for life is Wafat (Death) is W F Y(وفى)

- Arabic English Lexicon, by E.W. Lanes. Vol 8, Page 3057: Fulfilled, fully compensated, kept, took or received it fully, fulfiller, performer, keeper.

One crucial point to note is that the terms "Wafat" (death), "Wafa" (fulfilment), and "Aufo" (completion of a covenant) all stem from the same root word and share the same dictionary definitions. Yet, they have been given disparate meanings in conventional Quranic translations. I believe this translation discrepancy is a misfortune and a recurring theme encountered with almost every root word in the Quran.

The Death of (Nafs) Psyche

Regarding the Psyche (Nafs), the Quran states in various verses (29:57, 21:35, 3:185) that every psyche will "taste" (ذَائِقَةُ) death. It's often assumed that these verses refer to the inevitable physical death each living being will face. However, the term employed is "Zaiqa," meaning "taste."

It's only logical to infer that one has to be alive to taste or experience something. Consider this: what would be the significance of tasting anything if you were to die immediately after the act? Would the notion of taste make sense to you once you've experienced physical death, a state from which you cannot return? Surely not. The Quran frequently speaks of the abstract (Bil-Ghaib) forces of the mind that comprise human psychology. Similar logic applies to other verses in the Quran that refer to tasting the Azab (pain) 37:38, tasting the Fitna (the trial) 51:14, tasting the Rahma (Mercy) 41:50, and so forth. All these concepts exist within human psychology; we must be physically alive to comprehend any of them. Otherwise, they lose their meaning.

Physical death is an indisputable reality. However, in the same way that many parables and abstract concepts in the Quran have been interpreted literally, death has been similarly misinterpreted outside of its Quranic context. In the Quran, death is likened to the state of sleep (39:42), a temporary cessation of intellectual activity and consciousness, almost as if one is in a state of death.

39:42 It is Allah that takes the souls (psyche) at death; and those that die not (He takes) during their sleep: those on whom He has passed the decree of death, He keeps back (from returning to life), but the rest He sends (to their bodies) for a term appointed verily in this are Signs for those who reflect.

It's intriguing to ponder why the human mind is so captivated by life after physical death. Perhaps it's due to the unresolved questions and unfinished business that constitute our lives. For example, a person may lead a life of crime, causing immense suffering to others, yet evade justice in this world. Alternatively, a person may endure a lifetime of hardship and misery, dying without experiencing any alleviation or justice. These scenarios and others like them compel us to question the perceived cruelty of the gods of our cultural, traditional, or religious narratives.

To address this dissonance and soothe the anxieties of their followers, religious and traditional concepts had to offer some form of resolution. Thus, I posit that the idea of an afterlife was born. Nearly all religions and traditions incorporate an afterlife into their doctrines to assuage the fundamental human fear and anxiety precipitated by worldly injustice. As reiterated in this book, I won't delve into religious and traditional concepts. I merely aim to stir intellectual curiosity in readers.

I argue that our perceptions of injustice are sometimes subjective. Human beings, whether as individuals or as collectives such as tribes or nations, typically adhere to the primal evolutionary principle of survival of the fittest. Here, might is right, and justice is a tool used to serve self-interest at the expense of the weak. Of course, there are countless arguments for and against this idea. However, the fact remains that human civilisation still needs to fully shed the basic evolutionary instinct of survival of the fittest. I will leave this thought here for readers to consider.

Let us analyse without biases what Quran objectively says about Death.

30:19 It is He Who brings out the living from the dead, and brings out the dead from the living, and Who gives life to the earth after it is dead: and thus shall ye be brought out (from the dead).

In the verse above, the Quran depicts life and death as cyclical. Just as the Earth, symbolic of our lower consciousness, experiences cycles of death and rebirth, so does our psyche. The Earth in the Quran serves as a metaphor for the stage upon which the drama of human emotions and roles plays out, aptly termed Dunya.

Within the Dunya, we assume numerous roles concurrently; one might be a parent, child, sibling, spouse, manager, or employee, each role carrying its emotional baggage. The interplay of these roles and their associated emotions can generate a cacophony in our minds. If left unmanaged, this noise can overwhelm an individual, pulling them from heightened awareness to a state of unconsciousness or unawakened mind.

Those with greater self-awareness or enlightenment often strive to extricate themselves from this worldly noise. They aim to connect with their higher consciousness, becoming astute observers of their psyche or Nafs. This oscillation between self-awareness (life) and unconsciousness (death) is a natural, recurring process. Just as the earth, once barren, springs to life with the touch of water, our consciousness oscillates between states of life and death. The water is the wisdom from higher consciousness which help us become self-aware in this context. This comparison serves to facilitate our understanding of these complex concepts. Take a moment to reflect on this.

67:2 He who (Khalq) evolved the Death and Life, to see who amongst you do best of deeds. He is the exalted in might and forgiving.

The Arabic term "Khalaq" is commonly translated as "create." However, its derivatives, such as "Ikhlaq" and "Ikhlaqiat," signify "morals." Morality, distinguishing between right and wrong or good and bad behaviour, is often subjective and can vary between cultures. Yet, universal ethical norms within societies serve as a foundation for a communal moral code. This code guides social behaviour for harmonious coexistence and evolves with new experiences, knowledge, and collective wisdom.

In the Qur'anic exposition on human psychology, particularly concerning the 'Nafs' (Psyche), the evolution of morality is conceptualised as a dynamic and individualised journey. As individuals traverse the varied terrains of life, they perpetually engage in discernment, refining their cognisance of ethical paradigms. This ceaseless introspective learning, in turn, moulds and nurtures the conscience, making it a reflection of one's cumulative experiences and moral choices

While it is essential to acknowledge that "right" and "wrong" can be subjective, there are universally accepted ethical norms. The collective human conscience also evolves with these shared beliefs and principles. In this particular discourse, it's imperative to recognise that the delineation between morality — the discernment of right from wrong and the adjudication of good versus evil — remains profoundly personal and can exhibit subjectivity at the individual level.

Despite claims by organised religions, my perspective is that religious texts, including the Quran, don't dictate morality. Morality evolves as societies mature and collective wisdom expands. For instance, same-sex marriages, long deemed heresy in both Eastern and Western cultures, are now recognised and protected by law in many countries. Similarly, the practice of child marriage, once accepted in some cultures, is currently criminalised in many parts of the world. These examples demonstrate that morality is shaped by societal consensus and evolves independently of religious dictates. It underscores morality as a dynamic concept refined in response to societal evolution and necessities.

In verse 67:2, death is interpreted as lacking self-awareness or disconnecting from one's consciousness, whereas life is associated with achieving self-awareness and becoming cognizant of one's psyche. This transformative process evaluates who can carry out the best deeds according to our internal mechanisms.

"Best of deeds" might sound judgmental, but in the context of the Quran, it is always tied to a person's psychological stability and inner peace. Those who perform "right" or "best" deeds, as guided by their conscience instead of the dictates of the Quran, tend to achieve mental peace and tranquillity. Since our thought processes, awareness, and learning evolve from our experiences, the more we understand and observe our Nafs (psychology), the more likely we are to make sensible decisions. These choices, in turn, contribute to a more stable, fulfilling, and contented life. Therefore, in this context, we are our judges.

29:57 *Every soul (Nafs/Psyche) shall have a taste of death. Indeed, you will comeback to us.*

21:35 *Every soul (Nafs/Psyche) shall have a taste of death:* and We test you by evil and by good by way of trial. to Us must ye return.

3:185 *Every soul (Nafs/Psyche) shall have a taste of death:* And only on the Day of Judgment shall you be paid your full recompense (wafat). Only he who is saved far from the Fire and admitted to the Garden will have attained the object (of Life): For the life of this world is but goods and chattels of deception.

The verses above metaphorise "tasting" death for the psyche (Nafs). To taste something, one must be alive, suggesting that this death is not a literal end of physical life but a state of disconnection from self-awareness or consciousness. The ability to tell the tale to recall the experience is critical to understanding this metaphorical use of "tasting death."

This type of death, therefore, refers to falling out of touch with our consciousness and not being self-aware. And the recovery from this state, the reawakening to life, can be achieved by consulting or returning (Ruju) to our internal systems of consciousness. This can be done through introspection, or "Quran", in the metaphorical sense of objectively analysing oneself. Thus, "tasting death" and returning to life, in this context, encapsulate the continuous journey of self-awareness, self-discovery, and personal development.

Day and Night with Life and Death.

The concepts of life and death in the Quran are referred to as cyclical processes within the human psyche, paralleling the ceaseless cycle of day and night (3:27, 23:80).

3:27 Thou causest the night to gain on the day, and thou causest the day to gain on the night; Thou bringest the Living out of the dead, and Thou bringest the dead out of the Living; and Thou givest sustenance to whom Thou pleasest, without measure.

23:80 It is He Who gives life and death, and to Him (is due) the alternation of Night and Day: will ye not then understand?

This continuous rotation encapsulates self-awareness (life) and unawareness (death), painting an image of consciousness as fluctuating and recurring instead of a static state.

'Life,' in this context, represents a state of heightened consciousness or self-awareness, where an individual is fully attuned to their internal self and surroundings. On the contrary, 'death' symbolises a period of diminished awareness or a metaphoric 'sleep' (39:42), wherein one's senses are dulled, and their connection with their inner consciousness is reduced.

39:42 It is Allah that takes the souls (psyche) at death; and those that die not (He takes) during their sleep: those on whom He has passed the decree of death, He keeps back (from returning to life), but the rest He sends (to their bodies) for a term appointed verily in this are Signs for those who reflect.

These states of 'life' and 'death,' akin to the oscillation between day and night, are inherent parts of human existence. 'Day' signifies a state of enlightenment and self-awareness, an active engagement with one's consciousness (or being alive). 'Night,' in contrast, is a metaphor for the murkiness of the unconscious mind and the uncertainties that can arise without self-awareness (or being dead).

Against the backdrop of this cyclical paradigm, a common human tendency to deny this fluidity of consciousness is brought to light (22:66).

22:66 It is He Who gave you life, will cause you to die, and will again give you life: Truly man is a most ungrateful (Kaafir, concealer) creature!

Humans often lean toward interpreting life and death in their literal, physical senses, thus overlooking the internal transitions between different states of consciousness.

However, maintaining this heightened state of self-awareness is not a permanent condition, as highlighted in 21:34/35.

21: 34 We granted not to any man before thee permanent life (here): if then thou shouldst die, would they live permanently?

21:35 Every soul shall have a taste of death: and We test you by evil and by good by way of trial. to Us must ye return.

Practices across different religious traditions often aim to sustain or elongate this state of self-awareness, indicating the human desire for extended periods of conscious living.

Further, the concept of 'death,' or transitioning into a state of unawareness, is portrayed as an 'experience' or 'taste' (29:57). This temporary 'taste' of unawareness is a tool to stimulate the return to our conscious selves.

In this context, 'returning to Allah' is a reconnection with one's higher consciousness. By maintaining this connection, one can dwell in peace, symbolically a 'Jannah,' until they drift into a state of lower consciousness or 'descend' again.

Lastly, the judgment that one's psyche faces (39:70) is viewed as a direct reflection of one's actions on their psyche, with Allah, understood here as the internal sacred inner consciousness, overseeing these impacts.

39:70 *And to every soul (psyche) will be paid in full (wafat) of its Deeds; and (Allah) knoweth best all that they do.*

This interpretation reframes life and death in the Quran as psychological phenomena instead of physical events. It underscores the fluidity of consciousness, the pursuit of self-awareness, and the imprint of our deeds on our mental state.

Summary

In this Quranic interpretation, the concept of life is associated with a mind or psyche that is fully awakened, observant, and self-aware. In contrast, a mentality (or psyche) that lacks these qualities, essentially existing in an unawakened, unobservant, or unaware state, is considered dead.

There are several key points to note here:

1. The awakened state of the mind or psyche is where it can realise and communicate with its internal sacred inner consciousness (Allah).
2. This state of awakened awareness is not permanent within any human being. Due to worldly experiences and situations (Dunya), the mind or psyche can become unobservant and unaware, leading to a state of unconsciousness referred to as Death (Maut).
3. The Quran correlates this with the alternation of day and night, demonstrating how two closely related yet distinct states can transition into one another.
4. Another analogy used in the Quran is that of the dead earth returning to life with the arrival of rain. This physical rejuvenation parallels the psychological cycle of moving from an unaware (dead) state to a self-aware (alive) state.
5. As one gets increasingly involved or affected by worldly situations, stress can accumulate within the psyche, potentially transforming into pain. This necessitates a return to the process of consciousness and self-observation to rebalance the internal state.
6. Therefore, the Quran mentions that every psyche will experience death, implying not a physical death but a transient experience or 'taste' of unawareness.

7. In this framework, Allah's role in bringing death from life and life from death is understood as the continuous cycle of transitions within human psychology, moving between states of awareness and unawareness.

This interpretation suggests that life and death in the Quran are not physical but psychological, marked by self-awareness and consciousness levels. The continuous shift between these states is part of the human psyche's ongoing journey.

2

The Practical Implications & EI

PART 2

THE PRACTICAL IMPLICATIONS OF QURANIC WISDOM

AND

ACHIEVING HIGHER COMPETENCE IN EMOTIONAL INTELLIGENCE - EI.

15

Thoughts A Quranic Perspective

Thoughts

"The happiness of your life depends upon the quality of your thoughts." - Marcus Aurelius

Thoughts are central to human cognitive processes. Individuals constantly engage with various thoughts, but when certain patterns become distressing or dominate our cognition, it may hint at underlying psychological concerns.

Excessive focus on specific thoughts can skew perceptions, destabilise emotional equilibrium, and hinder daily functions. This includes persistent self-criticism, undue anxieties about the future, or the inability to move past prior experiences.

When such cognitive disruptions impact the quality of life, consulting mental health professionals is prudent. Equipped with expertise, they guide individuals in comprehending and steering their thought patterns, fostering healthier cognitive behaviours and bolstering psychological health.

Addressing these cognitive challenges is pivotal for self-awareness and personal evolution, emphasising the role of mental health in our self-understanding and realisation journey.

While thoughts lack tangible form, they can evoke palpable physiological reactions, exemplified by anxiety-induced alterations in blood pressure. An unchecked mind can spiral into detrimental thought patterns, affecting emotional and physical health. Yet, with intention and guidance, one can nurture constructive thought habits, enhancing emotional stability and physical well-being. Such tenets underpin numerous philosophical doctrines and techniques endorsed by motivational orators, spiritual guides, and personal development experts.

Our thinking processes are moulded by myriad elements: personal experiences, acquired knowledge, cultural heritage, individual convictions, and more. As life progresses, experiences prominently sculpt our beliefs, not just religious ones but our broader perspectives.

William James's statement, "You're not what you think you are, but what you think, you are," encapsulates the transformative power of thoughts on identity and worldviews. Recognising and channelling this profound influence is integral to fostering positivity and well-being.

Nevertheless, it is imperative to intervene before our thoughts evolve into maladaptive patterns that detrimentally affect our mental and physical well-being. Proactive conditioning and training of the mind are essential to curtail excessive rumination.

This book fosters awareness of this intricate process, aiming to illuminate the inner workings of individual thought patterns through the lens of Quranic wisdom. Doing so equips readers with insights and corrective strategies to achieve a harmonious psychological equilibrium.

Thought Patterns: A Quranic Perspective.

Thought patterns, often referred to as cognitive patterns or thinking patterns, describe the habitual ways individuals process information, often related to their responses to specific situations or their interpretation of events. These can be positive or negative, adaptive or maladaptive.

Beck and Ellis have eloquently delineated this concept in their respective scholarly works.

> "Habitual, structured ways individuals process information or situations, often linked to their emotional responses and actions. These patterns can be constructive or destructive, often influencing individuals' perceptions, attitudes, and reactions". (Beck, A. T. (1979). Cognitive Therapy and the Emotional Disorders. Meridian).

> "Recurring mental behaviours or habitual ways of processing information that can influence one's overall perception, behaviour, and worldview." (Ellis, A., & Harper, R. A. (1975). A New Guide to Rational Living. Wilshire Book Co.).

Setting aside the preceding discussion momentarily, it is widely acknowledged in cognitive studies that individuals cultivate distinct cognitive patterns based on their interpretations of events and circumstances. These patterns, influenced by one's inherent disposition, whether optimistic or pessimistic, reflect dominant thought processes that determine their recurrent modes of thinking.

It's common for most individuals to rapidly construct a mental framework or assessment of a situation, informed by their inherent biases and shaped by their habitual cognitive leanings. The brain's intricate capacity enables it to spontaneously associate and produce related ideas, supporting the initial perception.

These interconnected cognitions, irrespective of their empirical or logical validity, solidify within our consciousness, subsequently influencing our behaviours. Challenging and revising these entrenched perceptions, even when confronted with contrary evidence, often proves to be a formidable task for many.

We must closely monitor our thought patterns, ensuring vigilance over reflexive responses. One must recognise the mind's prodigious capacity to swiftly amass corroborative thoughts and ideas, which often bolster our initial, impulsively formed conclusions that lack deliberate contemplation.

These interconnected and interrelated thought patterns in the Quran are referred to as "Quam" translated as "Nations or Communities", which is contextual meaning.

Etymological and Lexical Analysis.

Qaum is a masculine noun and is in the nominative case (مرفوع). The noun's triliteral root is qāf wāw mīm (ق و م) or Q W M. The further derivatives of this word are Qaim, Aqim, Qayam etc.

- EWL Vol 8: Page: 2995: Stood still, established, set up, put up, set upright.
- Hens Wehr Page 934: To get up, stand up, stand erect, to rise, exist, to be existent.

In the context of its root word, the term 'Qaum' or 'Aqim' denotes establishment or longstanding constructs. In the Quranic parlance, this is often rendered as 'community.' Conceptually, these 'thought communities' denote an assemblage or confluence of interrelated thoughts and ideas. We can think of each 'Qaum' within our mind as a collection of related thoughts or ideas, each contributing to our overall understanding or perspective on a particular topic or issue. These communities of thoughts could represent various aspects of our lives, such as our beliefs about self, interpretations of experiences, values, moral principles, goals, biases, etc.

For example, when we face a challenging situation, the 'Qaum' of thoughts that get activated might include ideas about our self-efficacy, expectations about the outcome, memories of similar past experiences, and coping strategies. Together, these thoughts form a coherent narrative or story that guides our response to the situation.

Similarly, our 'Qaum' of thoughts about a particular person might include our memories of past interactions with them, judgments about their character, feelings associated with them, and expectations for future interactions. This 'Qaum' forms our overall impression or understanding of that person and influences how we interact with them.

These 'Qaum' or communities of thoughts are not static; they evolve and change based on our experiences and learning. When we encounter new information that contradicts our existing thoughts or beliefs, we may experience cognitive dissonance, a mental discomfort that motivates us to resolve the contradiction. This can lead to updating or revising our 'Qaum' thoughts, enabling us to adapt and grow.

The Quran employs theophanic description, where human-like attributes are given to abstract concepts for better comprehension. It's worth noting that while the 'Qaum' metaphor can provide valuable insights into the nature of our thoughts and ideas, it should not be taken to imply that all thoughts within a 'Qaum' are equally valid or beneficial. Some thought communities may be based on faulty reasoning or biases, leading to negative emotions or unhelpful behaviours. Hence, it's crucial to regularly examine our 'Qaum' of thoughts, challenge unhelpful or inaccurate thoughts and beliefs, and strive to cultivate a more accurate and constructive mindset. This process of self-reflection and growth is a central theme in many spiritual and psychological traditions, including the Arabic Quranic teachings.

All internal conflicts are waged within the lower consciousness (فِي الأَرْضِ) of individuals, while guidance is sought from our higher consciousness (السَّمَاوَاتُ). These mental battles are won or lost based on which thoughts we feed and nurture. We are the creators of both our benevolent and malevolent thoughts. The harmonious and discordant communities within us are the creators of both peace and hate. The task then is reconciling the internal thought community or 'Qaum'.

Each sense and the inherent messenger or inner voice, as discussed in previous chapters, has an associated group of thoughts, referred to as a 'Qaum' in the Quranic context. These senses are ever-present within us, and we need to activate and heed the right ones. The body is only functional when the self (Nafs or Psyche) is aware of the thoughts it should nurture and those it should eliminate. However, we often undervalue our potential and seek guidance from weaker external sources. We must utilise our senses and the inherent prescription (Kitab 21:10) that guides our daily needs.

21:10 *We have revealed for you (O men!) a book in which is a Message for you: will ye not then understand?*

The Quran criticises this ignorance and lack of trust (Iman) in our innate abilities.

The Negatives and Positive Thoughts Within

Thought processes are intrinsic to human cognition. Inherently, humans experience a confluence of both positive and negative thoughts. The cornerstone of psychological equanimity is cultivating an environment where positive thoughts are nurtured and propagated. Conversely, it is imperative that the mind is adeptly conditioned to recognise, acknowledge, and critically assess negative thoughts and related patterns. Employing rational discernment and empirical evidence, one should actively counter these detrimental thought patterns.

Subsequently, this work delves into various thought communities (Quams) as discussed in the Quran.

The Deniers or Kaafirs: The interpretation of "Kafir" as an infidel or a non-believer is widely known. Yet, an analysis with a psychological perspective can bring out a more profound and insightful understanding. The term "Kufr" in Arabic signifies the act of hiding or covering something deliberately. It implies that the person involved is conscious and knowledgeable about what they are concealing (Arabic English

Lexicon, by E.W. Lanes. Vol 7, Page 2620; The Hens Wehr Dictionary of Modern Arabic, by The Hans Wehr. Page 957).

From this understanding, we can extrapolate the idea of a "Kafir" as an individual who willingly ignores or covers up truths they are aware of. These truths could emerge from our internal book (Al-Kitaab) of experiences, knowledge, and self-awareness, which undergoes constant evolution and modification based on our life experiences.

3:70 *Ye People of the Book! Why reject ye the Signs of Allah, of which ye are (Yourselves) witnesses?*

5:86 *But those who reject Faith and belie our Signs,- they shall be companions of Hell-fire.*

2:99 *We have sent down to thee Manifest Signs (ayat); and none reject them but those who are perverse.*

Quranic verses like 3:70, 5:86, and 2:99 emphasise our inherent knowledge and understanding of these truths and signs and our propensity to ignore or cover them up. This act of wilful denial, or Kufr, has significant implications for our thought processes and mental well-being.

For instance, a recurring Kufr or cover-up attitude towards our inner signs of anxiety, fear, or warning can develop a negative thought pattern, as described in 30:44.

30:44 *Those who reject the Faith (Kufr) will suffer from that rejection (kufr): and those who work righteousness will spread their couch (of repose) for themselves (Nafs/Psyche) (in heaven):*

Note: in general, Kufr is translated as "rejection of faith" in translations (which is a contextual meaning rather than an accurate translation).

This psychological phenomenon can manifest itself in impulsive behaviours, where individuals act without much consideration for the potential consequences. When the outcomes are undesirable, they are left with psychological repercussions, including further anxiety and depression.

Conversely, acknowledging these inner signs and truths, referred to as 'Salihoon' or correction, can help break these negative thought processes and resulting patterns. It involves acknowledging our mistakes, learning from our experiences, and being guided by our higher consciousness (10:86, 3:147).

10:86 And deliver us by Thy Mercy from those who reject (Qaum-al-Kafireen).

3:147 All that they said was: "Our Lord! Forgive us our sins and anything We may have done that transgressed our duty: Establish our feet firmly, and help us against those that resist Faith (Qaum-al-Kafireen)".

As put forth in verse 30:44, those who engage in Kufr or cover up suffer from the very act, while those who perform 'Salihan' or corrections attain guidance for their psyche. It's an ongoing struggle within us, where we are the first ones to deny our inner voices and consciously ignore the guidance of our higher consciousness. In such a scenario, we become the "Awwal Kaafir", or the first denier (2:41), and the greatest denier resides within us.

2:41 And believe in what I reveal, confirming the revelation which is with you, and be not the first to reject Faith therein, nor sell My Signs for a small price; and fear Me, and Me alone.

The Quranic teachings regarding Kufr (deniers or those who covered/concealed) and Salihan (those who do corrections) provide a roadmap for personal growth and mental health. They urge us to confront our truths, accept our shortcomings, learn from our experiences, and strive to improve ourselves. It may be challenging but rewarding, leading to enhanced self-awareness, comprehension, and overall psychological well-being.

The Oppressor or Unjust (Zaalim): In the Quran, the term "Zaalim" is typically translated as "Oppressor" or "Unjust". The concept of Zulm (oppression or injustice) in the Quran often refers to the actions of individuals who disregard or suppress their inner guidance system, thereby harming their psyche. This oppression is self-inflicted, not imposed by external forces or divinity.

The Quran repeatedly emphasises that people are responsible for their own actions and their resulting psychological or spiritual state. Key examples of such teachings include verses 10:44, 21:64, 7:177, 2:57, 23:62, 45:22, 7:23, 28:16, 30:9, 14:45, 2:54, and 43:76. These verses underline the principle of individual responsibility and the consequences of ignoring inner guidance and wisdom.

10:44 Verily Allah will not deal unjustly with man in aught: It is man that wrongs his own soul.

21:64 So they turned to themselves and said, "Surely ye are the ones in the wrong!

7:177 Evil as an example are people who reject Our signs and wrong their own souls.

Moreover, verses like 7:23 and 28:16 portray prayers where individuals acknowledge their wrongdoings to their psyche and ask for forgiveness, signifying the need for self-realisation and corrective action.

In the context of the Quran, prayer is interpreted as an internal appeal to the wellspring of our consciousness, a call for assistance triggered by the acknowledgement of our deficiencies and missteps. It signifies a conscious shift towards self-awareness, a pivot towards understanding our fallibility.

However, this internal appeal only resonates when we connect with our higher consciousness. It is not simply a matter of acknowledging wrongdoing but also necessitates a commitment to rectification and self-improvement. In Quranic terms, this self-reformation process is called "Islah" or correction. It involves taking tangible steps towards rectifying our wrongdoings and aligning our actions with the insights gained from self-reflection.

Thus, prayer, in this perspective, goes beyond a ritualistic invocation. It is an active and dynamic process of self-examination, self-correction, and growth, echoing the broader Quranic ethos of individual responsibility and self-directed moral development.

The Quran urges introspection and informed decision-making based on consultation with inner wisdom and considering signs or messages from within. Ignoring these signs and acting hastily leads to self-oppression and harm. Therefore, true peace and comfort can only be found by acknowledging mistakes, seeking forgiveness, and amending behaviour.

The Perverse (Faasiq): In the Quran, the term "Fasaq" is typically translated as "deviation from the right course" or "immorality" (Hans Wehr Pg. 835). The correct course is often interpreted as the path that aligns with human conscience, morality, and common sense and doesn't cause psychological distress such as anxiety, fear, or pain.

2:99 We have sent down to thee Manifest Signs (ayat); and none reject them but those who are perverse.

4:135 O ye who believe! stand out firmly for justice, as witnesses to Allah, even as against yourselves, or your parents, or your kin, and whether it be (against) rich or poor: for Allah can best protect both. Follow not the lusts (of your hearts), lest ye swerve, and if ye distort (justice) or decline to do justice, verily Allah is well-acquainted with all that ye do.

Quranic verse 2:99 emphasises that disregarding clear signs leads to deviating from the right course. This idea is echoed in 4:135, which urges believers to stand firmly for justice, even against themselves, their parents, or their kin. It advises against following personal desires that could lead to unfairness or swerving from justice. The verse underscores that acting justly, even when challenging, can lead to long-term psychological benefits, while hastily choosing the unjust path can result in continuous inner conflict and the creation of lies to justify wrongdoing.

59:19 And be ye not like those who forgot Allah; and He made them forget their own souls! Such are the rebellious transgressors!

Verse 59:19 posits that forgetting Allah equates to ignoring one's psyche. When one disregards their inner psychological state, they stray from the right path. The right path involves continuously observing one's psychological well-being and considering the impact of life's choices and actions on personal peace. Those who ignore these signs and constantly cause psychological pain to themselves are seen as transgressors or perverse.

Ultimately, the Quranic teachings highlighted here are not tied to any specific religion or tradition but to a universal approach to maintaining psychological peace and well-being. They encourage introspection and mindful decision-making based on rationality and common sense.

The Mischief (Mufsideen): The term "Mufsideen" refers to thought processes that exhibit bad, evil, or corrupt characteristics as a dictionary (Hans Wehr Pg 834/835; EWL Volume 6 pg 2396). These traits result in improper, dishonest, and harmful decisions and actions, especially when entrenched in one's psyche and daily habits.

These negative traits, which include cover-up/ignore (kufr), injustice/darkness/oppression (zulm), and lying/deceiving (kazb), inevitably lead to immoral and incorrect choices. When these choices are taken hastily, disregarding personal wisdom and intelligence, they often result in mischief or corruption (fasad) on earth (2:8-12), i.e., in the individuals' daily lives and environments.

2:8 *Of the people there are some who say: "We believe in Allah and the Last Day;" but they do not (really) believe.*

2:9 *Fain would they deceive Allah and those who believe, but they only deceive themselves, and realise (it) not!*

2:10 *In their hearts is a disease; and Allah has increased their disease: And grievous is the penalty they (incur), because they are false (to themselves).*

2:11 *When it is said to them: "Make not mischief on the earth," they say: "Why, we only Want to make peace!"*

2:12 *Of a surety, they are the ones who make mischief, but they realise (it) not.*

These wrong actions remain ingrained in the individual's conscience even if justified falsely to others. The mind, functioning even during sleep, keeps revisiting these actions, leading to overthinking and stress. Over time, these negative psychological states can cause physical health issues due to the connection between mental states, chemical reactions, hormonal responses, and emotions.

When deception becomes an inherent trait, individuals may start believing their lies and may not even realise the harm they inflict on themselves. They deceive themselves more than anyone else, causing moral decay in their lives and environments while claiming to be reformers. The Quran highlights that these individuals are corrupt and unsound but remain oblivious to their condition due to their self-deception.

In the context described, such psyches evolve into habitual deceivers to the extent that the aforementioned verses characterise this behaviour as a psychological disease. This affliction impacts their lower consciousness (Al-Ard) and pervades their overarching psyche. Consequently, these individuals perpetually exist in internal discord and contention with others in their surroundings.

The Associators (Mushrikeen): As we delve into the psychological underpinnings of Quranic philosophy, let's explore the term "Shirk" and its associated implications in this context. Traditionally, "Shirk" refers to the sin of associating any deity with Allah. However, the psychological interpretation of "Shirk" in the Quranic context offers a different perspective.

The dictionary definitions from Hens Wehr (Page: 547) and EWL (Vol 4: Page: 1541) suggest meanings such as "to share", "to participate", "to be or become a partner", "to associate", and so on.

4:116 "*Allah forgiveth not the association with Him, but He forgiveth whom He pleaseth other than this: one who joins with Allah, hath strayed far, far away (from the right)*".

Interpreting "Allah" as our sacred inner consciousness, "Shirk" could imply associating or contaminating our rational thought processes, which arise from our higher self-awareness, with impulsive and negative thoughts. These irrational thought processes, fueled purely by impulses and devoid of wisdom, disconnect us from our higher consciousness and rationality. Mixing (associating) negative thought processes with those based on rationality and wisdom contaminates and pollutes the psychologically balanced state.

In this sense, "Shirk" refers to the contamination and pollution of our thought processes received from higher consciousness in the self-awareness state with these negative thought processes. The verse emphasises the gravity of this act, stating that such association can cause severe disturbances to our psychological balance, distancing us from our inherent wisdom and source of rationality. Therefore, it's crucial to recognise and prevent such associations to maintain a healthy state of consciousness and uphold our connection with our higher self.

Negative Communities of Thoughts: In exploring our psyche through the lens of Quranic philosophy, numerous communities of negative thoughts, or 'Quam', are illuminated. These negative thought processes can manifest within our consciousness if they aren't mindfully observed and rectified. The Quran discusses these potential communities:

1. Perverse (Fasiqoon) - 51:46
2. Liars (Kaziboon) - 26:117
3. Oppressors (Zalimoon) - 23:94
4. Self-deniers (Munkiron) - 23:94
5. Corrupt (Mufsideen) - 29:30
6. Those who conceal or cover up (Kafiroon) - 10:86
7. Procrastinators (Akhareen) - 44:28
8. Transgressors or tyrants (Taghoon) - 51:53
9. Criminals (Mujrimoon) - 44:22
10. Losers (Khasiroon) - 7:99

11. Those who are excessive (Musrifoon) - 43:5
12. Arrogant or proud (Aaleen) - 23:46
13. Misguided or astray (Daaleen) - 23:106
14. Those fascinated or unthinkingly following (Masahoroon) - 15:15
15. Enemies (Aadoon) - 26:166
16. Ignorant (Jahiloon) - 11:29
17. Scattered, divided or confused (Yafraqoon) - 9:56
18. Antagonistic or adverse (Khasimoon) - 43:58
19. Self-guided (Haad) - 13:7
20. Blinded (Aameen) - 7:64
21. Wicked thoughts (Boora) - 48:12.

Each category delineates a unique pattern of negative thought processes that could emerge if not attentively regulated. These adverse mental trajectories are collectively termed as 'disease' (مَّرَضٌ) in the Quranic philosophy. Through cultivating mindfulness of these predispositions, individuals can strive to dispel or transmute these potential impediments to their ascent towards higher consciousness.

Positive Communities of Thoughts: In parallel with examining potential negative thought processes, the Quran also elucidates a series of positive thought patterns or communities, or 'Quam', that individuals can cultivate within their psyche. The exploration of these positive thought processes reveals the following:

1. Remembrance, Recollection, or Reconnection with Inner Intellect (Zakiron) - 6:126
2. Submission to Higher Consciousness or Awareness (Abidoon) - 21:106
3. Wisdom or Intellect (Yaqiloon) - 29:35
4. Assurance or Certainty (Yuqinoon) - 45:20
5. Knowledge (Yalamoon) - 41:3
6. Security or Faith (Youminoon) - 29:24

7. Self-reflection or Contemplation (Yattafakkaroon) - 45:13
8. Listening or Understanding (Yasmaoon) - 10:67
9. Self-correction or Rectification (Saliheen) - 5:84
10. Gratitude or Thankfulness (Yashkaroon) - 7:58.

These categories represent diverse positive thought processes or patterns that can be fostered within one's consciousness. Encouraging these positive tendencies can aid individuals in achieving a higher state of consciousness and a more balanced psychological state.

The Arabic Quran calls for a war against our negative thoughts to attain inner peace. However, we sometimes mistakenly kill the good thoughts when we should focus on eliminating the harmful ones.

Intrinsic Propensity towards Impulsivity (Hawa)

As humans, we all possess inherent predispositions and desires to obey our whims. This spontaneous inclination or instinctual response is called (Hawa) in the Quran. The verb's triliteral root is hā wāw yā (ه و ي), Hens Wehr Page: 1219 (inclination, desire, whim, fancy, arbitrary views on based on personal opinion), EWL Vol-8 Page:3046 (inclination of mind/soul, blameable inclination, inclination of the soul to that in which the animal appetites take delight). Those prone to instinctual and impulsive decision-making often place themselves in psychological imbalance due to acting without adequate consideration, as mentioned in 25:43. One cannot aid such behaviour unless corrective measures are undertaken.

25:43 Seest thou such a one as taketh for his god his own passion (or impulse)? Couldst thou be a disposer of affairs for him?

30:29 Nay, the wrong-doers (merely) follow their own lusts, being devoid of knowledge. But who will guide those whom Allah leaves astray? To them there will be no helpers.

52:23 These are nothing but names which ye have devised,- ye and your fathers,- for which Allah has sent down no authority (whatever). They follow nothing but conjecture and what their own souls desire!- Even though there has already come to them Guidance from their Lord!

30:29 highlights that individuals who follow their whims without the application of conscious thoughts and wisdom are neither guided nor can they be assisted. This is because these personalities often have to confront the repercussions of their psychological and physical actions.

53:23 reveals that the naming (Asma) without proper evidence from the source of consciousness indicates that sometimes we attempt to rationalise our impulsive decisions based on reasoning, for which we lack accurate data and verification. These are nothing more than conjecture (Zunna) of the psychological self (Nafs) and impulsive desire (Hawa).

This occurs when we have not established proper checks and balances on our negative thought processes, leading to various negative thought patterns. These patterns invariably lead to impulsive decision-making. Therefore, the key is to establish proper checks and balances on our negative thoughts.

The Firewall Within

Within each individual, both positive and negative thought patterns coexist. The distinction between a self-aware individual and one who is not lies predominantly in their respective abilities to manage these thought processes. Generally, those dominated by negative emotions and thought patterns erect a formidable psychological barrier akin to a technological firewall. Each component of this psychological barrier correlates with one or more negative thoughts or thought communities. This self-erected blockade hampers their intellectual potential, obstructing a high-level, comprehensive understanding of situations, and consequently, decisions are frequently driven by emotion alone. These individuals channel their mental energy and intellectual capacities towards justifying impulsive decision-making.

The Firewall Within

The Lower Consciousness

The Wall of All and Negative Thought Processes and Patterns.

Each brick in this wall represents the interrelated negative thoughts or communities.

Constant Inner Conflicts. Source of all our psychological disturbance and pains. The hell-fire.

The Higher Consciousness

Innate Book (الكتاب)
The source of all Human Intelligence and Wisdom available through Self-Reflection, Deep thinking, Introspection and Self-Awareness (القرآن).

The Lasting Peace and Tranquility.

Break this wall through Self-Correction(عمل صالح), Strive(جهاد), Qitaal(القتال) and Purification(ذكاة).

The Psychological Wall

Conversely, the wisdom propagated in the Quran advocates a

differing approach. Emotions, intrinsic to human nature, should be regulated by employing our wisdom and intelligence.

The more robust the psychological barrier erected in our minds, the more arduous the path towards self-correction and heightened self-awareness becomes. It is a widely acknowledged observation that individuals with predominantly negative thought patterns and impulsive thinking constructs often possess an incredibly resilient and impenetrable mental 'firewall'. Such individuals harbour a level of ego that forestalls any consideration of fallibility. They resist all internal or external assistance, immobilising themselves within a self-perpetuating cycle of psychological turmoil that their self-constructed firewall perpetuates, barring any form of rational thinking.

Summary

Our psyche is like a complex ecosystem composed of a multitude of thoughts, both positive and negative. These thoughts don't exist in isolation but form interconnected communities, shaping our attitudes, behaviours, and overall mental health.

Positive thought communities include hope, optimism, love, gratitude, job and others. Nurturing these thoughts increases self-confidence, resilience, and a sense of well-being. They also foster healthy relationships, productivity, and an open mindset receptive to growth and learning.

Negative thought communities comprise fear, anger, guilt, jealousy, despair etc. These can lead to anxiety, depression, low self-esteem and negatively affect physical health.

Balancing these communities of thought is crucial. The goal is to manage them effectively and prevent them from becoming overpowering. This is what killing these 'Quam' or communities of negative thought processes, in essence, means in the Arabic Quran. This involves nurturing positive thought communities, creating a buffer against adversity and encouraging a healthier, more balanced mindset.

16

Types of Personalities in Quran

The Mental States

"Mental pain is less dramatic than physical pain, but it is more common and also more hard to bear. The frequent attempt to conceal mental pain increases the burden: it is easier to say 'My tooth is aching' than to say 'My heart is broken.'" - C.S. Lewis

A person's mental state reflects the thought processes that drive their thought patterns. There is always a thin line between the balanced and unbalanced state of mind; how to achieve and keep it intact is the sole focus of Quranic wisdom. Suppose this delicate balance is disturbed and left unchecked. In that case, it causes the mind to fall into a vicious cycle of wayward thinking and an endless sense of wandering, often resulting in mental stress, depression, anxiety, and other mental disorders. The people who are self-aware and watch their thoughts and the impacts on their emotions generally have control over their mental states. In this world, there are situations which hit us unexpectedly and can have a severe effect on our balance state of mind. But self-aware people quickly tackle the problem by controlling their thought patterns. They are generally aware of the negative and positive thought patterns and their impact on general health and state of mind.

Based on various thought patterns we discussed in the previous chapters, a person can possess positive and negative personalities or psychologies.

There are following three kinds of psychologies mentioned in the Quran.

Evil-inclined Personality/Psyche "النَّفْسَ لَأَمَّارَةٌ" (Nafs-e-Ammara)

12:53 *"Nor do I absolve my own self (of blame): the (human) soul/psyche is certainly prone to evil, unless my Lord do bestow His Mercy: but surely my Lord is Oft-forgiving, Most Merciful."*

The verse above employs an emphatic prefix and noun. The prefixed particle lām, typically translated as "surely" or "indeed," adds emphasis. The indefinite noun, which is feminine and in the nominative case, has the triliteral root hamza mīm rā (أ م ر). According to Hens Wehr (page 33), it denotes command, bidding, instruction, commission, entrustment, investment with authority, or ascension to power.

While this verse was usually referred to in the context of Prophet Yousuf (Joseph), this analysis will avoid its Judeo-Christian biblical interpretation. The focal point here is the kind of psyche portrayed in verse: one that habitually commands, instructs, or inclines toward the improper, erroneous, evil, or immoral path. This disposition is the psyche's default behaviour. However, a crucial aspect highlighted in the verse is the grace of Allah/Rab, which can curb this intrinsic behavioural tendency. As previously observed, every psyche receives divine assistance through inherent messengers, wisdom, and intelligence. This mechanism represents a built-in mercy.

Self-aware and observant individuals, fostering positive thought patterns, harness this mercy. Conversely, those who disregard their inner messengers, wisdom, intelligence, and the perpetual signs from their internal book tend to succumb to their psyche's default behaviour, resulting in dishonest, corrupt, and incorrect life choices and psychological stress and pain.

This psyche is entirely governed by emotions, seldom invoking rational thought processes. Depending on an individual's emotional state, the impacts and severity of decisions and choices made by such a personality can range from high to medium to low.

Blaming Personality/Psyche "بِالنَّفْسِ اللَّوَّامَةِ" *(Nafs-e-Lawwamma)*

75:2 proclaims, "And I do call to witness the self-reproaching soul/psyche: (Eschew Evil)."

The term "lawwama," a feminine adjective in the genitive case, traces back to the triliteral root lām wāw mīm (ل و م). According to Hens Wehr's dictionary (page 1037), it signifies blaming, rebuking, scolding, or reproaching. It refers to a stern critic or severe censurer.

This term characterises a psyche that incessantly reproaches others or itself. Typically, individuals with this psychological disposition tend to live in perpetual discontent. They habitually attribute their failures, mistakes, blunders, and misdeeds to others, eschewing personal responsibility. Conversely, an extreme manifestation of this psyche is steeped in self-reproach, engendering a severe inferiority complex. These individuals internalise external disappointments, failures, and regrets, leading them into a vortex of self-reproach and deep-seated depression.

Unchecked, this psychological pattern can result in persistent mental disorders, as the individuals trapped within this self-reproaching cycle find it challenging to escape the perpetuating depressive state and constant self or external blame. This represents a disturbed or unbalanced psyche, which invariably manifests as an unstable personality.

Moreover, these individuals often exhibit an emotional personality devoid of rational thinking, especially in decision-making contexts. Their decisions predominantly stem from instincts rather than careful reasoning, contributing to their enduring unbalanced personality. Thus, this verse sheds light on the crucial role of self-awareness and emotional intelligence in maintaining psychological equilibrium and the potential psychological ramifications of persistently blaming others or oneself.

Satisfied Personality/Psyche "النَّفسُ المُطمَئِنَّةُ"
(Nafs-e-Mutmainna)

89:27 proclaims, "O (thou) soul, in (complete) rest and satisfaction!"

The term "mutma'inna," a feminine, active participle in the nominative case, traces back to the triliteral root ṭā mīm nūn (ط م ن). Hens Wehr's dictionary (page 666) defines it as quieting, calming, appeasing, pacifying, soothing, allaying, and assuaging.

The term describes individuals or psychologies that are predominantly content with their lives. These personalities exhibit satisfaction both internally and with their social surroundings. Having mastered self-awareness, emotional self-regulation, and advanced emotional intelligence, they enjoy greater success in various life facets than their counterparts. Their mental energies are not drained by anxieties, depression, and other mental disorders induced by negative thought patterns and clusters.

Human beings invariably harbour negative thoughts and clusters. However, the distinguishing factor between balanced and unbalanced personalities is their ability to control these negative thoughts. Balanced personalities have learned to condition their minds to think positively, consistently monitoring their thoughts and emotions. On the other hand, unbalanced personalities surrender to their negative thoughts, lacking the capability to govern their negative thought patterns and clusters.

The thought patterns and clusters that proliferate and dominate our psychology profoundly influence our personality types. Hence, pursuing psychological tranquillity and satisfaction necessitates intentional thought management and emotional regulation.

Cogitation, Consciousness, and Daily Existence.

The intricate dynamics between our thoughts, emotions, and physical bodies hold immense potential for shaping our day-to-day lives. It's a truism: "You're not what you think you are, but what you think, you are," by William James. But how does this reality manifest itself in practical, everyday life?

Our mind, a hub of ceaseless thoughts, propels us through life. Our thoughts are instrumental, from the simplest tasks like choosing what to wear to more complex decisions like choosing a career path or dealing with interpersonal relationships. However, the relationship between our thoughts, bodies, and emotions is a complex web that weaves through our daily lives, often unnoticed.

Take, for instance, a common scenario: getting stuck in traffic. It's a situation most of us have encountered, and it's a prime example of how our thought processes can have immediate and tangible effects on our physical state and emotional well-being. One person might approach the situation with frustration, letting their mind be filled with thoughts of wasted time, the injustice of the situation, and the incompetence of other drivers. The body responds to these negative thoughts - blood pressure rises, the heart rate accelerates, and a headache begins to throb. Emotionally, they may feel irritable, angry, and stressed for the rest of the day.

However, another person might approach the same situation differently. Instead of dwelling on the negative, they might see it as an opportunity - to listen to an audiobook, catch up on phone calls, or take a few moments to breathe and relax. Physically, they remain calm and collected. Emotionally, they may feel at peace, even content. Same situation, but an entirely different experience. This simple example underscores the profound impact our thought processes can have on our day-to-day lives.

It's essential to recognise that our thoughts are not static; they are constantly shaped and influenced by various factors, including our experiences, knowledge, cultural backgrounds, personal beliefs, and more. As we navigate life, our accumulated experiences significantly mould our thought patterns and, consequently, our belief systems.

For example, imagine you are a young professional embarking on your career. You've been handed your first big project, and it's daunting. If your thoughts tend to veer towards the negative, you might start panicking immediately. You might convince yourself that you're incapable, that you'll mess up, and that your boss should never have trusted you with such a responsibility. These negative thoughts trigger anxiety and stress, which can manifest physically through sleepless nights, poor appetite, and even lead to illness. You may underperform not because you are incapable but because your thoughts convinced you that you were.

Conversely, if your thought patterns tend towards the positive, the same situation could have an entirely different outcome. Yes, the project is daunting, but you see it as a challenge, an opportunity to learn and prove yourself. Your positive thoughts fill you with excitement and motivation. Physically, you're energised and ready to tackle the tasks at hand. You perform well not just because you are capable but because your thoughts reinforce your self-belief and ability.

This extends beyond the individual level to communities and societies. The collective thought patterns of a group can significantly influence the emotional climate and overall well-being of the group. A community plagued by negative thought patterns might be rife with conflict, unhappiness, and stagnation. In contrast, a community that cultivates positive thinking might enjoy harmony, progress, and shared satisfaction.

Implementing Strategies for Achieving Equilibrium in Life.

So, how can we apply this understanding to enhance our everyday lives?

Awareness: The first step is awareness. Recognising the power of our thoughts and their effect on our emotions and physical well-being is crucial. We must monitor our thought patterns, consciously identify the negative ones, and strive to replace them with positive alternatives.

Resilience: Next, we need to cultivate resilience. Life will invariably throw challenges our way. Our ability to bounce back from these setbacks largely depends on our thought patterns. Instead of dwelling on the problem, we can train our minds to focus on solutions, learn from the experience, and move forward.

Empathy: Another critical aspect is fostering empathy. By understanding how our thoughts and emotions are interconnected, we can better appreciate others' perspectives. This improves interpersonal relationships and contributes to a more harmonious community and society.

Continuous Self-Improvement: We ought to pursue relentless intellectual expansion and self-enhancement. As we assimilate more knowledge, our horizons expand, leading to more nuanced and well-rounded thought processes. Such progress not only elevates our personal well-being but also amplifies our positive impact on society.

Compassion: Lastly, but most importantly, we must remember to practice self-compassion. Negative thought patterns often stem from self-criticism and feelings of inadequacy. We can disrupt these negative patterns and nurture a healthier mindset by treating ourselves with kindness and understanding.

In conclusion, the complex interplay between our thoughts, emotions, and physical bodies offers a compelling framework for personal growth and well-being. By harnessing the power of our thoughts, we can not only enhance our individual experiences and contribute to a healthier, more harmonious society. This understanding of our inner mechanics, illuminated by the saying, "You're not what you think you are, but what you think, you are," is not just philosophical rhetoric but a practical guide for everyday life.

Summary

Personality is the direct reflection of our psyche. The psyche has multiple dimensions; we hide a hidden dimension from others, while the other dimension is exposed automatically through our persona. The psyche is the accumulation of the thoughts, experiences and learnings collected by our five senses. All these accumulations get stored in our memory, becoming our inner book (2:2 Al-Kitaab, which has no doubt in it.).

The default position of mind is always Evil Inclined mind (i.e. Nafs-e-Ammara), which always gives the command to take immediate and instinctive actions without conscious thought. This default mind position has to be appropriately conditioned regularly. The activities/choices we take are based instinctively or with proper deliberate consideration. By applying our wisdom, intellect will define what type of personality we will have, i.e., a Satisfied or Self-Reproaching personality.

As humans, we naturally tend to fear anything we conceive as dangerous for us physically or our self-image/persona or a threat to our interest in any shape or form. This natural tendency can lead to various personality disorders if left unchecked and uncontrolled. In its unbridled form, this natural tendency results in a Nafs-e-Ammara and the Psyche that are always inclined towards evil, immoral, and corrupt practices. It is the core of all sorts of negative psyches. This includes but is not limited to Nafs-e-Lawwama. The self-reproaching personality or psyche. This type of psyche is consumed by self-pity or projection syndrome, which blames others for their failures, shortcomings and problems. Any negative mentality will cause the bearer to remain in pain, depression, anxiety, and multiple other personality disorders.

The people who are self-aware and continuously condition their minds to think positively through continuous striving/Jihad and observe the negative thought communities and kill/restrict them to get a foothold in their psychology are the ones who develop a balanced and satisfied psyche.

THE HIDDEN WORLD ~ 271

The States of Mind

Satisfied Personality/Psyche
(النَّفْسُ الْمُطْمَئِنَّةُ)
Nafs-e-Mutmainna

The ideal state of Peace and Tranquility State and Peaceful State of Mind Depicted as Garden of Eden/Jannah/Paradise

It is imperative to discern our position on this spectrum. One may find oneself at either end or perhaps somewhere intermediary.

The ultimate objective is to attain Nafs-e-Mutmainna: a state of mental tranquillity and a harmonious personality.

Rash Decisions and Unconscious Choices: A Trajectory from Equanimity to Psychological Turmoil.

Recognition and Acceptance: The Path to Rectification (Islah) and Fostering Vigilance (Taqwa).

Evil-Inclined, Blaming Personality/Psyche
(النَّفْسُ اللَّوَّامَةُ، النَّفْسُ الأَمَّارَةُ)
Nafs-e-Lawwamma
Nafs-e-Ammara

The worst state of Pain/Anxieties and Depressions Unstable and Painful State of Mind Depicted as Hell Fire

The Psychological States

17

Pathways to Cognitive Rectification

The Psychological Warfare

"The greatest battles of life are fought out daily in the silent chambers of the soul". - David O. McKay
"The real battlefield is the mind". - Thich Nhat Hanh
"If there is no enemy within, the enemy outside can do us no harm". - African Proverb

As we embark on the profound journey towards achieving higher consciousness and attaining self-awareness, we inevitably confront the daily challenges and battles that arise within our minds. These internal struggles are primarily against our negative thoughts and the resultant detrimental impulsive thought patterns. Navigating these internal conflicts significantly shapes our mental state and overall mental health. Now, let us delve into this intriguing psychological battlefield from the perspective of the Arabic Quran.

The Quran outlines a framework for understanding and managing these internal battles, often symbolically representing them as a form of Jihad or striving. In this context, Jihad is not a physical war but a psychological struggle against our negative thoughts and behaviours. This interpretation resonates strongly with many contemporary psychological approaches, such as cognitive-behavioural therapy, which also emphasises the importance of recognising and challenging our negative thought patterns.

The Quran strongly emphasises the role of self-awareness and self-regulation in this internal struggle. It teaches that by becoming more aware of our thoughts and emotions, we can begin to understand and control them, ultimately leading to a more peaceful and balanced mental state. Furthermore, it encourages us to use our wisdom and intelligence - our mental "wealth" - in this endeavour, equipping us with the necessary resources to manage our internal conflicts effectively.

The Quran offers a unique perspective on mental health and personal growth by presenting this psychological struggle in a spiritual context. It provides a rich framework for understanding the complexities of the human mind. It offers valuable insights into how we can navigate our inner psychological battles and emerge as more robust, more self-aware individuals.

Jihad (Strive)

The term "Jihad" has been a subject of intense discussions and sometimes controversies due to its various interpretations, particularly in religious and political contexts. As this book focuses solely on the psychological aspects elucidated by the Quran, the term "Jihad" is only examined in its literal and Quranic contexts.

The Arabic term "Jihad" derives from the root "J-H-D", which denotes striving, exerting effort, or struggling. As Hens Wehr Dictionary (Page 168) points out, it corresponds to "endeavour, strive, labour, take pains, fatigue, exhaust, strain, exert etc." Similarly, in the Arabic-English Lexicon by Edward William Lane (Vol 2, Page 473), it has been described as "he strove, laboured, or toiled, exerted himself or his power, or efforts, or endeavours, or ability, employed himself vigorously, strenuously, laboriously, diligently, studiously, sedulously, earnestly etc."

Contrary to the popular misconception associating "Jihad" predominantly with physical warfare or "holy wars", the Quranic usage entails only psychological context. It involves personal struggles, striving against negative inclinations, and working diligently towards personal and spiritual growth. It is a perpetual process of self-improvement, maintaining inner peace, and fostering positive thought patterns. It signifies the continuous endeavour of a person to control their thought processes and identify and correct any negative mental patterns. In this sense, "Jihad" represents the mental and spiritual "struggle" or "effort" a person exerts to achieve personal and spiritual growth.

The context of Jihad/strive in Quran is related to human psychology. In this perspective, Jihad is posited as an internal exertion against one's negative propensities. This can be seen in the exegesis of the verses following verses.

25:52 Therefore follow Not to the Deniers(Kaafir), but strive (Jihad) against them with the utmost strenuousness (Jihad Kabeer), with the it (Qur'an).

25:52 appears to direct one to engage in an internal struggle, or Jihad, against their internal negativities or inclinations towards denial (Kaafir), which serve to occlude one's wisdom. The psychological Jihad referred to here denotes the inner tumult that individuals undergo when they must exercise thoughtful deliberation despite the potential for their emotional impulses to steer them towards a less-considered path.

29:6 And if any strive(Jihad), they do so for their own souls (Nafs/Psyche): for Allah is free of all needs from all creation.

47:31 And We shall try you until We test those among you who strive (Mujahideen) their utmost and persevere in patience; and We shall try your reported.

Further, 29:6 and 47:31 assert that the pursuit of strive/Jihad is intended for the individual's personal and spiritual evolution and the transformation of one's psyche or Nafs. The verses articulate that this struggle isn't for Allah but is needed for the individual's psychological equilibrium. Furthermore, these verses underscore the virtue of patience, or "Sabar", as a vital component of this process. It suggests that the capacity to curb impulsive decisions and properly analyse situations is a crucial facet of Jihad for self-betterment.

Next, let's explore the term "Amwal". This is traditionally construed as referring to material wealth or physical possessions. The juxtaposition of "Amwal" with the Psyche or Nafs (بِأَمْوَالِهِمْ وَأَنفُسِهِمْ) in the

Quran might indicate a deep-seated connection to human psychology. This would imply that "Amwal" could denote an individual's mental faculties, intelligence, and wisdom. This understanding aligns with the dictionary definitions where "Amwal" includes the concepts of resources and gains, which can be extended to have intellectual and emotional resources in a psychological context.

Thus, the term "Amwal", in a psychologically-informed interpretation of the Quran proposed, refers to the internal assets that one must leverage during the process of Jihad for personal and spiritual growth. This interpretation remains coherent with the broader psychological and spiritual interpretation of the Quran, where Jihad is conceptualised not as a physical conflict but as a struggle for personal growth and self-improvement.

"Sabeel" has a tri-letter root word "S B L" that means the path, the way, access etc. In the Quranic context, the term "Sabeel Allah" refers to the path of achieving complete self-awareness and connecting with your own higher consciousness.

29:69 of the Quran elucidates that the path (Sabeel) towards heightened self-awareness and elevated consciousness is navigated through striving (Jihad) within oneself. This echoes the principles of introspective struggle for self-improvement.

61:11 That ye believe in Allah and His Messenger, and that ye strive (your utmost) in the Cause of Allah, with your property and your persons: That will be best for you, if ye but knew!

Further substantiating this, 61:11 intimates that those who are psychologically secure with Allah (interpreted here as a symbol for a sacred inner consciousness) and their inner guide (the messenger) and strive (Jihad) in the way of Allah (signifying the quest for higher awareness/consciousness), utilising all the cognitive resources (Amwal) of their psyche, will find themselves in a superior state (Khair) of existence, if they could comprehend this reality.

In this context, true wealth, as posited by the Quran, is not materialistic but the wisdom and knowledge gained through introspection in a state of elevated self-awareness. This mental wealth, a treasure trove of discernment, must be utilised in the struggle against our impulsive behaviours and thought patterns. In this internal battle, this psychological Jihad, we find our personal growth and spiritual enhancement.

Zakah (The Purification)

The term "Zakah" in the Quranic context means the purification of something. In the framework of Quranic psychology, this refers to purifying our thought processes from harmful influences. This act of cleansing one's thought processes is seen as a crucial step towards achieving success - defined here as attaining a balanced mental state and inner tranquillity.

91:9 Truly he succeeds that purifies it,

87:14 But those will prosper who purify themselves

Specifically, verses 91:9 and 87:14 of the Quran assert that those who have managed to purify their thoughts will indeed find success.

4:49 Hast thou not turned Thy vision to those who claim sanctity for themselves? Nay-but Allah Doth sanctify whom He pleaseth. But never will they fail to receive justice in the least little thing.

Meanwhile, verse 4:49 points out those who mistakenly believe they have purified their psyches when, in reality, they have not yet achieved the necessary level of higher consciousness. This suggests a common self-deception, where individuals are in a state of denial about the purity of their thoughts and overall psychological well-being. However, their lives and mental states provide clear evidence of whether they have genuinely achieved this internal purification.

The Quranic emphasis on purifying one's thoughts underscores the importance of mental hygiene in one's journey towards self-awareness and higher consciousness. It suggests that we must first recognise and address negative influences on our thought processes to achieve mental peace and equilibrium. Doing so can purify our minds, paving the way for inner peace and success.

2:151 A similar in that We have sent among you a Messenger of your own, rehearsing to you Our Signs, and sanctifying (purifying) you, and instructing you in Scripture and Wisdom, and in new knowledge.

The Quran details the process of purification in verse 2:151. It starts with the messages conveyed by our inner voice or inner messenger. These messages offer signs derived from our innate script, which provides us with knowledge and wisdom. When we apply this acquired knowledge and wisdom to our negative thought processes, we effectively purify them.

This process means that instead of making impulsive decisions dictated by our emotions, we pause, reflect, and employ our wisdom and intelligence to make decisions. By aligning our feelings with intellect, we make better, more considered decisions, demonstrating high emotional intelligence. This is the fundamental process of thought purification, as described in the Quranic context. This purification contributes to our overall mental well-being, facilitates self-awareness, and guides us towards achieving a balanced state of mind and inner peace.

Indeed, the term (وَآتُوا الزَّكَاةَ) "give or offer purification" appears numerous times within the Quran, stressing the importance of purification in our thought processes. This phrase is commonly interpreted as a call for the giving of physical charity in conventional exegesis. Although charitable acts are undoubtedly commendable and essential, they do not capture the full extent of the Quranic idea of "Zakah."

In the Quranic philosophical context, "Zakah" refers to the inner purification process, cleansing the thought patterns within our psyche. It does not solely pertain to external, tangible acts of charity but to the internal, intangible processes that lead to a more balanced, self-aware state of mind. It emphasises the need to regularly scrutinise, purify and control our thoughts, thus helping us manage our emotions and make better decisions, ultimately leading to emotional well-being and psychological harmony. The process of Zakah is, therefore, integral to cultivating emotional intelligence and maintaining mental equilibrium.

The Qitaal (Killings)

The term "Qitaal", often coupled with "Jihad", has been controversial, particularly in interpretations and discussions about the Quran. As our analysis focuses on the psychological perspective, we will approach these terms from this angle.

80:17 قُتِلَ الإِنسَانُ مَا أَكفَرَهُ

80:17 Woe to man! (Qatal al-Insaan) What hath made him reject (Kufr) Allah;

A noteworthy verse in this context is 80:17, which mentions the concept of an individual (Insaan) being "killed" (Qatal) as a concealer (Kaafir). Traditional translations often avoid the term "killed" in this verse, as it may seem inappropriate or not fitting. However, considering the Quranic psychological context, we can comprehend that the Quran discusses the presence of various negative thought patterns within the human mind, embodied in terms such as Kaafir (one who conceals or suppresses), Kazib (liars), Munkir (deniers), Zaalim (oppressors), and so forth.

In this perspective, the Quran encourages us to "kill" or extinguish these negative thoughts through purification. Therefore, "Qatal" or "killing" does not refer to a physical act of violence but metaphorically refers to the transformative process of overcoming and eliminating negative thought patterns. This purification is achieved by harnessing our inherent intellect and wisdom, a point discussed in a previous section. The goal is not to obliterate or ignore our thoughts but to refine, manage, and channel them positively, thereby attaining a balanced psychological state and improved mental well-being.

61:4 *Truly Allah loves those who fight (Qatal/Kills) in his path in battle array, as if they were a solid cemented structure.*

Per the Quranic psychological philosophy, the "path of Allah" denotes a journey towards self-awareness, connecting with our inherent wisdom encapsulated in the inner script, or Al-Kitaab, and attaining a heightened consciousness. In this endeavour, the term "Qital" (commonly translated as killing) represents a metaphorical struggle or a transformative process where individuals work to eradicate or rectify their negative thought patterns and purify their psyche.

This mental battle against negativities is not a one-time event but a persistent struggle that requires constant vigilance and effort. The essence of these verses lies in emphasising this ongoing struggle and the importance of maintaining a balanced and purified state of mind. One must continuously confront and rectify these detrimental thought processes to uphold this equilibrium and keep advancing toward higher consciousness.

2:190 *Fight in the cause of Allah those who fight you, but do not transgress limits; for Allah loveth not transgressors.*

2:191 *And slay them wherever ye catch them, and turn them out from where they have Turned you out; for tumult and oppression are worse than slaughter; but fight them not at the Sacred Mosque, unless they (first) fight you there; but if they fight you, slay them. Such is the reward of those who suppress faith.*

2:192 *But if they cease, Allah is Oft-forgiving, Most Merciful.*

2:193 *And fight them on until there is no more Tumult or oppression, and there prevail justice and faith in Allah; but if they cease, Let there be no hostility except to those who practise oppression.*

Let's delve into verses 2:190-193, oft-quoted yet arguably misinterpreted due to a literal and traditional perspective. However, through the prism of the psychological lens of the Quranic understanding that this text has thus far embraced, the true essence of these verses can be unravelled.

2:190 signifies the 'killing' or purging of detrimental thought processes in the pursuit of higher consciousness or the path of Allah. It illuminates the idea that if such thoughts are uncontrolled, they can disrupt our inner tranquillity and mental balance.

Continuing to 2:191, the Quran advocates an ongoing process of self-correction and purification. This implies that whenever one recognises a negative thought creeping into consciousness, one must arrest and 'kill' or purge it. In this context, 'killing' equates to eliminating negative thought processes through a method of purification elaborated upon earlier.

Moving to 2:192, it offers the wisdom that if such negative thoughts cease to exist or, more pragmatically, if they cease to disrupt one's inner peace and balance, they may be left as they are. This reflects the human condition, which is inherently predisposed to negative thinking owing to our evolutionary history.

Finally, 2:193 underscores the need to act only when these detrimental thought processes perturb one's mental peace or lead to life choices that might negatively impact one's psychological well-being.

Therefore, these verses are not about physical violence or aggression. Instead, they metaphorically address the psychological battle within oneself, exhorting a constant strive towards purging negative thoughts that disturb our mental equilibrium. Per Quranic philosophy, this is the path towards achieving higher consciousness and inner peace.

Another couple of verses, in a literal and traditional context, show the violence, whereas they completely blend perfectly with the psychological philosophy of the Quran.

9:5 But when the forbidden months are past, then fight and slay the Pagans wherever ye find them, an seize them, beleaguer them, and lie in wait for them in every stratagem (of war); but if they repent, and establish regular prayers and practise regular charity, then open the way for them: for Allah is Oft-forgiving, Most Merciful.

9:5 delves into the notion of 'polluted thoughts' - those that are compromised by our negativity and intrude upon our rational thought processes. It suggests that these contaminated thoughts should be captured, or 'Khuzo', whenever they surface in our psychological landscape. When we become aware of these thoughts creeping into our mind, we are advised to encircle, or 'Hisaar', them with principles - 'Waqudu', a term derived from 'Qaida', meaning principles of rational thinking and reasoning.

This iterative process should persist until these thoughts either revert or repent, signifying 'Tauba', or cease to arise in our psyche. Alternatively, this could continue until the thought processes morph into a pattern where they first initiate their purification.

Thus, this verse underscores the importance of self-awareness and actively mitigating negative thought processes. It advocates for constant vigilance in identifying and curbing these destructive thoughts by applying principles of rational thinking, thereby paving the way for mental purification and achieving higher consciousness.

9:29 *Fight those who believe not in Allah nor the Last Day, nor hold that forbidden which hath been forbidden by Allah and His Messenger, nor acknowledge the religion of Truth, (even if they are) of the People of the Book, until they pay the Jizya with willing submission, and feel themselves subdued.*

9:29 traditionally conveys a sense of religious intolerance or violence directed towards non-believers or those not following the Islamic faith. This interpretation can be seen as promoting an "us versus them" mentality and hence might be construed as promoting hostility.

However, a different interpretation emerges if we reframe this verse within the psychological context of the Quran. Instead of promoting religious intolerance, the verse is a metaphor for an inner struggle against the negative impulses and thought patterns within one's psyche.

"Allah" can be understood as the individual's inner sacred consciousness. "Belief in Allah" then refers to being mindful and aware of one's thoughts, feelings, and actions. To "not believe" signifies being unreflective, impulsive, or emotionally driven.

The phrase "بِالْيَوْمِ الْآخِرِ" or "the last day" metaphorically refers to the consequences of our choices and actions. Those who deny "Yaum-al-

Akhir" act impulsively without considering the repercussions of their actions, which can harm their mental health and overall well-being.

The verse's reference to "those who do not forbid (Haram) what Allah and His messenger have forbidden (Haram)" is pointing to those who go against the wisdom of their higher self or consciousness, resulting in poor decision-making.

In this context, the call to "kill" is a metaphor for challenging and altering one's negative thought patterns. The idea of "recompensation" or "Jizya" refers to restoring balance within one's mind through rational thinking.

In conclusion, this interpretation presents Verse 9:29 not as a call to physical violence against non-believers but as a call to an inner struggle against detrimental thought patterns that can harm our mental and emotional health.

The Harb (Warfare)

The psychological conflict within oneself is referenced as "Harb" in Quranic literature, a term that shares its tri-letter root (H R B or ح ر ب) with the word "Mehrab" (الْمِحْرَابَ). As per the EWL dictionary (Page 541), "Mehrab" is conceptualised as a "private chamber" or the "highest chamber in the house," whereas "Harb" (الْحَرْبِ) is indicative of a state of excitement, agitation or war, as per EWL Page 540. These seemingly disparate definitions coalesce beautifully upon a nuanced analysis.

The highest recess or chamber within our psychological construct symbolises the state of self-awareness and realisation of our elevated consciousness (Mehrab). This heightened self-awareness stirs and excites our deep-seated thoughts and self-reflective processes (Harb).

47:4 Therefore, when ye meet the Unbelievers (in fight), smite at their necks; At length, when ye have thoroughly subdued them, bind a bond firmly (on them): thereafter (is the time for) either generosity or ransom: Until the war lays down its burdens. Thus (are ye commanded): but if it had been Allah's Will, He could certainly have exacted retribution from them (Himself); but (He lets you fight) in order to test you, some with others. But those who are slain in the Way of Allah,- He will never let their deeds be lost.

47:5 Soon will He guide them and improve their condition,

47:6 And admit them to the Garden which He has announced for them.

This interplay is evident in verses 47:4-6. The verse 47:4 suggests that whenever one encounters negativity (Kufr) within oneself, one should tackle/strike it (30:58 through introspection) at its roots (Riqab), signifying the root causes of the negativity. Once these causes are acknowledged and addressed, leading to the cessation or purification of such thoughts, these no longer excite or stir up (Harb) negative emotions within the psyche.

Verse 47:5 underscores the ramifications of the aforementioned actions, delineating their immediate consequences. This procedure offers guidance intrinsically linked to the notion of "Islah" (correction). Consequently, 47:4 encapsulates nothing but the internal psychological process of rectification. In parallel, 47:6 conveys the outcome of this rectification: the attainment of a state of peace and tranquillity symbolically referred to as "Jannah.", a concept previously introduced to them.

Such internal confrontations with negativity constitute a test from Allah of the individual's psychological resilience. This test juxtaposes the positive and negative thoughts that coexist within us. The thought processes to which we yield control end up defining our personality. The negativity eradicated in the quest for higher consciousness (Allah's path) doesn't go to waste.

Therefore, the conflict or warfare alluded to in the Quran is always psychological. There are no implications of physical violence. The focus rests solely on the internal struggles within the Nafs (human psyche), the conflict between varying thought processes, and the endeavour to connect with one's higher consciousness for a peaceful and harmonious life (Dunya).

Applied Narratives: Stories of the Real-World Solutions

Integrating Life's Puzzles: Drawing upon Quranic wisdom, let us explore how to navigate and make sense of our daily tribulations. The following vignettes present hypothetical day-to-day scenarios we might encounter, illustrating how to harness the timeless insights of the Quran for practical application in our contemporary world.

Runaway Thoughts and Their Toll: Each of us, at times, grapples with relentless ruminations, whether stemming from personal relationships, our broader social environment, professional concerns, health, or any matter that sends our minds into incessant spirals.

At its core, such unbridled thinking can manifest as anxiety and depression. If not addressed, it may evolve into lasting psychological and physiological afflictions.

Harnessing Quranic Insight: Begin by recognising your inner compass and embarking on a journey of reflective analysis.

17:14 Read thine (own) record: Sufficient is thy soul (Psyche) this day to make out an account against thee.

Seek clear, objective evidence when confronted with overwhelming thoughts. For instance, if suspicions about a relationship's fidelity consume you, strive for unbiased proof rather than surrendering to unbridled fantasies.

49:12 O ye who believe! Avoid suspicion as much (as possible): for suspicion in some cases is a sin: And spy not on each other behind their backs. Would any of you like to eat the flesh of his dead brother? Nay, ye would abhor it...But fear Allah: For Allah is Oft-Returning, Most Merciful.

24:12 Why did not the believers - men and women - when ye heard of the suspicion,- put the best construction on it in their own minds and say, "This (charge) is an obvious lie"?

Should unsettling news about a loved one unsettle you, it's imperative to validate the information first-hand. You'll often find that unchecked reactions and rampant imaginings amplify situations without any grounded justification.

By seeking facts and evidence in situations that trouble you, you'll frequently discover that many of these concerns are merely figments of the mind. The mind often fabricates scenarios so convincingly that they become tangible realities within our consciousness. This is echoed in 49:12, which cautions against certain suspicions or detrimental imaginings, deeming them sins. Unlike traditional interpretations of 'sin', the Quranic perspective defines sins as anything that plunges one's psyche into distress. Thus, unchecked imagination is labelled as a 'sin' in the aforementioned verse.

Monitor your thoughts, encompass them, and cleanse (Zakah) them with concrete evidence, effectively neutralising (Qatal) any negative notions. This act of self-refinement is what constitutes self-correction (Islah). Engaging in this mental discipline and reshaping one's mindset embodies the true essence of Jihad (Strive) and Harb (traditionally known as warfare, but also understood as an excited state of mind).

Embrace Honesty, Even When It Reflects on You: Often, we deceive ourselves, overlooking our own flaws and repeating the same errors, trapped in a loop without resolution. Mistakes, by definition, are actions that yield undesired outcomes or errors in thought, comprehension, or decision-making.

Harnessing Quranic Insight: The journey to clarity begins with introspection. Recognising and addressing patterns in our thought processes that lead to distress is pivotal. Therefore, a candid evaluation of our psyche, acknowledging our own shortcomings, is of paramount importance."

4:135 O ye who believe! stand out firmly for justice, as witnesses to Allah, even as against yourselves, your parents, or your kin, and whether it be (against) rich or poor: for Allah can best protect both. Follow not the lusts (of your hearts), lest ye swerve, and if ye distort (justice) or decline to do justice, verily Allah is well-acquainted with all ye do.

Furthermore, as the verse underscores, we must champion what is right, regardless of whether it opposes us, our dearest ones, or differentiates between the affluent and the indigent. Bypassing this fundamental moral tenet to remain steadfast in our choices may offer a fleeting escape, but our inner conscience always recognises the misdeed. Habitual deviation births a weight of guilt, embedding discontent in our psyche and casting shadows on our demeanour, leading to a restless and perturbed disposition.

Battling Intrinsic Pessimism and Rashness (The Negativity): Rooted in our evolutionary history is a predisposition towards negativity. For the untrained mind, these adverse thoughts often take precedence. The Quran elaborates on these intertwined negative tendencies, terming them as communities and their profound impact on human psychology. Mastering this innate pessimism enables one to channel their cognitive resources most effectively, reaping personal benefits.

Such detrimental thought patterns fuel our internal unrest and disarray, analogised as a psychological 'hell-fire'. This relentless inferno scorches us from within. Hence, it becomes vital not just to recognise these pessimistic thought cycles, as detailed in this work, but to actively target and suppress their origins through introspection, objective analysis and a common sense approach.

As mentioned previously, fire is not physical but mental due to the disturbed mindset.

8:14 Thus : *"Taste ye then of the (punishment): for those who resist Allah, is the penalty of the Fire*

32:20 *As to those who are rebellious and wicked, their abode will be the Fire: every time they wish to get away therefrom, they will be forced thereinto, and it will be said to them: "Taste ye the Penalty of the Fire, the which ye were wont to reject as false*

As alluded to earlier, "fire" is metaphorical, representing a tumultuous mental state rather than a physical manifestation. This interpretation is underscored in verse 8:14, which references "taste the punishment of fire." Delving deeper, verse 32:30 elaborates on negative mentalities such as "Fasaq" (Rebellious) and "Kazab" (Deniars) of inner psychological conditions, suggesting that those entrenched in these mindsets will "taste the hell-fire" due to their persistent adherence to such behaviours. It stands to reason, after all, that if one remains resistant to personal growth and change, their circumstances will inevitably stagnate.

Furthermore, discerning these patterns in others is equally crucial. A mind in turmoil can ripple its unrest outward, potentially unsettling our own equilibrium.

11:113 *And incline not to those who do wrong, or the Fire will seize you; and ye have no protectors other than Allah, nor shall ye be helped.*

As highlighted in the preceding verse, individuals who habitually deceive themselves and harbour self-destructive tendencies typically cultivate negative thought patterns, disrupting their inner psychological harmony. Engaging with such personalities can sometimes perturb our own mental tranquillity. While it's true that we may find ourselves bound to these individuals, possibly due to close ties, completely distancing ourselves for the sake of our mental well-being isn't always feasible. In such instances, while it's essential to extend assistance and help them navigate their mental turmoil, one must tread cautiously to ensure one's own mental equilibrium isn't jeopardised. Striking a delicate balance is crucial in these interactions.

In any circumstance, the guiding principles remain consistent. You must remain attuned to your inner cognitive patterns (Al-Kitaab), pinpointing specific, often persistent negative tendencies such as Concealers/Kaafirs, Self-Deniers/Kaazib, the Corrupt/Fasiq and others mentioned previously. Vigilantly monitor your psyche (Nafs), engage in objective introspection (Al-Quran), and embark on a determined effort (Jihad) to challenge and neutralise (Qitaal) these adverse thoughts. Initiate corrective measures (Islah) through unprejudiced analysis and refine (Zakah) your cognitive landscape.

Summary

In the context of the Quran's psychological philosophy, warfare and striving aren't physical but internal, taking place within the individual's psyche. This understanding offers a fresh interpretation of the Quranic references to "Harb" (warfare), which are not about physical conflicts but the cognitive battles within our psyche, the struggles between divergent thought processes.

Central to this concept is the notion of 'killing' (Qatal) negativity, which literally represents an internal process of dealing with negative thoughts and impulses. It's about the psychological transformation of the individual, who 'kills' or neutralises negative thought patterns through introspection, correction, and the implementation of rational thinking.

This process is intimately tied to the concept of purification (Zakah), or the conscious cleansing of the mind from detrimental thoughts that might pollute the individual's mental equilibrium. The emphasis here isn't on eliminating all negative thoughts — an impossibility given our evolutionary history — but rather on managing and mitigating their influence, especially when they pose a risk to our peace and mental stability.

Finally, the idea of Jihad, in this context, is seen as the individual's 'strive' or struggle against their negative impulses. It's a quest for higher consciousness, a self-awareness journey involving the continuous engagement with and regulation of one's thought processes to maintain mental balance and tranquillity. This understanding positions Jihad as a personal, introspective journey rather than a communal or externally directed endeavour.

In conclusion, the Quran's psychological philosophy presents an internal, cognitive landscape where the battle between positive and negative thoughts unfolds. It outlines a process of combating negativity, purifying the mind, and engaging in an introspective struggle — a psychological Jihad — to achieve peace, stability, and higher consciousness.

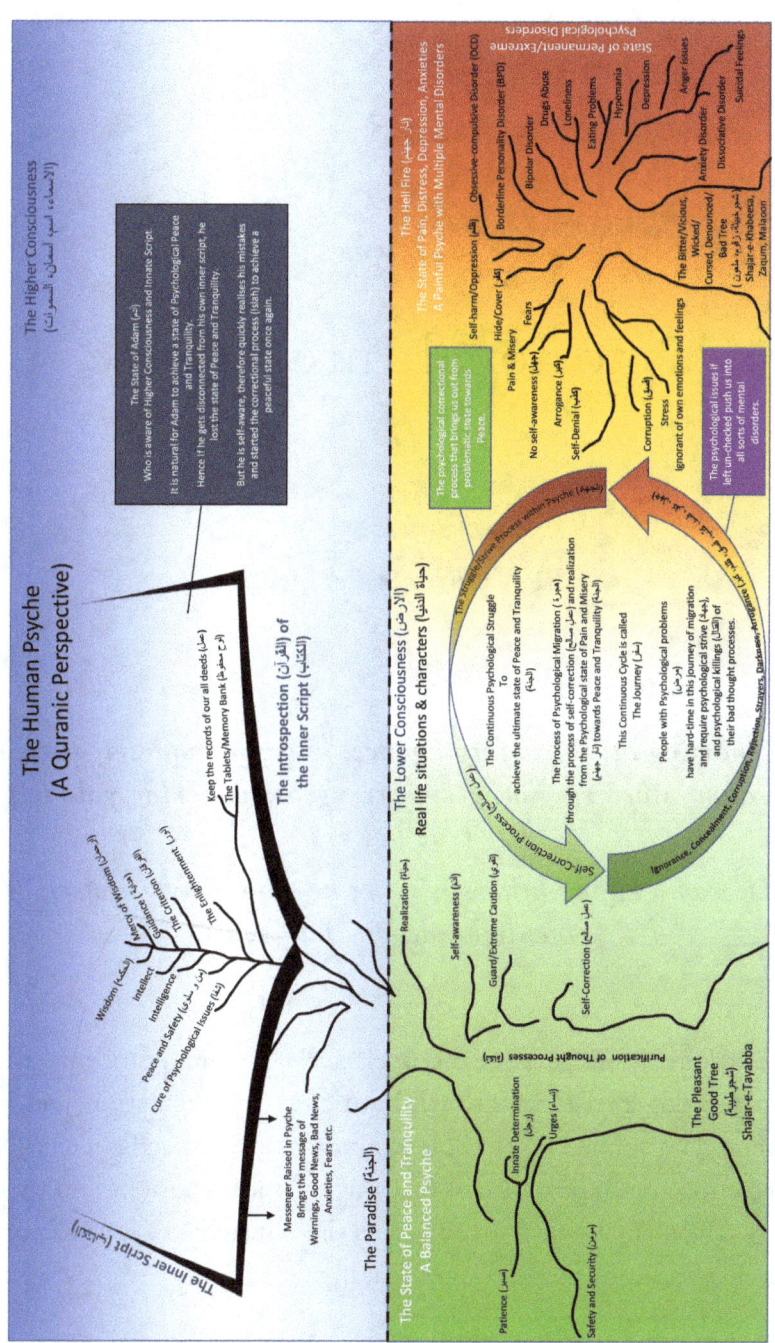

The Quranic Map of Human Psyche (Nafs)

18

Emotional Intelligence

EI A Quranic Perspective

"Knowing others is intelligence; knowing yourself is true wisdom. Mastering others is strength; mastering yourself is true power".
"He who knows others is wise; he who knows himself is enlightened". - Lao Tzu

Emotional Intelligence (EI) is a relatively contemporary construct in psychology. It delves into self-awareness, self-regulation, and social awareness. Grounded in psychological reactions to specific scenarios, EI underscores the importance of recognising one's emotions and those of others. The ultimate goal is to harness these insights to lead to positive outcomes and informed decision-making.

EI comprises four key elements: self-awareness, self-management, social awareness, and relationship management (Goleman, 1995). Self-awareness refers to an individual's ability to identify and understand their emotions and how they affect their behaviours and thoughts (Mayer et al., 2008). This understanding also extends to the emotions of others, fostering empathetic responses.

In summary, emotional intelligence is a crucial aspect of human cognition that significantly impacts individuals' personal and professional lives. Given the positive outcomes associated with high levels of EI, it is essential to foster and cultivate emotional intelligence through deliberate practice and interventions.

Emotional Intelligence (EI) is a modern psychological construct deeply rooted in various religious and spiritual traditions, including Arabic Quran. From a Quranic perspective, EI can be discerned from several verses and teachings that promote self-awareness, self-regulation, empathy, and effective interpersonal relationships.

Indeed, when addressing the topic of Emotional Intelligence (EI) within this framework, it isn't an attempt to affirm or harmoniously unify modern psychological theories with the Quran. One must be wary of the prevailing tendency among some traditional religious commentators to imperatively reconcile scientific revelations with scriptural texts, aiming to bolster their divine veracity. The primary motive behind invoking EI here is to shed light for the readers on how the intrinsic wisdom of the Arabic Quran can be comprehensively understood and applied using the principles of EI. This perspective serves as a bridge, allowing a nuanced interpretation that remains true to the essence of the scripture while resonating with contemporary psychological insights.

The Self-Observervance

Self-awareness is the cornerstone of emotional intelligence. The Quran echoes this sentiment in multiple verses.

59:19 And be ye not like those who forgot Allah; and He made them forget their own souls (Psyche)! Such are the rebellious transgressors!

This passage underscores the significance of self-awareness in acknowledging your intrinsic consciousness (Al-Kitaab), which leads to an upright life when remembered and observed.

75:14 Nay, man will be evidence against himself (Nafs/Psyche).

Further, 75:14 highlights our inherent capacity for self-reflection, proclaiming, "Indeed, mankind has insight into his soul." The term Basirah, used here, implies our ability to observe our psyche's contents.

17:14 "Read thine (own) record (the internal book): Sufficient is thy soul (Psyche) this day to make out an account against thee."

In 17:14, it says, "Read your record. Your self is sufficient as a reckoner against you this day." Here, the Quran emphasises the importance of reading our internal book (Al-Kitaab) embedded in our psyche. This introspection encompasses the comprehension of emotions, intelligence, and various thought communities/Qaum, both negative and positive. By understanding these thought processes, one can effectively manage emotions and the impacts of life's decisions.

2:44 Do ye enjoin right conduct on the people, and forget (To practise it) yourselves (own Psyche), and yet ye study the Scripture (the book)? Will ye not understand?

2:44 questions, "Do you order righteousness of the people and forget yourselves while you recite the Scripture? Then will you, not reason?" Here, the word Amar, meaning command, is utilised. The verse suggests that commanding your persona (Naas) to do something incompatible with your self-reflection can harm your psyche. In essence, preaching without practising, significantly when aware of the repercussions, can profoundly impact your psyche.

However, it is essential to note that self-awareness is merely the first step towards emotional intelligence. It is the conscious acknowledgement of one's emotions and the ability to introspect. However, managing those emotions and applying wisdom judiciously in different situations is entirely different. It is akin to knowing the benefits of a healthy lifestyle and leading one. Thus, knowing is one thing, but putting it into practice is a different challenge.

Being Cautious, Self-Management (Muttaqi)

Undeniably, managing our emotions necessitates becoming an observer of our psyche. This initial step prompts us to analyse how our emotions influence our decisions and to be cautious of our feelings' interplay within our psychology. This is the essence of the Quranic term "Taqwa." The word, derived from the Arabic root "W Q Y," translates to being cautious or guarded. It refers to preserving, shielding, or protecting oneself, especially one's consciousness (Lane et al., Vol. 8, Page 3059).

This preservation does not denote fear in the negative sense but rather the act of protecting and guarding one's consciousness. Upon gaining self-awareness and understanding the various aspects of our psychology, the higher and lower consciousness, the inner messenger, the balance and imbalance within, and the introspection derived from analysing our internal book (Al-Kitaab), we move on to self-management.

Self-management pertains to controlling our actions and decisions based on our emotions' self-awareness. The objective is to protect our mental state and maintain its balance. Without proper management of feelings and emotions, our psychological well-being can be significantly affected, regardless of our knowledge. This aspect of self-regulation is heavily emphasised in the Quran, particularly in managing emotional responses during difficult situations, as epitomised in 3:134.

3:134 *Those who spend (freely), whether in prosperity, or in adversity; who restrain anger, and pardon (all) men;- for Allah loves those who do good;-*

In the aforementioned verse, the exhortation to "spend freely" can be understood as an allegory for the judicious employment of one's intellectual faculties—namely, wisdom and discernment. Those who exercise restraint, avoiding hasty and irrational judgments, are exemplary in their conduct. It is these individuals, characterised by such thoughtful deliberation, whom Allah holds in high regard.

6:155 *And this is a Book which We have revealed as a blessing: so follow it and be righteous, that ye may receive mercy.*

In 6:155, the Quran speaks of the revealed book as a blessing and cautions us to follow its teachings to receive mercy: "And this is a Book which We have revealed as a blessing: so follow it and be cautious, that ye may receive mercy." Again, this mercy is not external but emanates from within us through self-management. Peace and psychological stability are achieved when we wisely manage our emotions using self-awareness.

29:6 *And if any strive (with might and main), they do so for their own souls (psyche): for Allah is free of all needs from all creation.*

In 29:6, the Quran advises that any struggle, or Jihad, is for our psyche's benefit: "And if any strive/Jihad, they do so for their souls/psyche: for Allah is free of all needs from all creation." In this context, the term Jihad refers to the ongoing inner struggle we face daily within our psyche. This struggle underscores our internal battles to make choices in life, highlighting the essence of emotional intelligence in our spiritual journey.

Self-regulation, or maintaining awareness of our internal mental state and reactions in various situations, is an enduring endeavour throughout our lives. Despite our knowledge and insight, humans are occasionally prone to impulsivity and unreflective actions. Such lapses can undoubtedly lead to psychological repercussions. However, swift recognition of these missteps, followed by timely corrective measures, can mitigate the personal psychological impact and alleviate strains within our social interactions.

Social-Awareness and Relationship Management

The fundamental architecture of human psychology and physiology is universally consistent across individuals, leading to shared emotional experiences. The distinguishing factor lies in individuals' ability to regulate mental processes and self-awareness. Such skills are particularly manifest in interpersonal interactions.

When an individual attains a certain level of self-awareness and introspective aptitude, it becomes crucial to utilise these skills to decipher the emotional responses of others in varying circumstances. An individual may have control over their emotions and display self-awareness, while others may not possess these abilities. In such instances, the emotionally competent individual possesses the potential to directly or indirectly influence the emotions of others through their actions or words. Understanding and perceiving the emotional undercurrents of others and subsequently assisting in managing their emotional responses forms a significant part of social awareness and relationship management.

One of the critical aspects of social competence and effective relationship management is managing personal emotional reactions, specifically anger (and or majority of impulsive reactions), and empathising with others. This requires imagining oneself in the place of others to understand the origins of their particular responses.

Quranic verse 3:134 addresses those who exercise restraint during periods of prosperity or adversity, control anger, and forgive others, indicating that Allah beloves such individuals. Here, 'spending' is not limited to its traditional interpretation of financial expenditure but extends to disseminating wisdom and knowledge acquired through self-awareness. Applying this knowledge to suppress adverse emotional reactions and anger in any situation is encouraged. The display of forbearance and the ability to diffuse conflicts with wisdom and calmness form a cornerstone of effective social relationships.

2:224 And make not Allah's (name) an excuse in your oaths against doing good, or acting rightly, or making peace between persons; for Allah is One Who heareth and knoweth all things.

2:224 emphasises the importance of maintaining peace and acting with righteousness, not using the name of Allah as an excuse to avoid doing good. Such peacekeeping efforts reflect the vigilance (Taqwa) gained through self-awareness. Constructive conflict resolution requires the removal of negative emotions and anger from the discourse and the application of wisdom and knowledge to reach mutually beneficial agreements.

49:6 O ye who believe! If a wicked person comes to you with any news, ascertain the truth, lest ye harm people unwittingly, and afterwards become full of repentance for what ye have done.

49:6 cautions against forming opinions based on unverified information or rumours. This is an essential consideration for maintaining harmonious social relationships. The verification of information, particularly when it may influence decisions and subsequent regret, is highlighted.

49:12 O ye who believe! Avoid suspicion as much (as possible): for suspicion in some cases is a sin: And spy not on each other behind their backs. Would any of you like to eat the flesh of his dead brother? Nay, ye would abhor it...But fear Allah: For Allah is Oft-Returning, Most Merciful.

49:12 warns against undue suspicion and spying on others, as these actions can potentially damage relationships. It emphasises the need for self-restraint and observing personal boundaries, underscoring that unchecked curiosity can lead to adverse outcomes. Understanding these Quranic verses and applying their wisdom can significantly enhance social awareness and relationship management.

Summary

As framed within the Quranic context, emotional intelligence is a multifaceted concept encompassing self-awareness, social awareness, and relationship management. These concepts are consistently embedded throughout various Quranic teachings, guiding individuals to navigate their emotions and interact effectively within society.

Self-awareness in the Quran is associated with introspection and controlling one's emotional responses. It pertains to understanding and regulating one's inner emotional landscape, allowing for more balanced decision-making and reactions, as illustrated in verse 3:134.

Social awareness, on the other hand, emphasises understanding and managing the emotional states of others. It encourages empathy and the ability to perceive the emotional undertones of a given situation, allowing individuals to respond appropriately and help put others at ease.

Relationship management underscores the importance of maintaining peaceful and effective interpersonal interactions. According to verses like 2:224 and 49:12, this involves controlling personal emotional reactions, specifically anger, forgiving others, avoiding undue suspicion and spying, and verifying information before acting on it.

The Quran fosters emotional intelligence by providing a comprehensive guide on managing personal emotions and interpersonal relationships, promoting a more harmonious and understanding society.

Epilogue

A JOURNEY BEYOND THE HORIZON OF CONSCIOUSNESS

In examining ancient sacred texts, when one extricates them from the layers of traditional interpretations, an enduring wisdom emerges that remains astonishingly pertinent and cogent. It is important to emphasise that this perspective doesn't necessarily assert the divine nature of these texts. Rather, I posit that they are manifestations of human creativity, a testament to the marvel of human consciousness.

A contextualised reading of the Quran, or any venerable sacred manuscript, devoid of historical predispositions and distanced from traditionalist and literal inclinations, brings to light that a large portion of their narratives, allegories, and precepts can be perceived as manifestations of innate human sensibility.

Our psychological construct is multifaceted, influencing the myriad dimensions of our persona. While we ardently project a certain character to the world, we simultaneously harbour emotions, judgments, and predispositions that we endeavour to conceal. Our psyche encompasses fervent desires, and an inherent will exists to act upon or resist these impulses.

A predominant catalyst for psychological complications stems from impulsive tendencies and a deficiency in self-awareness and self-regulation. The nucleus of these complications can be traced back to our thoughts. While thoughts are an intrinsic element of our psyche, if left unmonitored, they can spiral, leading to the formation of distinct cognitive patterns and processes, culminating in either a harmonious or tumultuous mental state.

Even when setting the Quran and the content of this manuscript aside, as humans, we invariably seek guidance from myriad sources to mould our mental framework. Often, we assimilate this counsel subconsciously, influenced by the sensory data and experiences we chronically accumulate, invariably coloured by our intrinsic biases.

Individuals with a paucity of self-awareness often exhibit knee-jerk reactions driven by their inherent biases and judgments. Conversely, those with heightened self-awareness harness their cognitive faculties, striving to extricate their biases and grounding their decisions in empirical evidence and sound rationale. It has been observed that such individuals generally cultivate a more prosperous, gratified, and equanimous mental disposition compared to their less self-aware counterparts.

In this light, the Quran is one among numerous resources that can aid in refining self-regulation and mastery when approached from this vantage point.

As we turn the final page of this immersive narrative, we find ourselves not at the end but on the precipice of a deeper understanding of the human psyche as portrayed through the Quranic lens. The narrative deftly weaves traditional exegesis with contemporary psychological perspectives, enriching the tapestry of insights that stimulate spiritual introspection and empirical reasoning.

The heart of this text pulsates with the exploration of the internal and the divine, particularly the profound interplay between the two.

This duality is exemplified by the nuanced discussions on "Hawa", our inherent inclination towards impulsivity, and the intricate dance of decision-making processes shaped by myriad internal and external forces.

One cannot help but appreciate the breadth and depth of the discussions on "Al-Kitaab", our inner book. It underscores the universality of human experiences and reaffirms the Quran's relevance as a scripture and an eternal compass for navigating the maze of human consciousness.

However, the journey continues. Our author provides tantalising hints of upcoming projects that promise to delve deeper into the vast ocean of Quranic knowledge. "The Concept of God and His Creations" promises to be a ground-breaking exploration of celestial narratives and their resonance in our lives. Furthermore, exploring the concepts of "Haram (restricted), Halal (allowed), and Morality" in the Quran will undoubtedly serve as a beacon for those seeking guidance in ethical and moral quandaries.

In sum, this book is not just an endpoint but a gateway. It beckons readers to continue their journey of discovery, to engage with their inner landscapes, and to find harmony in the blend of the spiritual and the empirical. As we eagerly await the next chapters in this enlightening series, we are reminded to constantly seek, reflect, and engage with the world within and around us. The journey is just beginning.

Notes

The Arabic Lexicons

There are multiple Arabic Lexicons and grammatical sources been used in this work.

- Fundamentals of Arabic Grammar provides an authoritative guide to Modern Standard Arabic (MSA) grammar. It has been organised to promote a thorough understanding of MSA grammar and presents its complexities in a cohesive and user-friendly format, filling many gaps left by other textbooks. Explanations are clear, full and accessible and extensive cross-referencing, two generous indices and six appendices provide users with easy access to the information they require. No prior knowledge of linguistic terminology is required.
- Barron's *501 Arabic Verbs* is printed in Arabic script with exemplary sentences in English for each verb. Verbs are arranged alphabetically in a table format, one verb per page with English translation, and conjugated in all tenses and forms.
- E.W. Lane's Arabic-English Lexicon (8 parts, London, 1863-93) is a major Arabic-English dictionary based on 112 sources, mostly medieval ones, along with al-Zabidi's Taj al-Aroos (also included in Lisaan.net). Lane died before he could finish the work, his great-nephew Stanley Lane-Poole finished it, publishing Volumes VI, VII and VIII from 1877–1893 using Lane's incomplete notes. Lane-Pool's work is of lower quality than Lane's. The work of Reinhart Dozy (see below) was meant as a supplement to Lane's work that covers modern Arabic (Lane focused on classical Arabic only). The digital text for the Lexicon was sourced from Tufts University under a Creative Commons Attribution-ShareAlike 3.0 United States License. We used a TXT version created by an internet user named Navid-ul-Islam. Lisaan.net's version of the

Lane Lexicon corrects various errors from both the Persues project (such as erroneous transcriptions of the Persian letter ژ) and the TXT version. Lisaan.net's version also provides helpful automatic annotations on the various abbreviations used by Lane.

- The Dictionary of Modern Written Arabic is an Arabic-English dictionary compiled by Hans Wehr and edited by J Milton Cowan. It is by far the best general Arabic-English dictionary available.
- *Tāj al-'Arūs* is *the* largest dictionary of the Arabic language ever written, comprising 11,800 pages. It is a commentary on the 15th-century *Qāmūs al-Muḥīṭ* of Firuzabadi. Murtaḍa al-Zabīdī (d. 1790 CE / 1205 AH) was a scholar of Islamic jurisprudence and the Arabic language from Belgram in West Bengal, India, from an Iraqi family that came from Wasit.
- Abū Mūsā al-Madīnī (d. c. 1185 CE / 581 AH), was one of the foremost scholars of his time and his knowledge and piety attained great renown. Among his students is 'Abd al-Ghanī al-Maqdisī, the great scholar of hadith. Al-Madīnī *Majmūʿ al-Mughīth* is a dictionary concerned with interpreting difficult and ambiguous words and expressions used in hadith and the Quran.
- *Muʿjam al-Lugha al-ʿArabīya al-Muʿāṣira* is a dictionary of contemporary Standard Arabic, 2500 pages in print. It was written by the Egyptian linguist Ahmad Mukhtar Umar (d. 2003 CE).
- *Muʿjam al-Ṣawāb al-Lughawī* is a 1000-page dictionary dedicated to correcting common errors in the usage of the Arabic language found in books, newspapers and television, written by the Egyptian linguist Ahmad Mukhtar Umar (d. 2003 CE) and his team.

Quranic Roots Words

Following are some of the Arabic Quran's root words and their variations used referred to in this book.

- The root Word (نفس) for Nafs or the Psyche/Soul, with all its variations, is used 298 times in 270 verses.

أَنْفُسَهُمْ أَنْفُسَكُمْ نَفْسِي نَفْسٍ أَنْفُسَكُمْ نَفْسًا أَنْفُسُكُمْ أَنْفُسِهِم لِأَنْفُسِهِمْ نَفْسَهُ وَالْأَنْفُسِ لِأَنْفُسِكُمْ بِأَنْفُسِكُمْ أَنْفُسِهِنَّ أَنْفُسِهِمْ أَنْفُسِكُمْ فَلِأَنْفُسِكُمْ نَفْسٌ وَأَنْفُسَنَا وَأَنْفُسَكُمْ نَفْسِي لِنَفْسِهِ أَنْفُسُهُمْ أَنْفُسَكُمْ لَأَنْفُسِهِمْ وَأَنْفُسِهِمْ نَفْسِكَ نَفْسَكَ وَأَنْفُسِهِمُ الْأَنْفُسُ نَفْسِي نَفْسُهُ النَّفْسَ بِالنَّفْسِ نَفْسِكَ نَفْسِي فَلِنَفْسِهِ بِأَنْفُسِهِمْ أَنْفُسِنَا أَنْفُسَنَا وَأَنْفُسَهُمْ لِنَفْسِي نَفْسِهِ أَنْفُسِكُمْ لِنَفْسِهِ نَفْسُكُمْ نَفْسِي نَفْسٍ لِأَنْفُسِهِمْ

الْأَنْفُسِ نَّفْسِهَا بِنَفْسِكَ نُفُوسِكُمْ نَفْسَكَ لِّنَفْسِهِ لِّنَفْسِهِ فَلِأَنفُسِهِمْ كَنَفْسٍ وَأَنفُسُهُمْ نَفْسَهَا نَفْسُكَ الْأَنْفُسَ لِأَنْفُسِكُمْ النُّفُوسُ تَنَفَّسَ لِنَفْسٍ فَلْيَتَنَافَسِ الْمُتَنَافِسُونَ النَّفْسُ وَنَفْسٍ

- The root Word (كتب) for Kitaab or the Book, with all its variations, is used 319 times in 279 verses.

الْكِتَابَ الْكِتَبَ يَكْتُبُونَ كَتَبَتْ الْكِتَابِ كِتَابَ كِتَابٍ وَالْكِتَابِ كُتُبٍ كَتَبَ فَاكْتُبُوهُ وَلْيَكْتُبْ كَاتِبٌ يَكْتُبُ فَلْيَكْتُبْ تَكْتُبُوهُ تَكْتُبُوهَا كَاتِبًا وَكُتُبِهِ كِتَابَ فَاكْتُبْتَا بِالْكِتَابِ كِتَابَ كِتَابًا سَنَكْتُبُ كَتَبْنَا كَتَبْتَ يَكْتُبْ وَكَتَبْنَا بِكِتَابٍ وَاكْتُبْ فَسَأَكْتُبُهَا مَكْتُوبًا كِتَابَ كِتَابَكَ كِتَابَهُ كِتَابَهُمْ كَاتِبُونَ لِلْكُتُبِ فَكَاتِبُوهُمْ اكْتَتَبَهَا وَكِتَابَ بِّكِتَابِي وَالْكِتَابَ كُتُبَ وَبِالْكِتَابِ وَنَكْتُبُ بِكِتَابِكُمْ لَكِتَابٌ سَنَكْتُبُ كِتَابِهَا كِتَابًا كَتَبْنَاهَا كِتَابِيَهْ كَاتِبِينَ كُتُبٌ

- The root Word (قرء) for Quran or the Reading/Introspection, with all its variations, is used 88 times in 79 verses.

الْقُرْآنَ قُرُوءٍ الْقُرْآنُ قُرِئَ وَالْقُرْآنِ يَقْرَأُ قُرْآنٌ قُرْآنٍ يَقْرَءُونَ قُرْآنًا وَقُرْآنَ وَالْقُرْآنَ قَرَأَتْ اقْرَأْ الْقُرْآنِ وَقُرْآنًا قُرْآنٍ تَقْرَؤُهُ لِتَقْرَأَهُ بِالْقُرْآنِ فَقَرَأَهُ وَقُرْآنٍ لَقُرْآنٌ اقْرَءُوا فَاقْرَءُوا وَقُرْآنَهُ قَرَأْنَاهُ قُرْآنٌ سَنُقْرِئُكَ

- The root Word (جنن) for Jinn/Jannah or the hidden one, with all its variations, is used 201 times in 196 verses.

جَنَّاتُ الْجَنَّةَ الْجَنَّةِ جَنَّةٍ جَنَّةَ جَنَّاتٍ وَجَنَّةٍ وَجَنَّةَ جَنَّاتٍ جَنٍّ وَجَنَّاتٍ الْجِنِّ وَالْجِنَّ الْجِنُّ الْجَنَّةُ جَنَّةِ الْجَنَّةُ جَنَّاتٌ لَمَجْنُونٌ وَالْجَانَّ وَالْجِنُّ جَنَّتَيْنِ الْجَنَّتَيْنِ جَنَّةٌ جَنَّتِكَ جِنَّةٌ جَنَّةٌ جَنَّةٍ جَانٌّ الْجِنُّ جَنَّتَانِ بِجَنَّتِهِمْ مَّجْنُونٌ الْجَنَّةُ بِالْجَنَّةِ الْجَنَّاتِ مَجْنُونٌ مَجْنُونٌ مَجْنُونٍ أَجِنَّةِ الْجَانِّ وَجَنَّتْ جُنَّةٌ بِمَجْنُونٍ جَنَّةَ جَنَّةَ جَنَّتِي

- The root Word (سمو) for Asma/Samawat or the higher consciousness, with all its variations, is used 493 times in 450 verses.

بِسْمِ السَّمَاءِ وَالسَّمَاءُ سَمَاوَاتٍ الْأَسْمَاءُ بِأَسْمَاءِ بِأَسْمَائِهِمْ السَّمَاوَاتِ اسْمُهُ مُسَمًّى سَمَّيْتُهَا السَّمَاوَاتُ اسْمَ السَّمَاءِ اسْمُ أَسْمَاءِ سَمَّيْتُمُوهَا الْأَسْمَاءُ أَسْمَائِهِ

سَمَاءُ أَسْمَاءً سَمُّوهُمْ وَالسَّمَاوَاتِ سَمِيًّا وَالسَّمَاوَاتُ سَمَّاكُمُ السَّمَاءُ سَمَاءٍ الِاسْمُ وَالسَّمَاءِ أَسْمَاءُ لَيُسَمُّونَ تَسْمِيَةَ بِاسْمِ تُسَمَّىٰ بِسْمِ

- The root Word (ارض) for Ard/Earth or the lower consciousness, with all its variations, is used 461 times in 440 verses.

الْأَرْضِ الْأَرْضَ وَالْأَرْضُ الْأَرْضُ وَالْأَرْضِ أَرْضُ أَرْضِ أَرْضِكُمْ أَرْضًا أَرْضَنَا أَرْضِكُمْ أَرْضِي أَرْضٍ أَرْضَهُمْ وَأَرْضًا وَأَرْضٌ وَلِلْأَرْضِ

- The root Word (نسو) for Nisa or the Innate Desires, with all its variations, is used 59 times in 53 verses.

نِسَاءَكُمْ نِسَائِكُمُ النِّسَاءَ نِسَاؤُكُمْ نِّسَائِهِمْ النِّسَاءِ نِسَاءِ وَنِسَاءَكُمْ وَنِسَاءَنَا وَنِسَاءً وَلِلنِّسَاءِ نِسَاءً نِّسَائِكُمْ نِّسَائِكُمْ وَالنِّسَاءِ نِسَاءَهُمْ نِسْوَةِ النِّسْوَةُ نِسَائِهِنَّ نِسَائِكَ النِّسَاءُ وَنِسَاءٍ وَنِسَاءَ نِسَاءُ نِسَاءٍ نِّسَائِهِم

- The root Word (رجل) for Rijal or the Innate determination, with all its variations, is used 73 times in 66 verses.

وَلِلرِّجَالِ فَرِجَالًا رِّجَالِكُمْ رَجُلَيْنِ فَرَجُلٌ رِجَالًا لِّلرِّجَالِ رَجُلٌ الرِّجَالِ الرِّجَالُ رِّجَالًا وَأَرْجُلَكُمْ رَجُلَانِ وَأَرْجُلِهِم رَجُلًا أَرْجُلِكُمْ رِجَالٌ رَجُلِ الرِّجَالِ وَأَرْجُلَكُمْ أَرْجُلَ رَّجُلَيْنِ وَرِجْلِكَ بِأَرْجُلِهِنَّ رِجْلَيْنِ أَرْجُلِهِمْ لِرَجُلٍ أَرْجُلُهُم بِرِجْلِكَ رَّجُلًا وَرَجُلًا لَّرَجُلٍ وَأَرْجُلِهِنَّ بِرِجَالٍ

About the Author

T. J. Roswell is a renowned author and scholar for his expertise in sacred texts, comparative religions, and philosophies. He boasts impressive academic accomplishments, including two master's degrees. He has made significant scholarly contributions, publishing influential papers in top-tier, internationally recognised and peer-reviewed journals. In 2023, he debuted his seminal work, "The Hidden World: Deciphering Sacred Text and Unveiling Mind". This book offers an innovative perspective, advocating for metaphorical interpretations of sacred scriptures and drawing connections to the realm of human psychology. The publication garnered widespread acclaim, earning commendations from various authors, journalists, and individuals across multiple religious backgrounds.

Index

abstract theories, 24
Adam, 3, 39, 42, 48, 57, 58, 60, 62, 66, 67, 103, 117, 118, 119, 120, 121, 122, 123, 125, 128, 129, 130, 131, 132, 133, 134, 135, 136, 137, 138, 140, 141, 142, 143, 144, 146, 147, 148, 149, 150, 152, 154
Adam and Eve, 39, 42, 58, 60, 62, 67, 72, 117, 118
allegory, 84, 125, 137, 156, 299
almighty creator, 34
anxieties, 164, 197, 222, 228, 240, 265
associated emotions, 229,

balanced whole, 121
behaviour and cognition, 56
belief systems, 24, 33, 41, 64, 98, 134, 193, 267
biblical, 30, 40, 48, 58, 60, 67, 117, 118, 119, 121, 123, 124, 262
Biblical narrative, 30, 48, 124

ceaseless thoughts, 266
Christianity, 4, 23, 30, 38, 147
common sense, 65, 250, 251, 290
concealed reservoir of wisdom, 129
concealed river of wisdom, 159
concept of guidance, 193
concept of religion, 1
contemplation, 2, 26, 65, 80, 183, 203, 209, 207, 243, 256
contradiction, 50, 54, 245
conventional interpretations, 18, 82, 95,
conventional notions, 71
correction process, 139, 157
creationist claims, 5

day and night, 113, 236, 209, 233

decision-making, 36, 58, 122, 125, 153, 198, 205, 207, 212, 213, 216, 217, 218, 219, 220, 250, 251, 256, 258, 264, 284, 288, 295, 303

depression, 90, 94, 95, 113, 164, 195, 196, 197, 198, 200, 248, 260, 261, 264, 270

desires and urges, 87, 93, 97,

disturbances and discomfort, 74

divine presence, 73, 95

divinities, 1

duality of the psyche, 66, 76, 121

ego, 109, 185, 259

elevated consciousness, 83, 103, 106, 107, 108, 109, 110, 113, 114, 115, 116, 120, 121, 123, 124, 131, 132, 135, 159, 209, 217, 229, 235, 248, 250, 254, 255, 272, 276, 278, 280, 281, 282, 283, 286, 292, 293

emotional biases, 106, 109

emotional intelligence, 28, 29, 35, 36, 51, 86, 114, 128, 129, 201, 202, 264, 279, 295, 296, 297, 298, 300, 303

emotions, and wisdom, 34

equilibrium, 51, 67, 74, 115, 121, 125, 127, 128, 154, 196, 240, 242, 264, 268, 275, 278, 279, 280, 282, 291, 290, 292

established beliefs, 3

eternal fate, 2

exaggerate, 81

existence, 1, 31, 32, 81, 101, 102, 108, 109, 112, 123, 140, 152, 156, 162, 168, 174, 178, 203, 230, 233, 266, 277

external blame, 264

external religious constructs, 115

faith, 1, 3, 4, 6, 7, 8, 9, 18, 19, 22, 23, 28, 33, 41, 69, 127, 146, 169, 170, 183, 186, 247, 248, 255, 281, 283

fallacy, 5

firewall, 258, 259

five senses, 170, 269

Forbidden Tree, 66, 117, 118, 137, 138, 141

God, 1, 2, 3, 12, 13, 14, 22, 23, 27, 32, 61, 72, 73, 80, 81, 98, 102, 103, 107, 109, 111, 138, 147, 228, 256, 307

governed by emotions, 82, 263

Habitual, 242, 243, 253, 263, 289

Heaven, 2, 5, 23, 57, 83, 84, 98, 99, 101, 103, 104, 105, 106, 109, 110, 111, 112, 113, 114, 115, 116, 120, 123, 140, 146, 147, 148, 149, 209, 249

Heavens and the Earth, 57, 99, 100, 101, 103, 104, 105, 109, 111, 140, 209 hidden, 61, 66, 67, 71, 75, 76, 77, 78, 79, 80, 82, 83, 86, 87, 116, 120, 124, 125, 126, 128, 129, 136, 137, 138, 142, 143, 150, 151, 152, 153, 158, 159, 160, 174, 209, 269

hidden aspects, 75, 77, 80, 83

Hinduism, 4, 8, 9, 27

historical teachings, 114

holy wars, 274

human cognition, 34, 246, 296

human endeavours, 26, 104

human interpretation, 39

human mind, 22, 43, 49, 52, 58, 60, 71, 94, 112, 114, 121, 128, 148, 157, 164, 198, 210, 220, 228, 273, 280

human nature, 75, 77, 87, 89, 119, 138, 194, 217, 259

human psychology, 2, 9, 10, 11, 13, 14, 16, 28, 32, 34, 35, 38, 41, 43, 44, 48, 51, 56, 60, 61, 71, 76, 80, 87, 89, 92, 93, 100, 101, 103, 104, 111, 115, 119, 120, 127, 134, 136, 151, 160, 211, 219, 227, 230, 237, 274, 276, 289, 301

humanity, 10, 14, 21, 22, 24, 25, 27, 33, 34, 56, 63, 68, 94, 146, 147

incessant flow, 152

incorrect choices, 252

inner balance and harmony, 205

inner script or innate wisdom, 208

inner voice, 181, 197, 213, 214, 215, 216, 217, 220, 221, 223, 245, 248, 278

Inspiration, 9, 79, 80, 81, 183, 214, 223

intellectual curiosity, 5, 228

intellectual faculties, 215

intelligence, 28, 29, 34, 35, 36, 51, 86, 114, 128, 129, 132, 133, 135, 137, 142, 151, 201, 202, 221, 252, 259, 263, 264, 276, 278, 279, 295, 296, 297, 298, 300, 303

internal script, 136, 166, 173, 182, 221

interpretations, 1, 8, 18, 19, 20, 31, 34, 37, 39, 40, 41, 42, 43, 46, 48, 50, 63, 73, 76, 81, 82, 84, 95, 98, 134, 135, 147, 148, 164, 170, 175, 212, 242, 244, 274, 279, 288, 305

interpreted literally, 40, 227

introspect, 53, 63, 111, 298

introspection, 2, 35, 53, 66, 73, 84, 87, 100, 103, 104, 105, 112, 151, 160, 165, 166, 167, 170, 172, 175, 177, 180, 182, 183, 184, 185, 186, 190, 191, 192, 193, 194, 195, 196, 200, 202, 201, 204, 205, 207, 208, 209, 211, 212, 232, 250, 251, 277, 285, 289, 290, 291, 292, 297, 299, 303, 306

Islamic tradition, 3, 39

Jinn, 44, 57, 66, 68, 69, 70, 71, 75, 76, 77, 78, 79, 80, 81, 82, 83, 85, 116, 120, 123, 124, 125, 150, 151, 152, 159, 160, 192

Judaism, 4, 23, 147

Judeo-Christian, 39, 40, 262

judgement, 52, 53
Judgement Day, 53, 174

Kafir, 246, 247
Kaafir, 113, 207, 234, 246, 248, 275, 279, 280, 291
Kufr, 3, 246, 247, 248, 249, 252, 279, 285

levels of consciousness, 105, 107, 111, 121, 160
Literalism, 31, 32, 39, 44
literalists and traditionalists, 40, 62, 78
logical evidence, 58
lower consciousness, 98, 105, 106, 108, 109, 110, 113, 114, 115, 116, 118, 120, 121, 132, 135, 136, 140, 159, 229, 235, 245, 253, 298, 312

male and female, 13, 61, 62
manufactured constructs, 22
manuscript, 18, 169, 305, 306
masculine, 61, 70, 90, 93, 102, 118, 124, 126, 130, 150, 166, 179, 210, 214, 225, 244
memories, 63, 64 66, 67, 95, 113, 163, 164, 165, 167, 172, 175, 184, 189, 205, 206, 214, 218, 244
mental energy, 196, 258
mental well-being, 176, 211, 247, 280, 291
messengers, 78, 79, 217, 220, 221, 263
metaphorically, 64, 105, 108, 115, 126, 129, 154, 155, 172, 280, 282, 283
metaphysics, 6, 24
moral judgment, 213
Muslim, 20, 40, 41, 50, 196

Naas, 57, 70, 71, 72, 74, 78, 86, 107, 108, 110, 111, 170, 171, 192, 298
Nafs, 42, 48, 49, 50, 52, 53, 54, 55, 57, 58, 59, 63, 67, 78, 93, 99, 105, 120, 152, 171, 192, 201, 227, 229, 230, 231, 246, 247, 257, 275, 286, 291, 297
Nafs-e-Wahid, 42, 60
Nisa, 57, 58, 88, 89, 90, 91, 92, 93, 94, 97, 116, 120

organised religions, 1, 23, 24, 34, 91, 230
orientation and relationships, 2
our destiny, 1

parable, 9, 43, 44, 51, 66, 72, 73, 89, 104 107, 108, 115, 120, 121, 135, 137, 142, 151, 152, 156, 157, 179, 180, 187, 191, 201, 213, 227
peace and tranquillity, 62, 128, 200, 231, 286
peaceful psyche, 74

peaceful state of mind, 87, 113, 136, 201
persona, 42, 43, 72, 73, 77, 78, 82, 84, 85, 95, 120, 159, 171, 182, 186, 298, 305
personal experiences, 100, 163, 168, 183, 187, 189, 214, 221
pessimistic thought cycles, 289
physical act of violence, 280
physical book, 60, 172, 186, 187
physical entity, 42
physical war, 273, 274
positive and negative thought, 258, 286
positive mindset, 62, 164
private chamber, 285
psychological barrier, 258, 259
psychological clothing, 142
psychological construct, 67, 285, 296, 305
psychological insights, 10, 28, 55
psychological Jihad, 275
psychological pain, 94, 155, 163, 251
psychological philosophy, 28, 44, 225, 280, 282, 292, 293
psychological well-being, 56, 74, 95, 104, 113, 115, 206, 210, 212, 214, 249, 251, 278, 282, 299
punishments, 2
purification, 64, 107, 277, 278, 279, 280, 281, 283, 286, 292

Quranic context, 60, 99, 100, 104, 105, 106, 110, 111, 122, 125, 126, 131, 172, 182, 188, 216, 225, 227, 245, 274, 276, 277, 278, 303
Quranic interpretation, 40, 129, 134, 135, 236
Quranic literature, 20, 54, 285
Quranic perspective, 59, 61, 81, 101, 106, 109, 112, 113, 240, 242, 288, 295, 296
Quranic Philosophy, 80, 114, 118, 122, 128, 143, 201, 253, 254, 282,
Quranic teachings, 29, 68, 106, 118, 130, 191, 249, 245, 251, 303

rational thinking, 110, 259, 264, 282, 283, 284, 292
reflections, 2, 15, 101
relationships, 2, 22, 35, 51, 61, 67, 78, 86, 87, 88, 89, 99, 155, 201, 266, 296, 302
religious intellectuals, 3
religious texts, 5, 18, 27, 39, 76, 103, 147, 148, 163, 170, 230
Religious traditionalism, 37
Rijal, 57, 58, 82, 88, 89, 90, 93, 94, 97, 116, 120

Satan, 3, 39, 44, 94, 107, 123, 126, 127, 128, 131, 133, 138, 140, 141, 142, 144, 155
scriptures, 9, 19, 24, 26, 27, 32, 33, 34, 37, 38, 39, 147, 148
self-awareness, 15, 73, 74, 75, 82, 85, 86, 87, 89, 97, 100, 104, 106, 110, 111, 112, 114,

123, 125, 128, 129, 130, 131, 132, 138, 139, 141, 142, 144, 151, 157, 158, 161, 165, 166, 171, 172, 173, 175, 181, 184, 298
  self-correction, 128, 136, 139, 152, 153, 157, 158, 199, 200, 222, 250, 256, 259, 288
  self-determination, 56, 90, 93, 94, 97, 116, 120, 121
  self-examination, 184, 205, 250
  self-improvement, 158, 160, 161, 165, 168, 175, 189, 199, 250, 268, 274, 276
  self-reproach, 263, 264, 269, 270,
  sexual, 2, 62, 92, 129
  signs, 62, 78, 99, 101, 111, 114, 129, 142, 187, 189, 203, 204, 205, 206, 207, 208, 209, 210, 211, 212, 214, 215, 216, 221, 223, 227, 233, 248, 247, 249, 250, 251, 263, 278
  skewed, 83, 221
  Soul, 12, 17, 42, 48, 49, 50, 52, 53, 54, 58, 59, 61, 105, 107, 108, 117, 143, 185, 187, 193, 201, 204, 207, 216, 220, 227, 231, 233, 234, 235, 249, 251, 256, 257, 262, 263, 265, 272, 275, 287, 297, 299, 300
  spiritual growth, 80, 89, 104, 187, 203, 210, 214, 276
  spiritual transcendence, 44
  spiritual wisdom, 76
  spiritualism, 21
  states of consciousness, 83, 84, 234
  striving, 15, 41, 64, 71, 89, 137, 165, 175, 199, 270, 273, 274, 276, 292, 306
  supernatural intervention, 121
  suspicions, 287, 288
  symbolic nature, 73, 89
  symbolism, 72, 77, 146

  tangible, 1, 43, 98, 112, 141, 147, 180, 186, 203, 209, 241, 250, 266, 279, 288
  thematic focus, 184
  theophanic, 245
  thought communities, 64, 246, 260, 270, 297
  thought patterns, 137, 138, 141, 195, 197, 198, 201, 204, 221, 241, 242, 246, 255, 257, 258, 259, 261, 262, 263, 267, 268, 269, 273, 274, 277, 279, 280, 283, 284, 290, 292
  thought processes, 56, 64, 94, 114, 136, 184, 231, 243, 246, 247, 248, 254, 255, 256, 258, 257, 260, 261, 263, 266, 267, 268, 274, 277, 278, 279, 280, 281, 283, 286, 289, 292, 297
  traditional interpretation, 40, 62, 67, 83, 103, 174, 288, 301, 305
  traditionalism, 31, 37, 38, 44
  traditional perspectives, 48
  traditionalist narratives, 50
  translations, 31, 40, 42, 50, 54, 55, 60, 76, 77, 90, 91, 98, 99, 108, 178, 248, 279
  tree, 66, 117, 118, 129, 134, 135, 137, 138, 141, 142, 143, 144

  warfare, 272, 274, 285, 286, 288, 292
  well-recognized phenomenon, 217

wellspring of wisdom, 10, 106, 152, 159
wisdom and guidance, 73, 89, 168

Zauj, 57, 59, 60, 76, 93, 120, 119, 128

www.ingramcontent.com/pod-product-compliance
Lightning Source LLC
Chambersburg PA
CBHW071218080526
44587CB00013BA/1415